Customizing macOS Sonoma

Fantastic Tricks, Tweaks, Hacks, Secret Commands & Hidden Features

Tom Magrini

Created in the United States of America
ISBN: 9798867370312
Independently Published

Terms & Conditions of Use

Some of the customizations contained in this book allow access to hidden system settings not visible in the macOS System Settings application. These customizations do not add to or change any part of the macOS operating system. They are additional system settings defined by Apple and built into macOS. All customizations are reversible and can be reset to their system default. The customizations were tested in macOS Sonoma, version 14.1. There is always the possibility that future updates to macOS could cause some of the customizations of hidden system settings to work as no longer expected.

While the author has taken every precaution in the preparation of this book, the author assumes no responsibility whatsoever for errors or omissions or for damages resulting from the use of the information contained herein. The information contained in this book is used at your risk. Any use of the information contained in this book constitutes your agreement to be bound by these terms and conditions.

Table of Contents

1

macOS Sonoma

Released in 2023, macOS Sonoma, officially macOS version 14, is Apple's latest operating system release for its Mac line of laptop and desktop computers. Keeping with its tradition of naming macOS releases after iconic California locations, Apple's latest release is named after Sonoma County.

Nestled in the heart of Northern California, Sonoma County is a captivating destination with its enchanting landscapes, rich history, and world-class wines. Sonoma's roots stretch back centuries, tracing a timeline of Spanish colonization, Mexican land grants, and the Bear Flag Revolt. It was the Mexican land grants, including one awarded to General Mariano Vallejo, that laid the foundation for the county's vineyards and winemaking.

The pivotal moment in Sonoma County's history came on June 14, 1846, when a group American settlers incited by U.S Army Brevet Captain John C. Fremont, staged the Bear Flag Revolt, declaring California's independence from Mexico. Led by William Ide and Ezekiel Merritt, 34 settlers captured the largely defenseless Mexican settlement of Sonoma, took Vallejo prisoner, and proclaimed California to be an independent republic. Using a cotton sheet and red paint, the "Bear Flaggers" created a makeshift flag of a grizzly bear, a red star, and the words "California Republic." Just three weeks later the California Republic quietly faded away as it became part of the United States. California adopted the Bear Flag as its state flag in 1911.

Today Sonoma County has over 400 wineries and more than 60,000 acres of vineyards. The diverse terroir, influenced by Pacific Ocean breezes and the warmth of inland valleys, provides the ideal conditions for a wide array of grape varieties. The Russian River Valley's cool climate produces world-class Chardonnay and Pinot Noir that are elegant, vibrant, and expressive of their terroir. The unique microclimate of the Dry Creek Valley yields Zinfandel grapes with bold flavors and spice. The Alexander Valley excels in producing Cabernet Sauvignon and Merlot while the Carneros region is known for its exceptional sparkling wines and Pinot Noir. Sonoma's wine culture emphasizes a laid-back, welcoming atmosphere, making it an ideal destination for wine enthusiasts of all levels of expertise.

While wine is undoubtedly a highlight of Sonoma County, the region is home to a plethora of charming towns, each with its own unique character and attractions. Nature enthusiasts will find solace in Sonoma County's stunning landscapes. The rugged coastline along Highway 1 offers breathtaking views of the Pacific Ocean, with opportunities for hiking, beachcombing, and whale watching. From its historical roots and world-renowned vineyards to its charming towns and natural beauty, Sonoma County captivates travelers with its timeless allure. Whether you're a wine aficionado, a history buff, or simply a seeker of beauty, Sonoma County is a place where memories are made, and the essence of California's wine country is savored in every sip and every sunset.

Why Customize macOS Sonoma?

macOS is widely considered to be one of the most popular and intuitive personal computer operating systems in the world. Known for its user-friendly interface, advanced security features, and smooth performance, macOS offers a wide range of features that make it easy to use and highly customizable. However, like any computer operating system, there are limitations to what you can do with it out of the box. This is where customization comes in. By customizing macOS, you can make your Mac work the way you want it to and get the most out of your Mac.

Whether you're a new user or a seasoned macOS pro, there are always ways to customize your Mac to make it work better for you. In this book, we will explore the many ways in which you can customize your macOS experience. From basic settings to advanced tweaks, I will guide you through the process of customizing your Mac to suit your needs.

There are many reasons why you might want to customize macOS. Perhaps you want to improve your productivity, optimize your workflow, or create a personalized computing environment that is tailored to your specific needs. Customizing macOS is also a great way to learn more about how your computer works. By exploring the underlying settings and preferences, you can gain a deeper understanding of the macOS operating system and how it interacts with your hardware. Whatever your reasons, there are countless ways to tweak macOS to suit your needs.

Customizing macOS Sonoma

Like previous macOS releases, Sonoma lets you completely customize your user experience until your Mac has a look and feel all your own. You can personalize your Mac, fine-tuning various aspects of the operating system to transform how you interact with it. Besides changing the look and feel, customizations allow you to be more productive and efficient by making macOS more closely match your personal computing style and how you work.

The default macOS settings that come out of the box make your Mac incredibly easy and efficient to use. And for most people, the defaults are all they'll ever need. But if you are reading this book, then you are not like most people. You want to tinker and tweak macOS to personalize it to the way you use your Mac. Besides, who wants their Mac to look, feel, and operate just like every other Mac? And of course, it's always cool to impress your friends when they notice your Mac does things theirs does not.

You don't need to be an Apple genius to customize macOS. Anyone with a little bit of familiarity with macOS can safely customize their user experience. Some customizations require a basic knowledge of how to use an application called Terminal. I'll teach you enough about Terminal in the next few pages to become truly dangerous (just kidding). My goal is to give you a foundation so you can execute simple Terminal commands to customize macOS. Once you have learned the basics of Terminal, you will be able to configure all the macOS customizations, hacks, and tweaks in this book to unlock the hidden features of macOS.

Each chapter focuses on customizing a particular aspect of macOS. We'll start first with a short introduction to some of the basics of macOS customization in this chapter. It's important to have a basic understanding of the tools and techniques you'll be using. I will first introduce the key tools and techniques you should be familiar with, including the System Settings and Terminal applications.

Next up, we'll cover Gestures and the Pointer in Chapter 2. If you are new to Macs and macOS, I will help you become an expert on gestures. Once we have covered the standard macOS trackpad and mouse gestures, I'll show you how to create personal, custom gestures. Creating a unique set of gestures is guaranteed to increase your efficiency and productivity.

The keyboard is the topic of Chapter 3. I know what you are thinking. "Why a chapter on the keyboard?" "Everyone knows how to use a keyboard." I'll show you a few keyboard customization tricks to change the behavior of the keys. You'll also learn how to create custom keyboard shortcuts, which can save you time, effort, and boost your productivity when working on your Mac.

In Chapter 4, you'll learn how to customize the Touch Bar, a dynamic input device with a strip of virtual keys that automatically change based on the running application. You will learn how to create custom Touch Bars.

We'll focus on the Desktop in Chapter 5. You'll learn how to customize the Desktop, personalize it, and make it more efficient, clean, and presentable. You will learn how to personalize your screen saver with the amazing, high-resolution screen savers of daytime and nighttime flyover footage you've seen on your Apple TV.

In Chapter 6, we'll tweak Mission Control, which provides a view of everything on your Mac – windows, apps in Full screen and Split-View mode, and Spaces. You'll learn how to increase your desktop real estate, declutter your desktop, and efficiently manage window clutter.

You'll learn to customize various options available in the Menu Bar and Control Center, in Chapter 7.

Next up in Chapter 8 is the Dock, one of the most iconic and recognizable macOS features, where you'll learn how to fine-tune the default macOS Dock to make it your personal, highly productive Dock.

Then we move on to Chapter 9, where you'll learn about Stacks, a cool feature of the Dock. You'll learn about a dozen tweaks guaranteed to increase your productivity, including how to create App Stacks.

Better searching is the topic of Chapter 10, where we'll customize Spotlight. I'll show you some tips and tricks for more accurate searches.

Next up is Siri, Apple's intelligent virtual assistant application, in Chapter 11.

Then we'll cover the Notification Center in Chapter 12. I'll teach you how to fine-tune this one-stop-shop that consolidates alerts and widgets.

In Chapter 13, we'll explore some tweaks to Launchpad, a macOS feature that blurs the line between macOS, iOS, and iPadOS.

Chapter 14 focuses on Finder, the macOS file manager application, which provides a user interface for managing files, disk drives, network drives, and launching applications. We'll customize Finder to make it more useful and more efficient.

Next, we will cover iCloud in Chapter 15. iCloud seamlessly integrates secure cloud storage with macOS, allowing you to store data, photos, documents, passwords, and contacts in iCloud and automatically synchronize them across all your Apple devices.

Windows are the focus of Chapter 16. You'll learn about Stage Manager. I'll also help those former Microsoft Windows users who miss Windows' window snapping feature. Everything is better on a Mac, including window snapping.

Customization of Safari is the topic of Chapter 17. You'll learn how to fine-tune Safari, change its appearance, and make it perform better.

The internet can be a dangerous place. We'll cover privacy and security in Chapter 18. You'll learn some tweaks to make your Mac a little more secure and keep your data safe.

Finally, Chapter 19 is a grab bag up of miscellaneous tricks, tweaks, and hacks.

How to Use This Book

There is no one way to use this book. If you want to impress your friends, and make them think you are an Apple genius, read it cover to cover, trying out each of the tweaks, hacks, secret commands, and hidden features.

You could start by focusing on a specific chapter that interests you, say, like the Dock. Another option is to review the contents and go directly to a tweak, hack, secret command, or hidden feature that interests you. No matter how you use this book, I hope that the tweaks, hacks, secret commands, and hidden features help you become more efficient and productive while having fun.

Before we get started, let's review some of the conventions used in this book.

Modifier Keys

Keyboard shortcuts allow you to perform actions that would normally require selecting a command from a menu or executing a gesture on a mouse or trackpad. Keyboard shortcuts require the use of one or more of the modifier keys listed below.

Fn	Function	⌃	Control	⌥	Option
⌘	Command	⇧	Shift	⊕	Globe
⎋	Escape	**F**	F(unction) key		

If you have an older Mac or older external keyboard, you're probably scratching your head wondering where the ⊕ key is. Depending on the age of your MacBook or external keyboard, you will have a key with an **fn** symbol or a key with both **fn** and ⊕ symbols. This key used to be called the Function key until Apple renamed it the Globe key in a previous release of macOS. To minimize confusion, Apple labels this key with both the **fn** and ⊕ symbols on new MacBook and external keyboards.

To make things even more confusing, Apple is inconsistent in the Systems Settings app. Sometimes Apple calls it the **fn** key while other times calling it the ⊕ key. Whenever I refer to the Function/Globe key in this book, I will use both symbols, as in the **fn** ⊕ (function/globe) key to minimize confusion.

To make things a bit more interesting, the **fn** ⊕ key can be found in two different locations depending on which external keyboard you own. On the smaller Magic Keyboards, the ones without a numeric keypad, the **fn** ⊕ key is in the lower left corner below the left shift key, the same place you will find it on a MacBook keyboard. However, if you have a Magic Keyboard with a numeric keypad, the Function/Globe key can be found between the alphabetic and numeric keypads in a group of 9 keys that include the **F13**, **F14**, **F15**, **home**, **page up**, ⌦ **delete** (forward delete), **end**, and **page down** keys.

Keyboard shortcuts are listed in parenthesis. For example, ⇧⌘G will be followed by (shift+command+G). To use a keyboard shortcut, you need to hold down the listed modifier key(s) while pressing the last key of the shortcut. For ⇧⌘G, you will hold down the shift and command keys while pressing the letter "G."

Note that when I refer to an **F** key, I am not referring to the key for the letter "F." I am referring to the function keys at the top of your keyboard that are labeled **F1** to **F12**. If you have an external keyboard with a numeric keypad, you'll also have **F13**, **F14**, and

F15 keys. You should also note that Macs are a little different than Windows PCs. On a Mac, each of the function keys is pre-configured to execute a specific action, such as increasing or decreasing the volume, launching Mission Control, or pausing and playing your music. If you want to use a function key as a plain old **F** key, you need to hold down the **fn** ⊕ (function/globe) key to avoid executing the assigned key command.

Command Typeface

When a tweak, hack, secret command, or hidden feature requires you to enter a command into the Terminal or Finder, I use a different typeface. When you see this typeface, these are commands that you will enter in the specified app.

```
defaults write com.apple.dock workspaces-edge-delay -float 0.5

killall Dock
```

By the way, don't let the "killall" command scare you. I'm not really asking you to kill your Dock. I wouldn't do that. I like the Dock. It is one of my favorite macOS features. The "killall Dock" command simply restarts the Dock so the previous command can take effect.

When a button needs to be clicked, the button name is bolded, as in "click the **Trackpad Options...** button."

Menus

Some commands in this book are executed using the Apple Menu. So, when you see this symbol: I'm referring to the Apple Menu located on the Menu Bar in the upper left-hand corner of your desktop.

When I ask you to execute a command using a menu, it will look like this: **> System Settings... > Desktop & Dock**. This is shorthand asking you to select the Apple Menu, then choose System Settings... from the pop-up menu, and finally, select the Desktop & Dock settings in System Settings. Hint: whenever you see this symbol: **>** I'm asking you to select from a menu.

In addition to the Apple Menu, I will ask you to make selections from other pop-up menus. In this example, **Finder > Settings...**, I am asking you to select the Finder menu, then select Settings. The Finder menu appears to the right of the Apple menu when Finder is the active application.

Graphical Controls

macOS uses graphical controls to enable, disable, tweak, and configure various features. Let's review the various graphical components in macOS Sonoma.

A slider allows you to choose any value between the pre-defined minimum and maximum values by dragging it anywhere within the range.

Keyboard brightness ━━━━━━━━━

Some sliders are stepped, meaning you can only select pre-defined values within the range.

Delay until repeat

Long   Short

Other sliders may offer an off option.

Magnification

Off   Small   Large

In macOS Sonoma, Apple replaced many of the checkboxes with switches to make the GUI look more like iOS and iPadOS. Switches offer only two options – on or off. I also use the terms enable and disable for on and off, respectively.

When a switch is on, the feature is enabled.

Minimize windows into application icon   ⬤

When a switch is off, the feature is disabled. Note that the switch turns gray when off.

Automatically hide and show the Dock   ◯

A checkbox turns a feature on or off. Checking the checkbox enables or turns the feature on while unchecking disables or turns it off.

Search results
Only selected categories will appear in Spotlight search results.

☑ Applications
☐ Bookmarks & History

Pop-up menus are denoted by the up and down arrows at the right end of the pop-up menu. Clicking anywhere in the field pops a menu of options from which to choose, thus the name "pop-up" menu.

	Always
	On Desktop Only
Menu Bar	In Full Screen Only
	✓ Never
Automatically hide and show the menu bar	
Recent documents, applications, and servers	20 ⌄

Radio buttons are sometimes used instead of pop-up menus, particularly when the available options are few. Selecting one radio button deselects another as only one option can be selected.

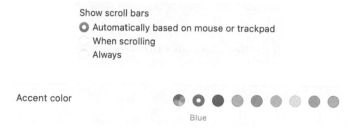

Buttons with an ellipsis (...) open other windows or configuration sheets when clicked. A configuration sheet appears on top of the main settings window, which will dim in the background. Configuration sheets are used to select and configure additional options.

Touch Bar Settings...   Keyboard Shortcuts...

Buttons without an ellipsis change the options in the settings window, turning white when selected.

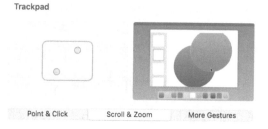

A blue border will appear around other buttons when selected.

When you see a greater than sign (**>**) next to an item, clicking on it will open another window.

A button with an **i** is an info button. Clicking it will provide more info about an item. Sometimes an ellipsis is used instead of an **i**.

Automatic updates   On ⓘ

Search fields are available in most windows and allow you to perform a search for almost anything on your Mac or on the internet.

 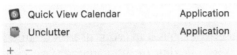

The red, yellow, green stoplight in the upper left corner of a window controls the window. Clicking on the red button closes the window. In some cases, it will also quit the app. The yellow button minimizes a window while the green button expands the window to full screen.

The **+** (add) button allows you to add an item to a list while the **–** (delete) button removes an item.

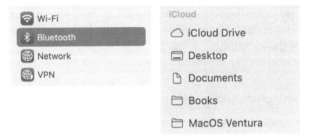

A sidebar allows you to select from multiple items and is found on the left side of a window.

A contextual menu appears when secondary clicking. Many contextual menus contain sub-menus.

System Settings

You'll do most of your customization work in the System Settings app. If you updated to macOS Sonoma from an earlier version of macOS, you are likely familiar with the System Preferences app. For macOS Sonoma, gone is the System Preferences app, replaced by a brand-new System Settings app that looks more like the Settings app in iOS and iPadOS. The macOS Sonoma System Settings app offers an extensive set of customization capabilities, allowing you to modify system-wide macOS behavior.

Throughout this book, I'll ask you to launch the System Settings application to customize specific macOS parameters. In macOS, there are often multiple ways to do the same thing, and there are several ways to launch the System Settings app:

1. Click on the System Settings icon in the **Dock**,
2. Launch System Settings using **Launchpad**,
3. Select > **System Settings...** from the Apple menu,
4. Open **Spotlight**, search for System Settings, and press the **return** key,
5. Launch **Finder**, open the **Applications** folder, and double-click on the System Settings icon, or
6. Launch **Siri** and ask it to "Launch System Settings."

Like iOS' and iPadOS' System Settings app, your username and picture will be displayed at the top of the sidebar. By clicking on your name, you can edit various parameters associated with your Apple ID, such as your name, phone, email, password, two-factor authentication, payment options, address, iCloud, purchases, Family Sharing, and the devices associated with your Apple ID. Any third-party settings will appear at the bottom of the sidebar.

Search System Settings

Sometimes finding the specific setting you want to modify is not intuitive. The Search field comes in handy when you know which setting you want to modify but don't know where to find it.

Click in the Search field or enter ⌘F (command+F) to go directly to the Search Field. As you type, macOS finds the settings that are most likely related to your search and displays a list of suggested items in the sidebar below the search field. Eventually, macOS zeroes in on the applicable settings.

If you don't know exactly what the macOS setting is called, Spotlight offers suggestions in the sidebar to help you find the right settings window. Click the highlighted settings or one of the items listed under the Search field to open the associated settings window.

Find a Setting Using Spotlight

Spotlight is the macOS search feature that allows you to search for items on your Mac and the internet. To open Spotlight, click on the magnifying glass in the upper-right corner of the Menu Bar or press ⌘**space** (command+space).

As you type in the Spotlight Search field, Spotlight provides results it thinks are likely matches, refining them as you type and organizing them into categories directly below the search field. Results are displayed in categories, with the Top Hit, the result Spotlight thinks is the most likely, highlighted at the top of the list. If you press the **return** key or double-click on the Top Hit, macOS opens it.

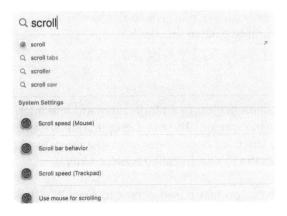

Terminal

 Apple offers customizations to change the behavior of macOS that are not accessible from System Settings. There is nothing really secret about these features other than the fact they are not directly accessible using the System Settings app. These hidden features require you to enter commands into an application called Terminal. Terminal provides a command line interface for you to interact with macOS directly, allowing you to take your macOS customization to an entirely new level not achievable using System Settings.

If entering commands into a command line interface sounds intimidating, it isn't. First, I'll show you how to use the Terminal application. Once you have learned the basics of Terminal, you will be able to configure all the macOS customizations, hacks, and tweaks in this book and unlock the hidden features of macOS.

The average Mac user may never know of the existence of the Terminal application, which is tucked away in the **Utilities** folder in the **Applications** folder. Those who know of Terminal's existence may avoid it because they find its archaic command line interface strange and intimidating. The modern computer user sees Terminal as a throwback to the old days of computing before GUIs became the norm. Terminal reminds us of a time when geeky computer scientists with thick glasses sat hunched over their keyboards, pounding away in a strange language more familiar to a computer than a human. As you'll see in the next few pages, Terminal may seem archaic, but it certainly isn't very intimidating.

Why bother using Terminal in the first place? While Terminal appears at first glance to be a relic more appropriate for a museum than your modern, beautiful, and elegant Mac, it is one of the most powerful, versatile, and useful applications in macOS. It has many uses beyond just customization of your macOS user experience. However, our focus in this book is customization and personalization of macOS, so I won't cover Terminal's other uses, which is a book all by itself.

Terminal can be used by users of all skill levels, even a novice Mac user who is learning about Terminal for the first time. We'll take some baby steps to build your confidence and learn the basics, enough so that you are able to configure any of the macOS customizations, hacks, and tweaks in this book.

What is Terminal?

Terminal is Apple's implementation of a Unix command line interface, commonly called a shell or command line interpreter. The macOS operating system, as well as its precursor NeXTSTEP, is based on Unix, an operating system first developed by AT&T in the 1970s. Apple macOS represents the largest installed base of Unix.

Essentially, Terminal gives you text-based access to macOS, allowing you to enter Unix commands, which let you configure various attributes that are not presented via the GUI. Other than its function as a command line interpreter, Terminal acts like any other application on your Mac.

Before You Begin

Some of the customizations require you to use Terminal to change preference settings, which are not visible in the macOS System Settings. These settings do not add or change any part of the macOS operating system. The settings described in this book are defined by Apple as part of macOS. All the customizations are reversible. While the Terminal commands in this book are safe to use, you must enter the commands exactly as shown. In Terminal, every character is important, including the spaces as well as any capitalization.

Launching Terminal

Let's launch the Terminal application. Like System Settings, there are multiple ways to launch the Terminal application. You can launch Terminal by any one of the following methods:

1. Open **Launchpad** and find the Terminal application and click on its icon,
2. Open **Launchpad** and type "Terminal" in the Launchpad search field and press the **return** key,
3. Open **Spotlight** and type "Terminal" in the Spotlight search field, and press the **return** key,
4. Launch **Finder**, open the **Applications** folder, open the **Utilities** folder, and double-click on Terminal, or
5. Launch Siri and ask it to "Launch Terminal."

Terminal provides a text-based user interface showing your username and the name of your computer, followed by a % sign. A gray rectangular pointer, called the prompt, waits patiently for your commands. Note that the name of the current user, the type of shell (macOS uses a shell called zsh), and the size of the window (80 characters by 24 lines) is shown on the window's Title Bar.

```
●  ●  ●                🖥 tmagrini — -zsh — 80×24
Last login: Sat Dec  2 07:11:35 on console
tmagrini@MacBook-Pro ~ % ▎
```

Terminal Basics

The first thing you'll notice about Terminal is the prompt. The prompt is where you will enter the commands shown in this book. When you open Terminal, the first two lines look something like this:

```
Last login: Wed Mar 2 12:40:04 on ttys000
tmagrini@Toms-MacBook-Pro: ~ % |
```

The first line tells you when you last logged in via the Terminal application. The second line contains the **prompt**. The prompt appears after the % sign. Depending on your selection in Terminal settings, which is accessed using the keyboard shortcut ⌘, (command+comma), the cursor may or may not blink and could appear as a block, an underline, or a vertical bar.

Commands are entered at the prompt. You do not have to use your mouse or trackpad as anything you type appears at the prompt. Once a command has been completely entered, you will press the **return** key to execute it.

Terminal provides no feedback when a command is entered correctly, behavior first-time Terminal users often find odd. Feedback is provided only when an invalid command is entered. And don't worry, macOS will not make any changes if the command is not valid. If a command is entered correctly, a new prompt appears on a new line awaiting your next command.

You will enter one command at a time into Terminal, pressing the **return** key after each to execute it. Note that commands shown in this book are case sensitive. Therefore, you must enter each one exactly as shown. Remember, every character is important in Terminal, including the spaces as well as capitalization.

So far, it sounds simple, doesn't it? The customizations that require the use of Terminal simply require you to type a few commands exactly as you see them in this book, pressing the **return** key after each command. Yes, it's that simple. Let's try a Dock customization to help you learn and gain more confidence using Terminal.

Your First Customization

macOS offers two standard animations when minimizing windows, the **Genie** and **Scale** effects, with the default being **Genie**. Unless you have changed the window minimization effect in the Dock & Desktop settings, you are using the default, Genie. Let's launch the Terminal application and check. Once Terminal has launched, enter the following command.

```
defaults read com.apple.dock mineffect
```

The command you just entered is a **read** command, which you just used to find out the current setting of the **mineffect**, short for minimization effect. If the output looks like the following, telling you that com.apple.dock mineffect does not exist, that is okay. All it means is that you have never changed the minimization effect in System Settings. Therefore, you are using Genie, the default.

```
Last login: Mon Feb 15 13:04:38 on ttys000
tmagrini@Toms-MacBook-Pro ~ % defaults read com.apple.doc
mineffect
2021-02-15 13:06:37.038 defaults[9946:220890]
The domain/default pair of (com.apple.doc, mineffect) does not
exist
tmagrini@Toms-MacBook-Pro ~ %
```

Now let's change the minimization effect using Terminal. First, minimize any open window so you can view the animation. If you minimized the Terminal window, click on it in the Dock to reopen it. This time you will enter a **write** command, which is used to change a setting. Enter the following two commands and press the **return** key after you enter each command. Be sure to capitalize the **D** in **D**ock.

```
defaults write com.apple.dock mineffect -string scale
```

```
killall Dock
```

Now minimize the Terminal window and note the change to the minimization animation. It is no longer set to the default of Genie. You can check this setting in the System Settings application. Launch System Settings, then click on the **Desktop & Dock** in the sidebar. Check out the setting next to **Minimize windows using**.

Wasn't that way cool? You just changed a macOS system parameter using the command line interface in Terminal.

If you want to change the window minimization effect back to Genie, you could simply select **Genie effect** from the pop-up menu next to **Minimize windows using** in the Desktop & Dock settings. But let's make the change using Terminal.

First, close the Desktop & Dock settings, then enter the following commands in the Terminal application.

```
defaults write com.apple.dock mineffect -string genie
```

```
killall Dock
```

Now check out the Desktop & Dock settings. Note that if you didn't follow my directions (shame on you) and left the Desktop & Dock settings open when changing back to the Genie effect, the change will not be reflected in the settings window. Close the System Settings app, launch it, and reopen the Desktop & Dock settings to see the change.

You could have also reverted to the default Genie animation using a **delete** command, as shown below. When you delete a setting, macOS reverts to the system default, in this case, the Genie effect.

```
defaults delete com.apple.dock mineffect
```

```
killall Dock
```

Congratulations! You just completed your first customization using the Terminal command line and reverted to the macOS system default. I told you it was easy!

Wait a minute. Why would you use Terminal to change the window minimization animation when it is so much easier to change it using System Settings? That is because some settings are not available in System Settings, like the third animation, the **suck** effect. System Settings allows you to switch between the Genie and Scale effects, but macOS has a third, hidden animation called **suck** that is not accessible in System Settings. It can only be changed using a command in the Terminal app. I'll show you how to configure the suck effect in the chapter on the Dock.

History Command

Before we finish our basic lesson on Terminal, I'll show you a few commands that will come in handy. The first command provides a history of all the commands you have entered. History comes in handy when you want to see what you did, or when you want to reuse a command. Using the history command allows you to not only see the commands you entered but to copy a command you wish to reuse. Copy and paste are supported in Terminal. Remember to copy only the command, not the prompt.

```
history
```

Now is probably a good time to remind you about the typeface. All Terminal commands are shown in the typeface shown above. When you see this typeface, it is your signal that these are commands you will enter at the Terminal prompt.

Up and Down Arrows

The **up** arrow key displays the last command you entered in Terminal. This lets you rerun the command by pressing the **return** key again or to backspace over part of the command to make changes. After you have entered several commands, pressing the **up** arrow lists each command in reverse order, essentially through your command history in reverse. Terminal beeps to let you know when you have reached the end of your history.

The **down** arrow moves you forward through your history of commands. The up and down arrows come in handy when you need to enter a previously used command again. Once you have found the command you want and it is displayed in Terminal, simply press the **return** key to execute it.

Clear

After entering lots of commands, the prompt will be at the bottom of the Terminal window, and the window will be full of commands. If you want to clear the window, enter this command. Don't forget to hit the **return** key.

```
clear
```

Note that using the clear command does not delete your command history. All the clear command does is clean up your interface.

Entering Long Commands

Some of the commands in this book are too long to fit on a single line in Terminal. A long command will flow onto the next line. A very long command can even take three lines in Terminal. Even though the command appears on multiple lines, it is still a single command and will not be executed until you press the **return** key. For example, the following command appears in one line in the book:

```
defaults write com.apple.screencapture disable-shadow -bool true
```

However, it appears on two lines in Terminal, as shown in the image on the next page. Remember, a command is executed when you press the **return** key, so do not press **return** until you have entered an entire command.

Let's Customize macOS Sonoma!

Now that you have learned the basics of the System Settings and Terminal apps, you now have the basic knowledge necessary to configure the customizations in this book. I told you it was that easy! Let's start with Gestures and Pointer Control.

―――――――――――

2

Gestures & Pointer Control

Hands down, Apple has the best multi-touch trackpad and mouse in the industry. No other computer manufacturer comes close. If you use a MacBook Pro or MacBook Air, you'll use your laptop's built-in trackpad every day. If you have a Mac desktop computer such as an iMac, Mac Pro, Mac Studio, or Mac Mini, I highly recommend you indulge yourself and purchase an Apple Magic Trackpad. A trackpad does more than just point and click. With a trackpad, you can take advantage of the full set of standard and custom gestures in macOS Sonoma. It will also look great next to your Apple Wireless Keyboard!

If you are using an Apple Magic Mouse, it also supports gestures, albeit a smaller number. macOS offers a total of six standard gestures for the Magic Mouse, while the Magic Trackpad supports a total of fifteen. While creating custom gestures can help alleviate this limitation, I find that I am far more productive using a trackpad than a mouse. Once you have mastered trackpad gestures, it's hard to go back to a mouse.

In this chapter, we'll first review the standard gestures for your trackpad and mouse as well as various attributes such as tracking speed, double-click speed, and Force Touch. Then I'll show you how to create custom trackpad and mouse gestures. Creating a unique set of gestures is guaranteed to increase your efficiency and productivity, giving you precise and completely natural control over your Mac.

If you are an experienced Mac user, you may be thinking about skipping this chapter since you are already familiar with gestures. If that's the case, I suggest you skim through this chapter as I introduce a few features that are not configured in the Trackpad or Mouse settings and then skip to the section on creating custom gestures.

If you are switching from a Windows PC, you may find gestures to be rather odd. Where is the right mouse button? Never mind that! Where is the left one?! However, with just a little practice, macOS gestures become completely natural. macOS gestures will become so natural that eventually you'll no longer think about which gesture does what. You'll rely on muscle memory, performing trackpad and mouse gestures without any conscious effort. Once you have mastered the built-in macOS gestures and have created a few custom ones, you'll never want to use a Windows PC again!

Trackpad Gestures

While an Apple trackpad provides 15 standard gestures, Apple leaves a few disabled by default, and one is hidden in another settings window. I suggest you turn on all trackpad gestures and spend about half an hour or so learning what each does. After a little practice, you'll find gestures will become completely natural, and you will no longer have to remember which gesture accomplishes what task.

To open the Trackpad settings, launch the System Settings app and scroll to the bottom of the sidebar and click on **Trackpad**. Look for the three buttons towards the top of the window for each of the gesture categories – **Point & Click**, **Scroll & Zoom**, and **More Gestures**. The currently selected button is white. The gestures are listed below the sliders for the tracking speed and click pressure, which we'll cover later in this chapter.

Besides enabling and disabling gestures, the **Trackpad** settings lets you to customize some of the gestures. The Trackpad settings also allow you to adjust the pointer tracking speed and Force Touch options. If you are setting up a new Bluetooth trackpad, you'll do that in the Trackpad settings too.

Let's start with the three **Point & Click** gestures – **Look Up & Data Detectors**, **Secondary Click**, and **Tap to Click**. Moving your pointer over each of the gestures changes the animation shown at the top of the Trackpad settings window. The animation on the left demonstrates how to perform the gesture on a trackpad while the animation on the right demonstrates what the gesture does.

Look Up & Data Detectors

Move your pointer until it is hovering on **Look Up & Data Detectors**. The animation at the top of the Trackpad settings window will change to demonstrate how to perform the gesture. A pop-up menu to the right of **Look Up & Data Detectors** gives you the option of disabling the gesture, using a one-finger Force Click, or a three-finger tap. You'll need a trackpad that supports Force Touch for the one-finger Force Click option to appear.

If you highlight a word in a document or webpage and use this gesture, macOS will look up the word in the dictionary, thesaurus, Wikipedia, Siri Knowledge, Siri Suggested Websites, or the Mac App Store. Depending on the word, you may see other options such as news, sports, TV, or movies. The Data Detector feature recognizes the type of data, such as dates and addresses. This is an extremely handy feature allowing you to quickly add a new event to Calendar or a contact to the Contacts app.

An advantage of selecting **Tap with Three Fingers** is that this setting also enables **Quick Look**, which allows you to preview a file in Finder using a three-finger tap on the file's icon. You can also use the three-finger tap gesture to preview a web link in Safari.

By default, macOS enabled a default set of reference sources – Wikipedia, Apple Dictionary, Oxford American Writer's Thesaurus, and the New Oxford American Dictionary. A reference source is used by macOS to look up the item you highlighted with the Look Up & Data Detectors gesture. macOS uses the language you chose when you first set up your Mac.

If you would like to change or add additional languages to the dictionary or add or remove reference sources, use the Look Up & Data Detectors gesture to look up a word in a document or on a webpage. When the Look Up window appears, click on the tiny gear next to **Configure Dictionaries**. This reveals a settings window where you can change or add languages and enable and disable reference sources. Note that you may have to scroll to the bottom of the window to find the gear icon.

The top of the window lists available reference sources. You can enable a reference source by checking the checkbox next to the source. You can configure the reference sources to appear in the order you desire by dragging them.

Your list of reference sources will look a little different than what is shown in the image to the right. This is because I dragged the four checked reference sources, which are the macOS defaults, to the top of the window.

You can enable other languages by checking the checkbox next to the language. If your desired language is not shown, use the pop-up menu next to **Other Languages** to select a language from the list.

Secondary Click

A secondary click is used to reveal context-sensitive menus. For those more familiar with a Windows PC, a secondary click is like clicking the right mouse button. macOS has three options to perform a secondary click on your trackpad – clicking or tapping with two fingers, clicking in either the bottom right or left corner, or disabling the gesture. The current selection has a checkmark next to it.

Make your selection from the pop-up menu next to **Secondary click**. If you select the **Off** option, you will need to hold down the ⌘ (command) key while clicking to perform a secondary click.

The second option is dependent upon whether you have enabled tap to click. With tap to click enabled, you'll have the option of **Click or Tap with Two Fingers**. With tap to click disabled, you are offered the option of **Click with Two Fingers** since tapping is no longer an option.

The final two options are to **Click in Bottom Right Corner** or **Click in Bottom Left Corner**.

Tap to Click

Enabling the **Tap to click** gesture allows you to gently tap the trackpad to perform a click instead of pressing firmly. The difference between a click and tap is the amount of force you use to perform the gesture. A tap is a gentle tap on the trackpad, while clicking requires you to press down on the trackpad with slightly more force.

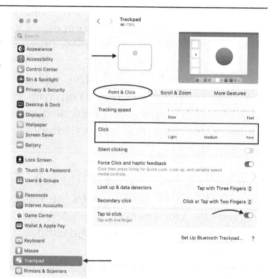

You can enable or disable Tap to Click by clicking the **Point & Click** button and flipping the switch next to **Tap to click**. Enabling this gesture does not replace the default click option as both are supported when tap to click is enabled.

The amount of pressure needed to enable a click can be adjusted using the slider next to **Click**. The default is medium. Move the slider left or right to configure how firmly you'll need to press the trackpad to perform a click.

Note that pressing down on the trackpad is still required to perform a click and hold to drag, move, or lasso items, although you can accomplish these actions using three fingers when three finger drag is enabled. See "Three-Finger Drag" later in this chapter.

Natural Scrolling

If you are switching from a Windows PC to a Mac, natural scrolling may appear to be a little strange at first. On a Windows PC, you scroll up to move your content down and scroll down to move your content up. Natural scrolling is exactly the opposite – your content moves in the same direction as your fingers, tracking the direction of your fingers on the trackpad. That is how scrolling works on an iPhone or iPad. If you have an iPhone or iPad, you have been scrolling naturally without even realizing it.

With natural scrolling, place two fingers on your trackpad and move them in the direction you want to move your content. If you want to move your content up, scroll up with two fingers. If you want to move your content down, scroll down with two fingers.

macOS lets you disable natural scrolling. Click the **Scroll & Zoom** button in Trackpad settings and then flip the **Natural Scrolling** switch off. When disabled, you'll scroll up to move your content down and scroll down to move your content up, like you would on a Windows PC.

Another difference between macOS and Windows is that scrollbars only appear along the edges of a window when you are scrolling. This is the default setting in macOS, which of course, is customizable. I'll show you scrollbar customizations in a later chapter.

Zoom In and Out

macOS uses the same gestures to zoom in or out as an iPhone or iPad – spread two fingers apart to zoom in and pinch two fingers together to zoom out. Zooming is enabled by default.

Place two fingers close together on your trackpad and spread them apart to zoom in. Be sure to maintain continuous contact with the trackpad while spreading your fingers apart. A rubber band animation lets you know when you have reached the maximum limit of a zoom. To zoom out, place two fingers apart on the trackpad and move them together in a pinching motion. The rubber

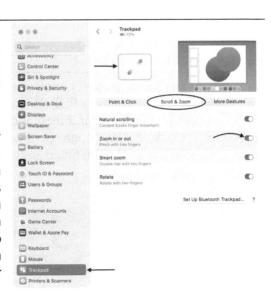

band animation lets you know when you have fully zoomed out. To stop zooming, stop moving your fingers and lift them off the trackpad.

When you have multiple tabs open in Safari, a two-finger pinch-zoom on a Safari tab executes the **Show All Tabs** command, displaying all webpages as a set of thumbnails. This is the same action performed if you were to use the keyboard shortcut ⇧⌘\ (shift+command+\). To take a tab back to full size, hover over it with the pointer and spread two fingers apart on the trackpad. You can also click on the thumbnail to restore the webpage to its full size.

Smart Zoom

Smart Zoom is another feature that macOS borrows from the iPhone and iPad. When you want to zoom in, double tap your trackpad with two fingers. Double tap again to zoom out. This feature is enabled by default.

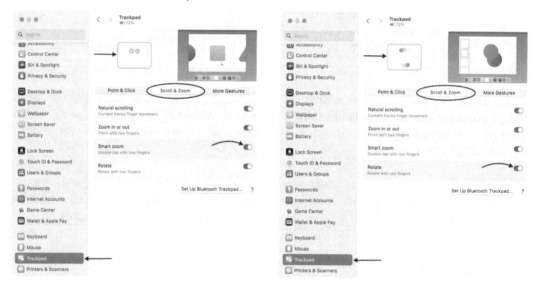

Rotate

Rotate is another handy feature I often use in the Photos application and when working with images in other formats or PDF documents. You can rotate an image or a page in a PDF document by placing your thumb and forefinger on the trackpad and rotating your fingers in a clockwise or counterclockwise direction while maintaining continuous contact with the trackpad. The rotate gesture is enabled by default.

Swipe Between Pages

Swiping between pages is very much like thumbing through pages in a book. A common use for this gesture is to move forward and backward through webpages in Safari.

There are four options available – scrolling left or right with two fingers, swiping with three fingers, or swiping with either two or three fingers, along with an option to disable this gesture. To configure, click the **More Gestures** button in Trackpad settings. Make your selection from the pop-up menu next to **Swipe between pages**.

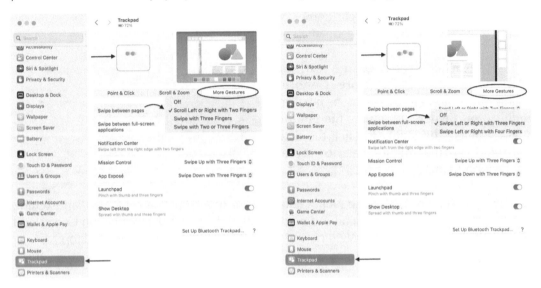

Swipe Between Full Screen Apps

Almost any application can be taken to full screen on your Mac. The macOS full screen feature expands the application window, hiding both the Menu Bar and the Dock, so that the window covers your entire desktop. This feature is great when you want to focus on the application you are working in while eliminating distractions that come with a desktop full of windows. To take a window to full screen, click on the green control button located in the upper left corner of the window's Title Bar. You can also use the keyboard shortcut ^⌘F (control+command+F) to take an app to full screen mode.

The swipe between full screen apps gesture lets you swipe between one or more full screen apps and Spaces, both of which I cover in more detail in the chapter on Mission Control, by swiping left or right. Click the **More Gestures** button in Trackpad settings. This gesture can be configured to use either three or four fingers or disabled from the pop-up menu next to **Swipe between full screen applications**.

Notification Center

The macOS **Notification Center** is a panel of widgets, notifications, and alerts hidden beyond the right edge of your desktop. The gesture to reveal Notification Center seems a little odd at first because you start off the right edge of your trackpad and swipe left with two fingers. Swiping in the opposite direction, pressing the **esc** key, or clicking anywhere on your desktop or an application window exits Notification Center, hiding it beyond the right edge of your desktop.

You can also make the Notification Center appear and disappear by clicking on the date and time in the upper right corner of your desktop's Menu Bar.

The Notification Center gesture can be disabled by clicking the **More Gestures** button and flipping the switch next to **Notification Center**. Disabling the gesture does not affect the ability to click the date and time in the Menu Bar to reveal Notification Center.

I'll show you how to customize Notification Center in a later chapter. Also, an exciting new feature in macOS Sonoma allows you to pull widgets out of Notification Center and place them on your desktop. We'll cover Widgets in the chapter on the Desktop.

Mission Control

Mission Control is a handy feature that allows you to create, delete, manage, navigate, and rearrange Spaces and the application windows that reside on them. Mission Control provides a view of every window running in each Space as well as applications in Full Screen or Split View. Using Mission Control, you can quickly jump to another Space, Full Screen app, Split View app, or a window. Mission Control allows you to drag windows from one Space to another. I'll cover Spaces in detail in the chapter on Mission Control.

You can configure the Mission Control gesture to swipe up using three or four fingers or disable it. Click the **More Gestures** button in Trackpad settings. Use the pop-up menu next to **Mission Control** to configure. When you select three or four fingers, the same number of fingers will be automatically configured for the App Exposé gesture. Refer to the next section for information on App Exposé.

You can also access Mission Control using the keyboard shortcut **^up** (control+up arrow), or by clicking the Mission Control icon in the Launchpad, Dock, Applications folder, or in the Touch Bar if your MacBook Pro is equipped with one. Disabling the gesture for Mission Control in the Trackpad settings has no effect on these other methods.

To close Mission Control, swipe down with the same number of fingers as the swipe up gesture, enter **^up** (control+up arrow), tap its icon on the Touch Bar, press the **esc** key, or click on any of the windows or Spaces displayed in the Spaces Bar at the top of Mission Control.

App Exposé

App Exposé lets you see all the windows of an app regardless in which Space the window resides. You can then jump quickly to a window by clicking on it. While Mission Control displays all windows in a Space, even if they are from different applications, App Exposé displays all windows of the selected app even if they are in different Spaces.

To configure the App Exposé gesture, click the **More Gestures** button. Next, select from the pop-up menu next to **App Exposé**. The App Exposé gesture can be configured to swipe down with three or four fingers or disabled. When you select three or four fingers, the same number of fingers will be automatically configured for the Mission Control gesture.

You can also access App Exposé using the keyboard shortcut **^down** (control+down arrow). Disabling the App Exposé gesture has no impact on the keyboard shortcut.

To close App Exposé, swipe up with the same number of fingers as the swipe down gesture, enter **^down** (control+down arrow), press the **esc** key, or click on a window.

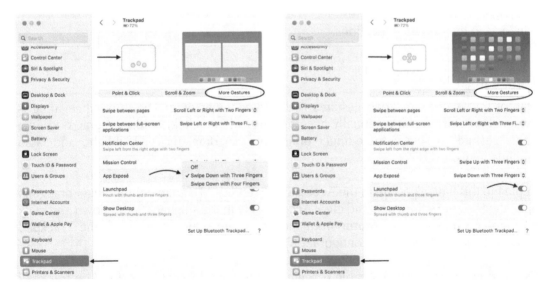

Launchpad

Launchpad is another feature macOS borrows from the iPhone and iPad. Launchpad allows you to see, organize, and launch your apps from a central location that displays all the apps on your Mac. Place your thumb and three fingers on your trackpad. Ensure your thumb and fingers aren't too close together. Now pinch your thumb and three fingers together to open Launchpad.

You can also access Launchpad by clicking on the Launchpad icon in the Dock or Touch Bar, or by launching it from the Applications folder. To exit Launchpad, press the **esc** key or use the **Show Desktop** gesture.

Show Desktop

The **Show Desktop** is used to clear all windows from your desktop. Starting with your thumb and three fingers placed close together on your trackpad, quickly spread them apart. Any windows will be moved to the left and right edges of your desktop. Reverse the gesture to restore your windows.

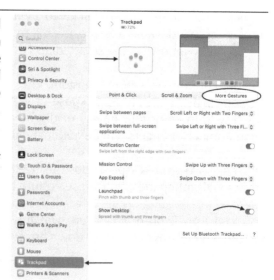

You can also toggle show desktop on and off by pressing **fn+F11**.

A new feature in macOS Sonoma lets you perform the Show Desktop command by clicking anywhere on your desktop wallpaper. Click again to restore your windows to their original locations.

Three-Finger Drag

One of my favorite trackpad gestures is the three-finger drag. The three-finger drag is extremely useful since it essentially accomplishes what a click, hold, and drag does in a single gesture. Using a three-finger drag, you can drag, move, highlight, and lasso multiple items.

Apple hid this handy gesture in the Accessibility settings. To enable three-finger dragging, open the System Settings app and click **Accessibility** in the sidebar. Scroll down and click on **Pointer Control** under **Motor** from the list at the right. Now click the **Trackpad Options...** button to reveal a configuration sheet.

On the configuration sheet, enable dragging by flipping the switch next to **Use trackpad for dragging** on. Next, select **Three Finger Drag** from the pop-up menu next to **Dragging style**. Click **OK** to finish.

To use a three-finger drag to move a window, position your pointer over the title bar, place three fingers on your trackpad, and move the window anywhere on your desktop or to another Space if you are in Mission Control. Lift your fingers off the trackpad to end the drag. This gesture can be used to move items in Finder by positioning your pointer over a file (or folder) and using a three-finger drag to move it to another folder or the Trash. If you hold down the ⌥ (option) key, the file will be copied to the new location. A three-finger drag can also be used to lasso a group of files in Finder.

The three-finger drag gesture is also handy for selecting text in Apple Pages or Microsoft Word. Position the pointer in your document and use the three-finger drag gesture to select text by dragging left or right. You can also use the gesture to lasso a group of emails in Mail, files in Finder, or pictures in Photos.

Three-Finger Double Tap Zoom

Another one of my favorite trackpad gestures is the three-finger double tap zoom. This gesture is like the smart zoom gesture but instead of zooming in on a single window, the three-finger double tap zooms the entire desktop. If you don't lift your fingers off the trackpad after the second tap, you'll see a magnifying glass that lets you scroll up and down to change the zoom level. Double tap again to zoom out.

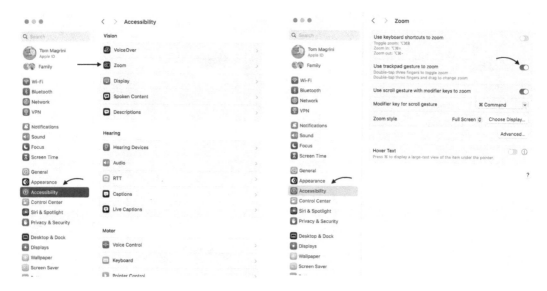

Apple hid this gem in the Accessibility settings. To enable the three-finger double tap zoom gesture, open the System Settings app and click **Accessibility** in the sidebar. Scroll down and click on **Zoom** in the **Vision** section. Flip the switch next to **Use trackpad gesture to zoom** on.

Drag Lock

When dragging an item, for example when moving a file to another folder, dragging ends when you remove your finger(s) from the trackpad. By enabling the **Drag Lock** feature, you can change this behavior so that the drag ends when you tap the trackpad upon reaching the destination.

The advantage of using drag lock is that if you accidentally lift your finger off the trackpad, the drag will not end prematurely. Drag Lock is handy when you're dragging an item from one side of a large monitor to the other as you often run out of trackpad space before completing your drag.

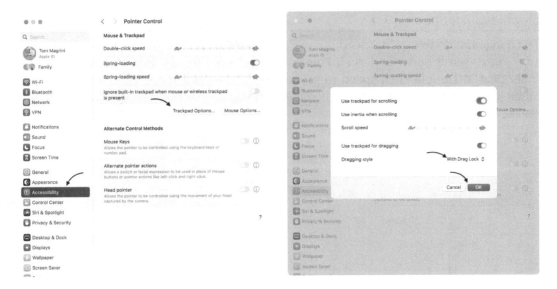

To enable Drag Lock, open the System Settings app and click **Accessibility** in the sidebar. Scroll down and click on **Pointer Control** under **Motor** from the list in the right pane. Next, click the **Trackpad Options…** button. Enable dragging by moving the switch next to **Use trackpad for dragging** on. Select **With Drag Lock** from the pop-up menu next to **Dragging style**. Click **OK** to finish.

With drag lock enabled, double tap an item without lifting your finger off the trackpad after the second tap. Keep your finger on the trackpad to drag the item to its new location.

Tracking Speed

If you are using your trackpad for the first time, you may notice that the pointer moves rather slowly. You can adjust the pointer tracking speed to make it move more slowly or more quickly.

From the Trackpad settings, click the **Point & Click** button. Move the slider next to **Tracking speed** to adjust the pointer tracking speed. The default setting is medium. Move the slider to the left to make the pointer move more slowly and to the right to make it move more quickly. Changes take effect immediately, so you can try out your new tracking speed and adjust if necessary.

Double-Click Speed

To change the double-click speed, open the **Accessibility** settings in the System Settings app. Next, scroll down and click **Pointer Control** from the list under **Motor**. Use the slider next to **Double-click speed** to adjust the double click speed from turtle (slow) to rabbit (fast). Changes take effect immediately, so you can try out your double click speed setting and adjust if necessary.

Ignore the Built-in Trackpad

When using my Apple Magic Trackpad with my MacBook Pro, I find it annoying when I accidentally brush against the built-in trackpad, and the pointer flies off into left field. There is a simple solution for this annoyance – configure macOS to ignore the built-in trackpad when a Bluetooth trackpad or mouse is connected.

To ignore the built-in trackpad, open the System Settings app and click **Accessibility** in the sidebar. Scroll down and click **Pointer Control** from the list under **Motor**. Flip the switch next to **Ignore built-in trackpad when mouse or wireless trackpad is present** on.

Connect a New Bluetooth Trackpad

To connect a new Bluetooth trackpad, first turn it on and open the **Trackpad** settings in the System Settings app. Click the **Set Up Bluetooth Trackpad...** button at the lower right. The Bluetooth settings window will open. Your Mac will search for any new Bluetooth devices and discover them automatically.

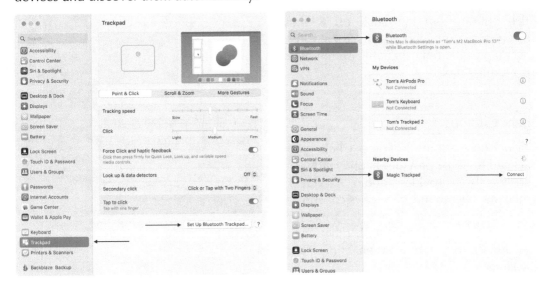

When your new trackpad is discovered, click the **Connect** button. If you don't see your trackpad, check to see that the Bluetooth switch at the top of the window is on. Once you have connected your new trackpad, you can close System Settings.

Force Touch

Force Touch is a pressure-sensitive multi-touch technology developed by Apple that first became available in its MacBook in 2015. A Force Touch trackpad has sensors underneath its multi-touch surface that can distinguish the amount of pressure being applied. This allows you to take advantage of additional functionality available in many app and in macOS. Apple's Magic Trackpad brings the same Force Touch technology in Apple laptops to the Mac desktops.

To perform a **Force Click**, press down on your trackpad's surface with more force and maintain that pressure for a moment before releasing. The trackpad's advanced sensors detect the increased pressure, identifying it as a Force Click gesture. You will receive haptic feedback, a subtle tactile response from the trackpad that simulates the sensation of pressing a physical button. Force Clicks trigger secondary functions or additional features based on the context in which they are used. For example, Force Clicking on a word might open a dictionary window with a definition.

If you don't want the Force Click feature, macOS allows you to option to disable it. Open Trackpad settings, click the **Point & Click** button, and flip the switch next to **Force Click and haptic feedback** off. Disabling Force Click removes the Force Click option from the **Look up & data detectors** gesture and reverts to a three-finger tap as the only available option other than turning it off.

Silent Clicking

When you perform a Force Click, your trackpad not only provides haptic feedback, but it also provides audio feedback, simulating the sound of a physical mouse button being pressed. If you don't like this sound or don't wish to disturb others, you can disable this feature by enabling **Silent Clicking**.

Open the Trackpad settings, click the **Point & Click** button, and flip the switch next to **Silent Clicking** on. Your trackpad will continue to provide haptic feedback but will do so silently.

Mouse Gestures

Apple's Magic Mouse supports only 6 gestures due to its limited multi-touch surface space. Gestures are also limited to one or two fingers for the same reason. For three- and four-finger gestures, you will have to create custom gestures, which I will show you how to do later in this chapter.

I suggest you turn on all mouse gestures and spend a few minutes learning what each does. After a little practice, you'll find the gestures will become completely natural, and you will no longer have to remember which gesture accomplishes what task.

To open the Mouse settings, launch the System Settings app and scroll to the bottom of the sidebar and click on **Mouse**. You'll notice two buttons towards the top of the window for each of the gesture categories – **Point & Click** and **More Gestures**. The currently selected button is highlighted. The gestures are listed below the slider for the tracking speed, which we'll cover later in this chapter.

Besides enabling and disabling gestures, Mouse settings lets you to customize some of the gestures. The Mouse settings also allow you to adjust the pointer tracking speed. If you are setting up a new Bluetooth mouse, you'll do that in the Mouse settings too.

Let's start with the three **Point & Click** gestures – **Look Up & Data Detectors**, **Secondary Click**, and **Smart Zoom**. Moving your pointer over each of the gestures changes the animation shown at the top of the Mouse settings window. The animation on the left demonstrates how to perform the gesture while the animation on the right shows you what the gesture does.

Natural Scrolling

If you are switching from a Windows PC to a Mac, natural scrolling may appear to be a little strange at first. On a Windows PC, you scroll up to move your content down and scroll down to move your content up. Natural scrolling is exactly the opposite – your content moves in the same direction as your fingers, tracking the direction of your fingers on the mouse. This is how scrolling works on an iPhone or iPad. If you have an iPhone or iPad, you have been scrolling naturally without even realizing it.

With natural scrolling, you move your fingers in the direction you want to move your content with your content tracking your finger movement. If you want to move your content up, scroll up with one finger. If you want to move your content down, scroll down.

macOS lets you disable natural scrolling by clicking by flipping the switch next to **Natural Scrolling**. When disabled, you'll scroll up to move your content down and scroll down to move your content up, like you would on a Windows PC.

Scrollbars only appear along the edges of a window when you are scrolling. This is the default setting in macOS, which of course, is customizable. I'll show you scrollbar customizations in a later chapter.

Secondary Click

A secondary click is used to reveal context-sensitive menus, like clicking the right mouse button on a Windows PC. macOS offers three options on an Apple Magic Mouse –

clicking on the right side, clicking on the left side, or disabling the gesture. The current selection has a checkmark next to it.

Make your selection from the pop-up menu next to **Secondary click**. If you select the off option, you will need to hold down the ⌘ (command) key while clicking to perform a secondary click. The other two options are to click on the right or left side of the mouse.

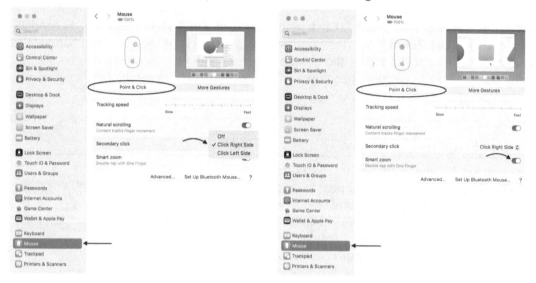

Smart Zoom

Smart Zoom is another feature that macOS borrows from the iPhone and iPad. When you want to zoom in, double tap your mouse with one finger. Double tap again to zoom out.

This feature is enabled by default and can disabled by clicking the **Scroll & Zoom** button and flipping the switch next to **Smart zoom** in the Mouse settings.

Swipe Between Pages

Swiping between pages is very much like thumbing through pages in a book. A common use for this gesture is to move forward and backward through webpages in Safari. There are four options available – scrolling left or right with one finger, swiping left or right with two fingers, or swiping left or right with either one or two fingers, along with an option to disable this gesture.

To configure swiping between pages, click the **More Gestures** button and select your option from the pop-up menu next to **Swipe between pages**. You can disable swiping between pages by selecting **Off** from the pop-up menu.

Note that if you configure swiping between pages with two fingers, macOS will disable swiping between full-screen apps since this gesture requires two fingers.

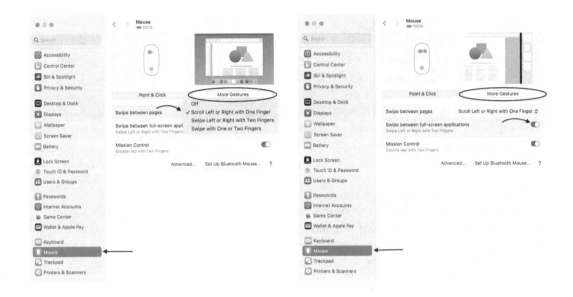

Swipe Between Full Screen Apps

Almost any application can be taken to full screen on your Mac. The macOS full screen feature expands the application window, hiding both the Menu Bar and the Dock, so that the window covers your entire desktop. This feature is great when you want to focus on the app you are working in while eliminating distractions that come with a desktop full of windows. To take a window to full screen, click on the green control button located in the upper left corner of the window's Title Bar.

You can also use the keyboard shortcut ^⌘F (control+command+F) to take an app to full screen.

The gesture to swipe between full screen apps, swiping left or right with two fingers, can be enabled and disabled by clicking the **More Gestures** button and using the switch next to **Swipe between full-screen applications**.

Note that if you enable swiping between full screen apps, the only valid options for swiping between pages are scrolling left or right with one finger or disabling the gesture.

Mission Control

Mission Control provides a view of every window running in each Space as well as applications in Full Screen or Split View. Using Mission Control, you can quickly jump to another Space, Full Screen app, or Split View app. Mission Control allows you to drag windows from one Space to another.

The mouse gesture for Mission Control is a double tap with two fingers, which is the only option other than disabling the gesture. Click the **More Gestures** button and use the switch next to **Mission Control**.

You can also access Mission Control using the keyboard shortcut **^up** (control+up arrow), or clicking the Mission Control icon in the Launchpad, Dock, Applications folder, or its icon in the Touch Bar if your MacBook Pro is equipped with one. Disabling the gesture for Mission Control in the Mouse settings has no effect on these other methods.

To close Mission Control, swipe down with the same number of fingers as the swipe up gesture, enter **^up** (control+up arrow), tap its icon on the Touch Bar, press the **esc** key, or click on any of the windows or Spaces displayed in the Spaces Bar at the top of Mission Control.

Tracking Speed

If you are using your Apple Magic Mouse for the first time, you may notice that the pointer moves rather slowly. You can adjust the pointer tracking speed to make it move more slowly or more quickly.

From the Mouse settings, click the **Point & Click** button. Move the slider next to **Tracking speed** to adjust the pointer tracking speed. The default setting is medium.

Move the slider to the left to make the pointer move more slowly and to the right to make it move more quickly. Changes take effect immediately, so you can try out your new tracking speed and adjust if necessary.

Double-Click Speed

To change the double-click speed, open the **Accessibility** settings in the System Settings app. Next, scroll down in the right pane and click on **Pointer Control**.

Use the slider next to **Double-click speed** in the right-hand pane to adjust the double click speed from turtle (slow) to rabbit (fast). Changes take effect immediately, so you can try out your double click speed setting on your mouse and adjust if necessary.

Ignore the Built-in Trackpad

When using my Apple Magic Mouse with my MacBook Pro, I find it annoying when I accidentally brush against the built-in trackpad, and the pointer flies off into left field. There is a simple solution for this annoyance – configure macOS to ignore the built-in trackpad when a Bluetooth trackpad or mouse is connected.

To ignore the built-in trackpad, open the System Settings app and click **Accessibility** in the sidebar. Scroll down and click on **Pointer Control** under **Motor** from the list in the right pane. Flip the switch next to **Ignore built-in trackpad when mouse or wireless trackpad is present** off.

Pointer Acceleration

Pointer acceleration is an ergonomic feature that tracks the speed you move your mouse. It boosts the speed at which your pointer moves across your desktop when you move your mouse quickly. Pointer acceleration allows your pointer to cover large physical distances, from one end of your desktop to the other, while allowing for precise movement when you move your mouse slowly. Pointer acceleration is enabled by default.

If you play games on your Mac, pointer acceleration can lead to inconsistent mouse speeds and impact your accuracy. If you move your mouse quickly, macOS will assume you want to move over a large distance, causing you to overshoot your target. You'll want to disable pointer acceleration when playing games.

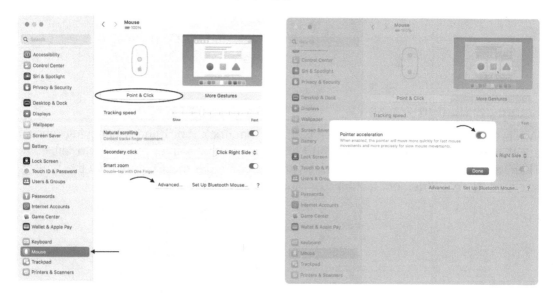

To disable pointer acceleration, open System Settings, select **Mouse** from the sidebar, and click the **Point & Click** button. Click the **Advanced...** button. In the next window, flip the switch next to **Pointer acceleration** on. Click the **Done** button to finish.

When you are no longer playing a game, you can flip the pointer acceleration switch on to take advantage of this macOS feature.

Connect a New Bluetooth Mouse

To connect a new Bluetooth mouse, first turn it on and open the **Mouse** settings in the System Settings app. Click the **Set Up Bluetooth Mouse...** button at the lower right. The **Bluetooth** settings window will open. Your Mac will search for any new Bluetooth devices and discover them automatically.

When your new mouse is discovered, click the **Connect** button. If you don't see your mouse, check to see that the Bluetooth switch at the top of the window is on. Once you connected your new mouse, you can close System Settings.

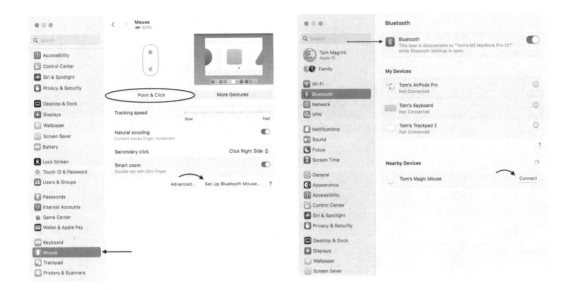

Custom Gestures

Now that you are familiar with the standard macOS gestures, let's learn how to create custom gestures. Creating gestures for common tasks helps you squeeze every drop of productivity from your trackpad or mouse and lets you truly personalize your Mac. While there are a few utilities that allow you to create custom gestures, my hands-down favorite is **BetterTouchTool**.

BetterTouchTool lets you assign actions to gestures using one, two, three, four, or five fingers combined with a tap, double-tap, tip-tap, swipe, or in combination with one or more modifier keys: ⇧ **fn** ⊕ ^ ⌥ ⌘ (shift, function/globe, control, option, and command). You can assign one of over 200 predefined actions, any keyboard shortcut, or a series of actions to your custom gestures.

BetterTouchTool is available for $10 for a standard license, which entitles you to two years of upgrades. A lifetime license costs $22. BetterTouchTool is offered with a a 45-day free trial. Download BetterTouchTool from https://folivora.ai/.

Privacy & Security Settings

The first time you open BetterTouchTool, macOS confirms that you want to open it since it is an app downloaded from the internet. This warning is an Apple security feature to ensure that you do not open an app that you may have accidentally or unintentionally downloaded from the internet. Any app that was not downloaded from the Mac App Store or is not from a certified Apple developer will trigger this warning.

After opening BetterToolTouch, it will ask you to authorize it in the **Accessibility** window in the **Privacy & Security** settings. Flip the switch next to **BetterTouchTool** on.

Configure Basic and User Interface Settings

Click the BetterTouchTool icon in your Menu Bar to reveal a pop-up menu and select **Configuration**. To access BetterTouchTool's preferences, click on the circled ellipsis in the upper-right corner of the BetterTouchTool configuration window, enter ⌘, (command+comma), or select **BetterTouchTool > Preferences**. Next, select **Basic** in the sidebar under **Standard Settings**.

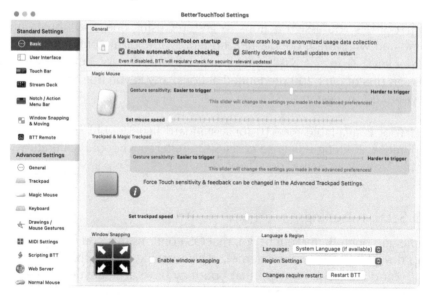

There are a few settings you should validate before creating your first custom gesture. Ensure the four checkboxes under **General** are checked. Doing so will ensure that BetterTouchTool runs each time you restart your Mac, updates are automatically downloaded and installed so you will always have the latest version, and crash logs and anonymized usage data collection helps to continually improve BetterTouchTool.

In the next two sections, you can adjust the sensitivity of your mouse and trackpad to make your gestures easier or harder to trigger. I have found that the default settings work fine for me. This window also allows you to enable window snapping; however, I recommend you consider another app, which I will introduce in the window snapping chapter.

Next, select **User Interface** in the left sidebar under **Standard Settings** and validate that the checkbox next to **Show Menubar Icon** is checked. The Menu Bar icon is a convenient way to quickly open the configuration window to create and make changes to your custom gestures, access documentation, or go to the Community Forum.

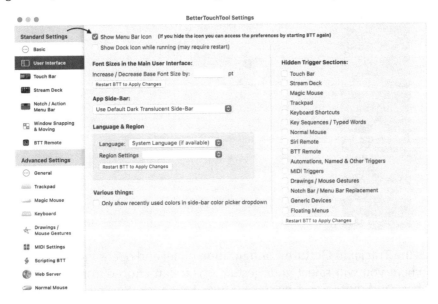

You can choose to not show the BetterTouchTool icon in your Menu Bar. You will have to launch BetterTouchTool each time you want to access the configuration window.

The BetterTouchTool icon does not appear in the Dock unless you have the Configuration window open. If you want the BetterTouchTool icon in your Dock, check the checkbox next to **Show Dock Icon while running**. You will have to restart your Mac for this change to take effect.

Custom Trackpad Gestures

Let's create your first custom trackpad gesture. Select **Trackpad** from the pop-up menu in the toolbar at the top of the BetterTouchTool configuration window. The sidebar contains the **App List**. Gestures can be created for a specific application or **All Apps**. A gesture created for a specific application will only work when that application is running. A gesture created for All Apps works in all applications.

By default, you will see 2 items listed in the App List, **All Apps**, and **Finder**. You can add other applications by clicking the **+** (add) button in the lower-left corner to select an app from your Applications folder or one that is currently running. You can also drag an application from your Applications folder into the App List.

In this example, let's create a custom gesture that will work in all applications. First, select **Trackpad** from the pop-up menu at the top of the BetterTouchTool configuration window. Next, click on **All Apps** in the sidebar. Then click the large blue **+** (add) button under **Add first Trackpad Gesture for All Apps**.

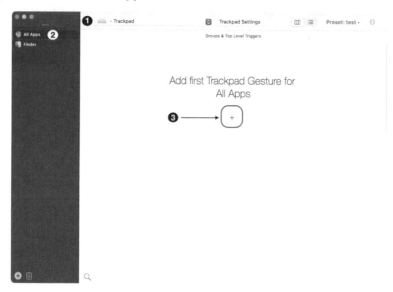

This reveals the **Trackpad Gesture Configuration** panel and opens the **Select Trigger** pop-up menu where you will select your gesture. You can choose from one-, two-, three-, four-, and five- and more finger gestures, Force Touch, or your own unique gesture. In this example, let's select the **Two-finger TipTap Left (1 Finger Fix)** as our trigger. To see the two-finger gestures, you'll have to scroll down through the one-finger gestures list and expand the two-finger gestures list.

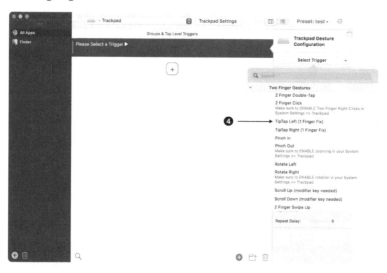

A tip-tap gesture is performed by placing the number of fingers selected, in this case two, on the trackpad and tapping with one finger, in this case the left finger, while the other finger remains on the trackpad. Conversely, to perform a two-finger tip-tap right gesture, you would place two fingers on the trackpad and tap with the right finger while the left finger remains on the trackpad.

Next, click the large blue + (add) button under **Assign First Action to Selected Trigger** to reveal the **Action Configuration Panel**. Open the pop-up menu under **Select a predefined action or keyboard shortcut** to select the action you want your gesture to perform.

In this example, the action we'll choose is to empty the trash. Enter "empty" into the search box to avoid browsing through the huge list of actions BetterTouchTool supports. If we browsed through BetterTouchTool's extensive list of available actions, we would have found empty trash under **System Actions**.

Actions available in the Action Configuration panel are grouped and categorized based on what they do. You can choose to have your gesture perform a keyboard shortcut or choose an action from 20 categories. Now try out your new custom gesture to empty the trash. Repeat the same steps to create more gestures.

Custom Mouse Gestures

Let's create our first custom mouse gesture. Select **Magic Mouse** from the pop-up menu in the toolbar at the top of the BetterTouchTool configuration window. The sidebar contains the **App List**. Gestures can be created for a specific application or **All Apps**. A gesture created for a specific application will only work when that application is running. A gesture created for **All Apps** works in all applications.

By default, you will see 2 items listed in the App List, **All Apps**, and **Finder**. You can add other applications by clicking the + (add) button in the lower-left corner to select an app from your Applications folder or one that is currently running. You can also drag an application from your Applications folder into the App List.

In this example, we'll create a custom gesture that will work in all applications. First, select **Magic Mouse** from the pop-up menu at the top of the BetterTouchTool configuration window. Next, click on **All Apps** in the sidebar. Then click the large blue + (add) button under **Add first Magic Mouse Gesture for All Apps**.

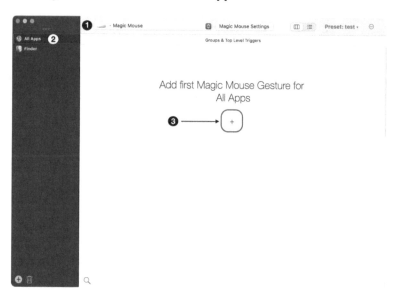

This reveals the **Magic Mouse Gesture Configuration** panel and opens the **Select Trigger** pop-up menu where you will select your gesture. You can choose from one-, two-, three, and four-finger gestures. In this example, let's select the **3 Finger Swipe Up** as our trigger. To see the three-finger gestures, scroll down through the gestures list and expand the three-finger gestures list.

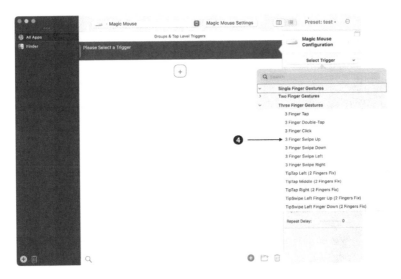

Next, click the large blue **+** (add) button under **Assign First Action to Selected Trigger** to reveal the **Action Configuration Panel**.

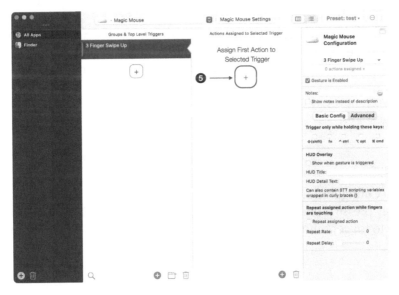

The pop-up menu under **Select a predefined action or keyboard shortcut** is where you will select the action you want your gesture to perform. In this example, the action we'll choose is to launch Mission Control. Enter "mission" into the search box to avoid browsing through the huge list of actions BetterTouchTool supports. Had we browsed through BetterTouchTool's extensive list of available actions, we would have found Mission Control under **macOS Functionality**.

You may recall that earlier in the chapter, we enabled a standard mouse gesture for Mission Control, double tapping the mouse with two fingers. I chose to configure a custom gesture to invoke Mission Control for two reasons. First, I wanted a mouse gesture that mimicked the trackpad gesture, a three-finger swipe up. Secondly, I wanted to demonstrate that you can create a custom gesture even if the action already has a pre-defined standard macOS gesture. We can now disable Mission Control in the Mouse settings and select another action for the two-finger double-tap in BetterTouchTool.

Now try out your new custom gesture to open Mission Control. Repeat the same steps to create more gestures.

Modifier Keys

The **Gesture Configuration** panel lets you configure an action to trigger only while simultaneously pressing one or more modifier keys. Using modifier keys, you can use the same gesture to trigger different actions depending on the key(s) you are holding.

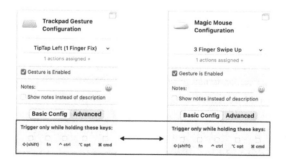

Check the checkbox above the ⇧ **fn** ⊕ ^ ⌥ ⌘ (shift, function/globe, control, option, and command) keys to select one or more modifier keys. Once you have configured one or more modifier keys, the keys will appear next to your gesture under Groups & Top Level Triggers.

Trigger Location

By default, any gesture you create will trigger regardless of where your pointer is located on your desktop. BetterTouchTool allows you to configure a gesture to only trigger when your pointer is over your Dock or Menu Bar or not over either your Dock or Menu Bar. This allows you to use the same gesture to trigger different actions depending on the where your pointer is located.

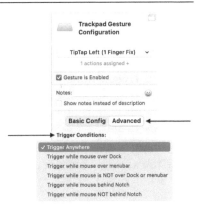

Click the **Advanced** button in the Gesture Configuration panel and choose from the **Trigger Conditions** options in the pop-up menu.

Multiple Action Gestures

BetterTouchTool doesn't limit your gestures to a single action. You can configure a gesture that will execute multiple actions. To create a multiple action gesture, we will repeatedly click the + (add) button in the **Actions Assigned to Selected Trigger** column for each additional action we want to add.

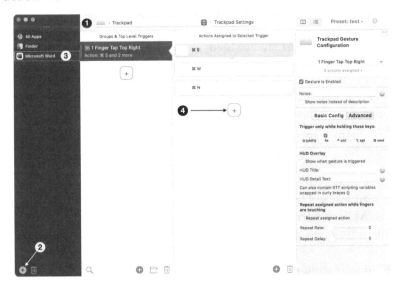

Let's create an application-specific trackpad gesture for Microsoft Word. First, select **Trackpad** from the pop-up menu at the top of the configuration window. Next, click the + (add) button at the bottom of the application sidebar. This gives us a choice of selecting an application using Finder or choosing a running application. Let's choose Microsoft Word from the list of running apps.

Click Microsoft Word in the application sidebar and create a 1-Finger Tap Top Right gesture on the trackpad combined with the **fn** ⊕ (function/globe) key. Next, enter the keyboard shortcut ⌘S (command+S), which saves your currently active document.

To add additional actions, click the large **+** (add) button in the **Actions Assigned to Selected Trigger** panel located under the ⌘S (command+S) action we just added. Next, add the keyboard shortcut ⌘W (command+W) to close your Word document. Then click the **+** (add) button again to add ⌘N (command+N), which opens open a new Word document. Now when I tap the top right corner of my trackpad while pressing the **fn** ⊕ (function/globe) key, BetterTouchTool will send three keyboard shortcuts to save and close my active Word document and open a new document.

Modify a Custom Gesture

To modify an existing gesture, first select the app from the App List and then click on the gesture in the **Groups & Top Level Triggers** panel. Next, click on the action in the **Actions Assigned to Selected Trigger** panel and select your desired action from the pop-up menu.

Disable or Delete a Gesture

BetterTouchTool lets you disable a gesture without deleting it. To disable a gesture, click on the gesture and uncheck the checkbox next to **Gesture is Enabled** in the **Gesture Configuration Panel.**

If you want to delete a gesture, BetterTouchTool offers three deletion options. You can delete the action associated with a gesture, delete the gesture, or delete an application and all its custom gestures.

To delete an action associated with a gesture, highlight the gesture in the **Groups & Top Level Triggers** panel, can on the action in the **Actions Assigned to Selected Trigger** panel, and click on the trash can icon at the bottom of the panel.

To delete a gesture, highlight the gesture in the **Groups & Top Level Triggers** panel and click the trash can icon at the bottom of the panel.

If you want to delete an application and all its gestures, highlight the application in the Applications sidebar and click the trash can icon at the bottom of the sidebar. Note that BetterTouchTool will not let you delete **All Apps** and **Finder** from the App List.

Import and Export Gestures

If you want to share gestures with your friends or create a backup of your gestures, you can export your gestures to a file.

Click **Preset** in the upper-right corner of the BetterTouchTool configuration window to reveal the Preset configuration window.

Select from the list of Preset names and click **Export Highlighted**. Select **Only Tiggers** or **Triggers & Settings** from the save dialog window. Name your file, choose the save location, and press **Save**.

To import a gesture file, click **Preset** and then click **Import** from the configuration sheet. Browse to the gesture file, select it, and click **Open**.

Finding a Lost Pointer

Have you ever lost the pointer? Sometimes finding the pointer is difficult, particularly when it blends into the desktop background. Most people either shake the mouse or move a finger back and forth on their trackpad, hoping they will see the pointer as it moves. Apple added a neat little feature that takes advantage of this behavior by making the pointer grow larger as you shake your mouse or move your finger back and forth on the trackpad.

To enable shake to locate, open the System Settings app, click on **Accessibility** in the sidebar and then click on **Display** in the right pane. Scroll down to display the **Pointer** options. Flip the switch next to **Shake mouse pointer to locate** on.

Now if you lose your pointer, move your finger rapidly back and forth on your trackpad or shake your mouse to find your pointer.

Pointer Size

While you can use the shake mouse pointer to locate feature to find a lost pointer, maybe the default macOS pointer is a little bit too small for you, especially if you're using a large monitor. If this is the case, you can change the pointer size to make it easier to locate.

To change your pointer size, open System Settings, click on **Accessibility** in the sidebar and then click on **Display**. Scroll down slightly to display the **Pointer** options. Use the slider next to **Pointer size** until your pointer is at your desired size.

Note that changing the pointer size also changes the cursor size in word processing applications and the crosshairs used to take screenshots.

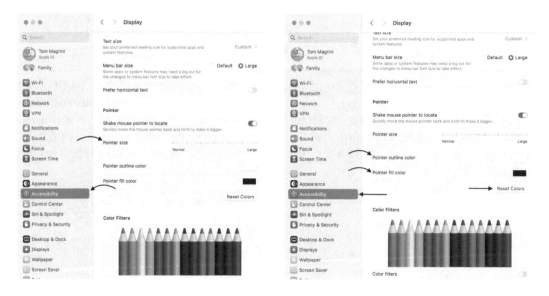

Pointer Color

If you do not like the default black pointer, you can change its fill and outline colors. To change the color of your pointer, open System Settings, click on **Accessibility** in the sidebar and then click on **Display**. Scroll down slightly to display the **Pointer** options.

The default fill color is black, and the default outline color is white. To change the fill or outline color, click the colored rectangle next to one you want to change to open a color picker window where you can select your desired color. Click the icons at the top of the window to change the type of color picker window from a wheel, sliders, spectrum, Apple colors, and colored pencils.

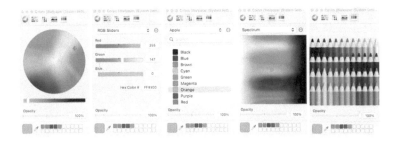

To return to the macOS default of a black pointer with a white outline, open System Settings, click on **Accessibility** in the sidebar and then click on **Display**. Scroll down slightly to display the **Pointer** options. Click the **Reset Colors** button.

3

Keyboard

I know what you are thinking. "Everyone knows how to use a keyboard." While I'll cover various keyboard shortcuts throughout this book, I'll show you how to create custom keyboard shortcuts in this chapter. You can use keyboard shortcuts to speed up everyday tasks, to open applications, and execute commands within applications. If you are looking for a productivity boost, keyboard shortcuts let you do most things faster with a few keystrokes.

Remap the Modifier Keys

macOS allows you to change the action performed by the modifier keys: ⌃ ⌘ ⌥ fn 🌐 (control, command, option, and function/globe). Why would you want to change the behavior of the modifier keys? You may want to remap the modifier keys if you are more familiar with a keyboard layout different from the one on your Mac, like a Windows PC. For example, the control key on a Windows PC keyboard is located where the function/globe key is on a Mac keyboard.

To change the mapping of the modifier keys, open System Settings, scroll down, and select **Keyboard** in the sidebar. Click the **Keyboard Shortcuts...** button to reveal a configuration sheet. Click **Modifier Keys** in the configuration sheet's sidebar. If you have multiple keyboards, select your keyboard from the pop-up menu at the top of the configuration sheet. Choose your desired key mapping from the pop-up menu next to each of the modifier keys. Click **Done** when finished.

If you want to restore the modifier key mapping to the macOS default, open System Settings, scroll down, and select **Keyboard** in the sidebar. Click the **Keyboard Shortcuts...** button to reveal a configuration sheet. Click **Modifier Keys** in the configuration sheet's sidebar. Select your keyboard from the pop-up menu at the top of the configuration sheet if you have multiple keyboards. Next, click the **Restore Defaults** button. Click **Done** when finished.

Caps Lock

Why should you disable the caps lock? Because things like thiS HAPPEN WHEN YOU ACCIDENTALLY HIT THE CAPS LOCK BEFORE REALIZING YOUR MISTAKE. Doh! If caps lock is driving you nuts, macOS lets you disable it.

To disable the caps lock key, open System Settings, scroll down, and select **Keyboard** in the sidebar. Click the **Keyboard Shortcuts…** button to reveal a configuration sheet. Click **Modifier Keys** in the configuration sheet's sidebar. If you have multiple keyboards, select your keyboard from the pop-up menu at the top of the configuration sheet. Choose **No Action** from the pop-up list next to **Caps Lock (⇪) key**. Click **Done** when finished.

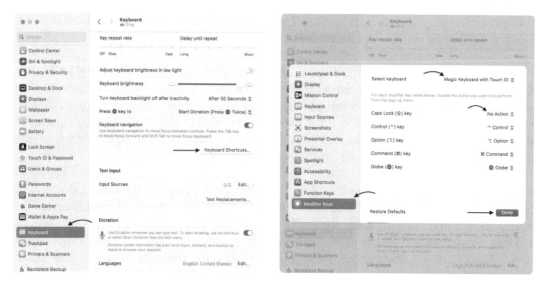

You also have the option to remap the Caps Lock to perform a different action, remapping it as a ⌃ ⌥ ⌘ ⊕ ⎋ (control, option, command, globe, or escape) key.

If you want to enable the caps lock key later, select **Caps Lock** from the pop-up list or click the **Restore Defaults** button. Click **Done** when finished.

A new feature in macOS Sonoma notifies you when caps lock is on by placing a caps lock icon below the text cursor.

Keyboard Brightness

One of the great features of Apple's laptops is keyboard backlighting is standard on all models. Anyone who has fumbled around in dim light on a cheap Windows PC keyboard knows the value of keyboard backlighting. Keyboard backlighting is on by default.

Your Apple laptop automatically adjusts your keyboard brightness in low light. You can disable this feature and manually adjust the brightness level of your keyboard backlighting, if desired.

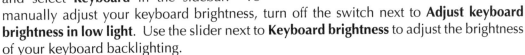

Open the System Settings app, scroll down, and select **Keyboard** in the sidebar. To manually adjust your keyboard brightness, turn off the switch next to **Adjust keyboard brightness in low light**. Use the slider next to **Keyboard brightness** to adjust the brightness of your keyboard backlighting.

If you want to dim your keyboard lighting when your MacBook has been idle for a while, select 5, 10, 30 seconds, or 1 or 5 minutes, or Never from the pop-up menu next to **Turn keyboard backlight off after inactivity**. Dimming the keyboard backlight when your MacBook is idle helps save power when running on battery.

If you have a MacBook Pro with a Touch Bar, you can control the keyboard brightness using the control on the Expanded Control Strip. If you hold down the ⇧⌥ (shift+option) keys while adjusting the keyboard backlight on the Touch Bar, the brightness will increase or decrease in quarter-segment increments. This trick also works when adjusting the display brightness and sound volume. See the chapter on the Touch Bar for information on how to customize your Touch Bar.

Function Keys

When you press an **F** (function) key, it executes the command associated with it (i.e., Mission Control, Launchpad, Play/Pause, Volume Up, Volume Down, Mute, etc.). On a Mac, you need to hold down the **fn** ⊕ (function/globe) key to use an **F** key as a standard **F** key, which is the opposite of how a Windows PC keyboard works. If you'd like the **F** keys to work as they do on a PC, macOS allows you to configure the **F** keys so that they act as standard function keys.

To make the **F** keys perform like function keys, open the System Settings app, scroll down, and select **Keyboard** in the sidebar. Click the **Keyboard Shortcuts...** button to reveal a configuration sheet. Click **Function Keys** in the configuration sheet's sidebar. Next, flip the switch next to **Use F1, F2, etc. keys as standard function keys** on. Click **Done** when finished.

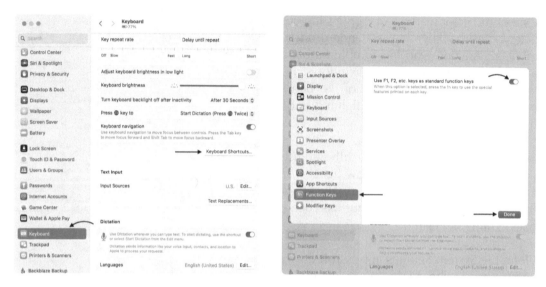

How do you increase the volume and use the other functions after making this change? Hold down the **fn** 🌐 (function/globe) key while pressing an **F** key.

If you have a MacBook Pro with a Touch Bar, you have the option of making the **F** keys appear in the Touch Bar when running certain apps.

If you have a MacBook Pro with a Touch Bar, you can configure the F keys to perform like function keys when running a specific application. Open System Settings, scroll down, and select **Keyboard** in the sidebar. Click the **Keyboard Shortcuts...** button to reveal a configuration sheet. Click the **+** (add) button, which will open your Applications folder. Select the application and click the **Open** button. Repeat to add another application. To remove apps, click the **–** (delete) button. Click **Done** to finish.

Keyboard and Character Viewer

The Keyboard Viewer comes in handy when looking for a special character like the cents symbol, ¢, which can be found at ⌥4 (option+4). The Keyboard Viewer shows you where characters for other languages, symbols, and special characters are located on your keyboard.

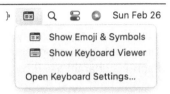

The Character Viewer is useful when you are looking for that perfect emoji that captures exactly how you feel. It shows you a vast selection of emoji and symbols, including math and currency symbols, flags, bullets and stars, arrows, letter symbols, parentheses, pictographs, and punctuation.

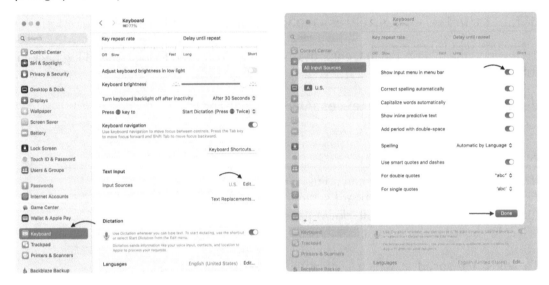

You can add a pop-up menu in the Menu Bar for quick access to the Keyboard and the Character Viewers. Open System Settings, scroll down, and select **Keyboard** in the sidebar. Click the **Edit...** button to reveal a configuration sheet. Flip the switch next to **Show input menu in menu bar** on. Click **Done** when finished.

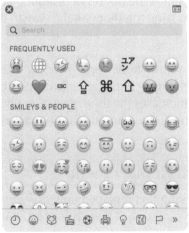

Key Repeat

By default, holding down a key in macOS does not activate key repeat as you might expect. Instead, a contextual menu appears, which allows you to insert diacritic characters (i.e., accented, and other non-English characters). To select a diacritic character, press the number under the character.

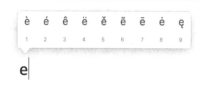

If you don't have a need for diacritic characters, you can enable key repeat, by launching Terminal and entering the following command. You will need to log out and log back in for this change to take effect.

```
defaults write -g ApplePressAndHoldEnabled -bool false
```

To revert to the macOS default, enter the following. You need to log out and log back in for the change to take effect.

```
defaults delete -g ApplePressAndHoldEnabled
```

Key Repeat Rate and Delay

If you enable key repeat, you can adjust the repeat rate and delay in Keyboard settings. Open System Settings, scroll down, and select **Keyboard** in the sidebar.

To adjust the speed at which a character repeats while holding its key down, adjust the slider under **Key repeat rate**. Moving the slider to the right increases the rate at which a character will be repeated while you hold down the corresponding key. This slider also offers the option of disabling key repeat by moving the slider all the way to the left to off.

To adjust how long macOS waits until repeating a character, adjust the slider under **Delay until repeat**. Moving the slider to the left increases the time macOS waits before repeating a character while moving to the right shortens the amount of time macOS waits.

Text Replacement

Creating text replacements saves you keystrokes, allowing you to enter a word or phrase by typing only a few characters. When you enter a text shortcut, macOS replaces it with the associated phrase listed in the Keyboard settings. macOS comes preconfigured with approximately a dozen text replacements such as "(c)" for © for copyright, common fractions, such as ¼ ½ ¾, and "omw" for "On my way!"

You can create your own text replacements, which will let you type a shortcut for longer phrases you commonly use. Some ideas include your email address or phone number, or short messages you frequently send through Apple's Messages app.

To create a text replacement, open the System Settings application, scroll down, and select **Keyboard** in the sidebar. Next, click the **Text Replacements...** button to reveal a configuration sheet. Click the **+** (add) button in the bottom left corner, which will open another configuration sheet where you can create your new text replacement. Enter your shortcut in the **Replace** field and the replacement phrase in the **With** field.

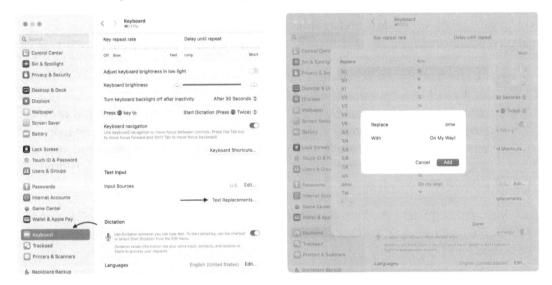

To remove a text replacement, open the System Settings application, scroll down, and select **Keyboard** in the sidebar. Click the **Text Replacements...** button to reveal a configuration sheet. Click the **–** (delete) button in the bottom left corner.

Text replacement will work across your Apple devices with iCloud, keeping your replacements up to date across all your devices.

Dictation

Dictation is an extremely useful feature that lets you quickly turn your thoughts into text. You can dictate in any application anywhere text can be entered. Essentially, if you can type it, you can dictate it. For macOS Sonoma, Apple added a new feature that allows simultaneous use of the keyboard and dictation. This feature allows you to seamlessly switch between typing and dictation. Start typing, hit the dictation keyboard shortcut, and finish your thought by dictating it. Similarly, you can switch from dictation to typing. In previous macOS releases, dictation would end the moment you began typing.

To turn Dictation on, open System Settings, scroll down, and select **Keyboard** in the sidebar. **Dictation** is at the bottom of the Keyboard settings, so you'll need to scroll down to see the available configuration options. Flip the **Dictation** switch on to enable dictation. If you need to change the language, click the **Edit...** button. Choose your microphone source from the pop-up menu next to **Microphone source**. Automatic punctuation is on by default and will insert commas, periods, and question marks as you dictate.

The default shortcut to start Dictation is the **F5** key. On older Macs, you would need to press the **fn** ⊕ (function/globe) key twice. The pop-up menu next to **Shortcut** provides additional options, including pressing the **F5** (microphone) key, ^ (control) key twice, ⊕ (globe) key twice, the right or left ⌘ (command) key twice, or either ⌘ (command) key twice. You also have the option to create your own shortcut by choosing **Customize...** from the pop-up menu.

Your Mac will beep, and the Dictation icon will appear to let you know macOS is ready to listen after you enter the shortcut. Enter the dictation shortcut again when you are finished dictating.

Screenshots

macOS has powerful, built-in screenshot and screen recording functions, so there is no need to purchase a separate app. You can take a screenshot of your entire desktop, an area of your desktop, a window, or your Touch Bar using a keyboard shortcut. Similarly, you can record a video of your entire desktop or a portion of your desktop.

To take a screenshot of your desktop, enter ⇧⌘3 (shift+command+3).

To capture a specific area of your desktop or a window, enter ⇧⌘4 (shift+command+4) to bring up a set of crosshairs. Drag the crosshairs across the desired area and release your hold when done.

To take a screenshot of a window, press ⇧⌘4, move the crosshairs over the window you want to take a screenshot of, press the **spacebar** to change the crosshairs to a camera, and click or tap your mouse or trackpad. Your Mac will take a screenshot of the entire window.

The Screenshot Utility is activated using the keyboard shortcut ⇧⌘5 (shift+command+5). It offers quick access to take a screenshot, record your screen, and several configuration options, including the save location and a timer.

The Screenshot Utility tools are separated into screenshot tools, screen recording tools, and options with a vertical separator between each group. The tools are, from left to right, Capture an Entire Screen, Capture Selected Window, Capture Selected Portion, Record Entire Screen,

Record Selected Portion, and Options. Once you have selected your choice, a **Capture** button appears at the Screenshot Utility's right end next to **Options**. To close the Screenshot Utility, click the **X** (close) button.

Options allow you to change your save location and set a timer for 5 or 10 seconds. Other options include Show Floating Thumbnail, Remember Last Selection, and Show Mouse Pointer.

If you own a MacBook Pro with a Touch Bar, you can take a screenshot of the Touch Bar using the keyboard shortcut ⇧⌘6 (shift+command+6).

The floating thumbnail appears in the lower lower-right-hand of your desktop after you take a screenshot. Swiping to the right on the floating thumbnail immediately saves your screenshot to your Desktop folder. You can also do nothing, and your screenshot will be saved to your Desktop folder. Clicking on the floating thumbnail opens your screenshot in the Markup app. Screen recordings open in QuickTime. You can also drag the floating thumbnail into a folder in Finder or the Mail, Messages, Preview, or Photos apps.

Secondary clicking on the floating thumbnail reveals a contextual menu with save and application options. You can choose to close or delete the screenshot or open the Markup app. You can also save the screenshot to the Desktop, Documents folder, or Clipboard, or open it in Mail, Messages, Preview or Photos. Screen recordings replace the Preview option with QuickTime.

In releases before macOS Mojave, screenshots were automatically saved to the Desktop folder without the Floating Thumbnail. If you prefer that behavior, you can disable the Floating Thumbnail feature by opening the Screenshot Utility by using the keyboard shortcut ⇧⌘5 (shift+command+5). Click **Options** to reveal a contextual menu. Select **Show Floating Thumbnail** to remove the checkmark. Screenshots will now be saved immediately to your Desktop folder or to your Documents folder or Clipboard, both of which can be selected from the **Options** menu.

You can also disable the Floating Thumbnail by entering the following command in Terminal.

```
defaults write com.apple.screencapture show-thumbnail -bool false
```

Enter the following command in Terminal to restore the Floating Thumbnail.

```
defaults write com.apple.screencapture show-thumbnail -bool true
```

Screenshot Keyboard Shortcuts

The predefined keyboard shortcuts for screenshots are listed below. Note that ⇧⌘6 (shift+command+6) and ^⇧⌘6 (control+shift+command+6) only work if you have a MacBook Pro with a Touch Bar.

⇧⌘3	Takes a screenshot of the desktop and saves it to the Desktop or another designated folder.
^⇧⌘3	Takes a screenshot of the desktop and saves it to the Clipboard.
⇧⌘4	Takes a screenshot of a user-defined area and saves it to the Desktop or another designated folder.
^⇧⌘4	Takes a screenshot of a user-defined area and saves it to the Clipboard.
⇧⌘4 + space	Takes a screenshot of a window and saves it to the Desktop or another designated folder.
^⇧⌘4 + space	Takes a screenshot of a window and saves it to the Clipboard.
⇧⌘5	Launches the Screenshot Utility
⇧⌘6	Takes a screenshot of the Touch Bar and saves it to the Desktop or another designated folder.
^⇧⌘6	Takes a screenshot of the Touch Bar and saves it to the Clipboard.

If you want to change the default keyboard shortcuts, you can redefine them in the **Keyboard** settings. You can also disable them if you do not need to take screenshots and want to use the keyboard shortcuts to perform other actions.

To disable or change the keyboard shortcuts for screenshots, open the System Settings app, scroll down, and select **Keyboard** in the sidebar. Click the **Keyboard Shortcuts...** button to reveal a configuration sheet. Select **Screenshots** from the sidebar. Uncheck the checkboxes next to the shortcuts you want to disable.

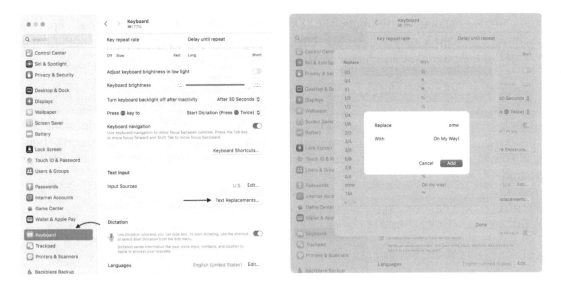

To change a shortcut, double-click on the key combination in the right column next to the shortcut you want to change and enter the new key combination in the field. Click **Done** when finished.

Clicking the **Restore Defaults** button will restore the default keyboard shortcuts.

Save to the Clipboard

Saving screenshots to a file is handy if you need to annotate the screenshot. However, sometimes you need to copy the screenshot directly into a document. In that case, it is much easier to save a screenshot directly to the Clipboard. Add the ^ (control) key to the screenshot keyboard shortcut, and macOS saves your screenshot to the Clipboard. You can then paste the screenshot into your document by selecting **Edit > Paste** or by using the keyboard shortcut ⌘V (command+V).

Destination Folder

By default, macOS saves screenshots to your Desktop folder. If you take a lot of screenshots, your Desktop can quickly fill up with clutter. macOS lets you change the default destination folder to something other than your Desktop folder.

To change the destination folder for screenshots and screen recordings, open the Screenshot Utility using the keyboard shortcut ⇧⌘5 (shift+command+5). Click **Options** at the end of the Screenshot Utility to reveal a contextual menu. Click your desired destination folder or application – Desktop, Documents, Clipboard, Mail, Messages, and Preview – from the contextual menu. If you want to save to a different folder, click **Other Location...** and navigate to your desired folder. You also have the option of creating a new folder by clicking the **New Folder** button. Click the **Choose** button once you have selected your desired destination folder.

You can also change the destination folder for your screenshots using Terminal. For this example, I created a folder called **Screenshots** in my **Documents** folder. The path I need to enter in the command to change the destination folder is:

`~/Documents/Screenshots/`

Launch Terminal and enter the following commands. Note that the first two lines are one command. Do not press the **return** key until you have entered the entire command. There is a space after location. Replace **~/Documents/Screenshots/** with the path to your desired folder.

```
defaults write com.apple.screencapture location
~/Documents/Screenshots/
```

```
killall SystemUIServer
```

Enter the following commands in Terminal to revert to the macOS default of saving screenshots to the Desktop folder.

```
defaults delete com.apple.screencapture location
```

```
killall SystemUIServer
```

Shadows

macOS inserts a gray shadow around an image captured by a screenshot. If you want to remove the shadow, launch Terminal, and enter the following commands.

```
defaults write com.apple.screencapture disable-shadow -bool true
```

To revert to the macOS default, enter the following commands in Terminal.

```
defaults write com.apple.screencapture disable-shadow -bool false
```

Timestamp

When you take a screenshot, macOS automatically adds the date and time the screenshot was taken to the filename. If you prefer to not have the timestamp included in the filename, open Terminal and enter the following commands.

```
defaults write com.apple.screencapture include-date -bool false
```

To revert to the macOS default, enter the following commands in Terminal.

```
defaults delete com.apple.screencapture include-date
```

Timer

The Screen Utility allows you to set a timer for screenshots. Open the Screenshot Utility using the keyboard shortcut ⇧⌘5 (shift+command+5). Click **Options** at the end of the Screenshot Utility to reveal a contextual menu. Select either 5 seconds or 10 seconds for your timer. Once you have set a timer, a capture button appears at the end of the Screenshot Utility with the timer you set. When you click the **Capture** button, the timer counts down until the screenshot is taken.

If you want to cancel the screenshot before the timer expires, move your pointer over the countdown timer and click **Cancel**. To remove the timer, open the Screenshot Utility, click **Options**, and select None under **Timer**.

Pointer

If you want the pointer to appear in your screenshot, open the Screenshot Utility using the keyboard shortcut ⇧⌘5 (shift+command+5). Click **Options** at the end of the Screenshot Utility to reveal a contextual menu. Click **Show Mouse Pointer**.

File Format

macOS saves screenshots in Portable Network Graphics (PNG) format, an open, extensible image format supporting lossless data compression. PNG was created as an improved, non-patented replacement for Graphic Interchange Format (GIF). macOS supports the ability to save screenshots in other formats.

If you prefer to save your screenshots in jpg format, launch Terminal and enter the following commands.

```
defaults write com.apple.screencapture type jpg
```

```
killall SystemUIServer
```

macOS also supports pdf, psd, gif, tga, tiff, and bmp formats.

To save screenshots in another file format, replace **jpg** in the above command with your desired format.

To revert to the macOS default, enter the following commands in Terminal.

```
defaults write com.apple.screencapture type png
```

```
killall SystemUIServer
```

Connect a New Keyboard

To connect a new Bluetooth keyboard, turn it on and open the System Settings application, scroll down, and select **Keyboard** in the sidebar. Click the **Set Up Keyboard...** button found at the bottom of the Keyboard settings window. The **Bluetooth** settings window will open, and your Mac will search for new Bluetooth devices and automatically discover them.

When your new keyboard is discovered, click the **Connect** button. If you don't see your keyboard, check to see that the Bluetooth switch at the top of the window is on position. Verify that you switched your new Bluetooth keyboard on, and that the battery is fully charged. Once you have connected your new keyboard, you can close System Settings.

Keyboard Shortcuts

Veteran Mac users know that keyboard shortcuts are a huge productivity booster, allowing you to perform routine and repetitive tasks more quickly and efficiently. Keyboard shortcuts are an alternative to executing a command through a pop-up menu using your mouse or trackpad. Keyboard shortcuts let you keep your fingers on your keyboard, reducing the number of times you must remove them you use your trackpad or mouse. If you learn and practice macOS Sonoma's keyboard shortcuts, soon muscle memory will take over and you'll start using keyboard shortcuts without any conscious effort.

You can use macOS keyboard shortcuts to quickly issue a command, open an app, or have macOS perform other tasks. For example, you can quit an application using the keyboard shortcut ⌘Q (command+Q) or close a window without quitting the active app using ⌘W (command+W). Keyboard shortcuts are much faster than using your mouse or trackpad to select **Quit** or **Close** from the Application Menu.

There are tons of keyboard shortcuts in macOS, and it is hard to remember them all. In the table below, I've listed what I feel are some of the essential keyboard shortcuts that every Mac user should know.

⌘N	Creates a new window or document
⌘O	Opens a file or document
⌘T	Creates a new tab in an existing window
⌘A	Selects all items
⌘F	Search
⌘G	Find the next occurrence of the searched item
⇧⌘G	Find the previous occurrence of the search item
⇧⌘N	Creates a new folder in Finder
⌘X	Cuts the highlighted item(s) and copies them to the clipboard
⌘C	Copies the highlighted item(s) to the clipboard
⌘V	Pastes the contents of the clipboard
⌘Z	Undo the previous command
⇧⌘Z	Repeat the previous command (undo's the undo)
⌘H	Hide the active app
⌥⌘H	Hide all apps except the active app
⌥⌘D	Hide or show the Dock
⌘W	Close the active window
⌘Q	Quit the active app
⌘P	Print
⌥⌘⏏	Opens the Force Quit window
⌘space	Opens and closes Spotlight
⌥⌘space	Search Finder for a file
^⌘F	Take the active window to full screen
🌐F	Toggle full screen mode on and off
⌘tab	Opens the application switcher
⌘,	Open the settings or preferences for the active app
⇧⌘P	Show or hide the preview pane in Finder
⌘S	Save a document or file
⇧⌘S	Save (a document or file) As
⌘M	Minimize a window into the Dock
^up	Launch Mission Control
^down	Launch App Exposé
^⌘Q	Lock screen
⇧⌘Q	Log Out
⇧⌘?	Open the Help Menu
⌘[	Navigate forward
⌘]	Navigate backward
⌘+	Zoom In
⌘−	Zoom out
⇧⌘delete	Empty the Trash

Custom Keyboard Shortcuts

I'm sure you noticed some pop-up menu items you frequently use in various applications do not have a keyboard shortcut. If you find yourself using a command that does not have a keyboard shortcut, macOS has a feature that allows you to create a custom keyboard shortcut.

Let's walk through the creation of a custom keyboard shortcut for a specific application. First, open the System Settings app, scroll down, and select **Keyboard** in the sidebar. Click the **Keyboard Shortcuts...** button to reveal a configuration sheet. Select **App Shortcuts** from the sidebar.

To create a new keyboard shortcut, click the **+** (add) button to reveal a configuration sheet. To create a keyboard shortcut that works in all applications, choose **All Applications** from the pop-up menu next to **Application**. This type of keyboard shortcut works in any application that has the menu item as an option.

If you want to create a keyboard shortcut for a specific application, select the application from the pop-up menu next to **Application**. In this example, we will create a keyboard shortcut for **Preview**, one of the apps included with macOS.

Enter the **Menu Title** exactly as it appears in the menu from the app. I am creating a keyboard shortcut for the command to **Adjust Size...** located in the **Tools** pop-up menu of the Preview app.

Adjust Size...

You may have to enter the complete menu hierarchy for your keyboard shortcut to work properly. I've found this to be hit or miss. Sometimes I do not need to enter the full menu hierarchy, other times I must for the shortcut to work.

Tools—>Adjust Size...

Note the **->** (hyphen+greater than sign) between the top menu item, **Tools**, and the submenu item, **Adjust Size...**. Do not enter any spaces between the menu and submenu items. If the command has an ellipsis (three periods) appended to it, enter the ellipsis (…) by typing 3 periods.

Enter your keyboard shortcut in the field next to **Keyboard Shortcut**. In the example, our new keyboard shortcut for the Adjust Size… command in Preview is ⇧⌘A (shift+command+A). Click the **Done** button to close the configuration sheet. Repeat to add more keyboard shortcuts. Click **Done** when finished.

To remove a custom keyboard shortcut, open the Keyboard settings. Click the **Keyboard Shortcuts…** button to open the configuration sheet. Select **App Shortcuts** from the sidebar. Highlight the keyboard shortcut you want to delete and click the – (delete) button. Click **Done** when finished.

Do Not Disturb

There isn't a keyboard shortcut for Do Not Disturb in macOS. Previous versions of macOS used ⌥⌘right (option+command+right arrow) as the keyboard shortcut to toggle Do Not Disturb on and off.

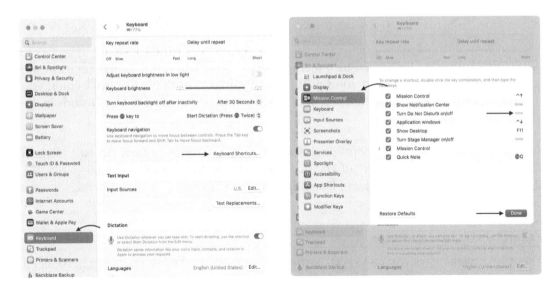

If you would like to assign a keyboard shortcut to enable and disable Do Not Disturb, open the System Settings app, scroll down, and select **Keyboard** in the sidebar. Click the **Keyboard Shortcuts…** button to reveal keyboard shortcuts configuration sheet. Select **Mission Control** from the sidebar. Ensure the checkbox next to **Turn Do Not Disturb**

On/Off is checked. Double-click **none** to the right of **Turn Do Not Disturb On/Off** and enter your keyboard shortcut. I'll use ⌥⌘**right** (option+command+right arrow) since I am used to it from previous versions of macOS.

Once configured, this keyboard shortcut acts as a toggle to enable and disable Do Not Disturb. When Do Not Disturb is enabled, you'll see a quarter moon icon in your Menu Bar. When it is disabled, the icon will be grayed out.

Apple also calls the Do Not Disturb feature **Focus**. You will see it called Focus in the macOS Control Center. When you select **Focus Settings...** from the Control Center, you can configure the Do Not Disturb settings. We'll cover Focus and Do Not Disturb in the chapter on the Menu Bar.

To disable this keyboard shortcut, uncheck the checkbox next to **Turn Do Not Disturb On/Off**. If you want to restore all keyboard shortcuts to their macOS defaults, click the **Restore Defaults** button. Click the **Done** button when finished.

Zoom Keyboard Shortcuts

There are several ways you can zoom in macOS Sonoma. In the last chapter, I introduced a trackpad and mouse gesture to perform a Smart Zoom of a window. I also showed you how to enable a three-finger double tap to zoom in and out on your desktop. Now let's enable a set of keyboard shortcuts to zoom.

To enable zoom keyboard shortcuts, open the System Settings app and select **Accessibility** in the sidebar. Click on **Zoom** in the **vision** section of the Accessibility settings window. In the window, flip the switch next to **Use keyboard shortcuts to zoom** on.

Once enabled, you can toggle zoom on and off using the keyboard shortcut ⌥⌘8 (option+command+8). If you want to zoom in, use the ⌥⌘= (option+command+=) keyboard shortcut. To zoom out, use ⌥⌘– (option+command+–).

Scroll with Modifier Key Zoom

Yet another method to zoom is to hold down a modifier key while scrolling on your trackpad or mouse.

To enable scrolling zoom, open System Settings and select **Accessibility** in the sidebar. Under **Vision** in the Accessibility settings window, select **Zoom**. Flip the switch next to **Use scroll gesture with modifier keys to zoom** on. You can select the modifier key using the pop-up menu next to **Modifier key for scroll gesture**. You have a choice of ^ ⌥ ⌘ (control, option, or command) with the ⌘ (command) key being the default.

To zoom in, hold down your chosen modifier key while scrolling up. Scroll down while holding down the modifier key to zoom out.

The default zoom style is a **Full Screen**, where the zoom takes up the entire screen. You can select a different style using the pop-up menu next to **Zoom style**. In a split screen zoom, the zoomed area is shown in a portion of the screen along the edge of your desktop. For a picture-in-picture zoom, think of a rectangular magnifying glass.

You can change the size and location of the zoom window for the split screen and picture-in-picture styles. Click the **Size and Location...** button. For split screen, drag the separator bar to resize the zoom area. You can also reposition the window by dragging to another edge of your desktop. For picture-in-picture, drag one of the edges or corners of the zoom window to resize it. You can reposition the picture-in-picture zoom window by dragging it to a new location. When you are satisfied with the zoom size and location, click the **OK** button. The picture-in-picture zoom area is shown in the image above.

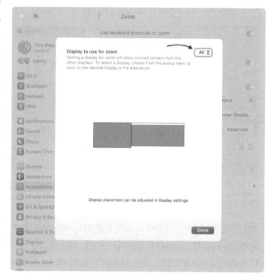

If you have multiple monitors, you can zoom the screen on another monitor by clicking the **Choose Display...** and selecting the display you want to use for zooming from the pop-up menu next to **Display to use for zoom**. Click **Done** when finished.

4

Touch Bar

Some MacBook Pro models feature a 2170 x 60-pixel touchscreen display called the Touch Bar, where the function keys are usually located. The Touch Bar is a dynamic input device with a strip of virtual keys that change based on the active application. The far-right end features a Touch ID that allows you to unlock your MacBook Pro, unlock apps that require a password, or authorize Apple Pay. The **Control Strip**, which contains four controls, is located on the right quarter of the Touch Bar. Some models of the MacBook Pro have the **esc** key integrated as part of the Touch Bar while the M1 and M2 MacBook Pro laptops feature a physical **esc** key.

By default, the Control Strip contains four controls for screen brightness, volume, mute, and Siri. Tapping the left arrow located at the Control Strip's left end reveals the complete set of controls usually found on the top row of a physical keyboard – brightness, Mission Control, Launchpad, keyboard backlight, media playback, and volume. When expanded, the Control Strip is called the **Expanded Control Strip**.

Holding down the **fn** ⊕ (function/globe) key reveals the standard set of function keys, **F1** to **F12**.

The Touch Bar also serves as a virtual keyboard, offering quick access to standard tools and other functionality that you would usually access from the Application Menu. These tools are displayed between the **esc** key and the Control Strip in an area called **App Controls**. The tools available in App Controls change as you change the active app.

macOS lets you customize the controls that appear on the Touch Bar, changing or rearranging the controls shown in the Control Strip and Expanded Control Strip. Let's first start with Touch ID and Apple Pay and then customize the Touch Bar controls.

Touch ID

Touch ID lets you unlock and log into your Mac using your fingerprint rather than your password. You can also use Touch ID to enter passwords on webpages and make purchases using Apple Pay. Touch ID supports multiple users, allowing other family members to use your Mac and make purchases.

To set up Touch ID, open System Settings, scroll down, and select **Touch ID & Password** from the sidebar.

Next, click the **+** (add) button above **Add Fingerprint** in the Touch ID & Password settings window to add your first fingerprint. Place your finger on the Touch ID button and follow the instructions to lift and rest your finger to capture your fingerprint. Ensure that your finger is clean and dry for the best results. Click **Done** to save your fingerprint. Repeat to add additional fingerprints. You can enter up to three fingerprints per user.

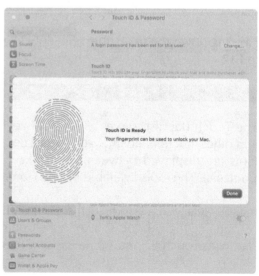

To delete a fingerprint, hover over the fingerprint icon with your pointer until an **X** (delete) button appears above and to the left of the icon. Click the **X** (delete) button to delete the fingerprint. You will be prompted to enter your password and confirm that you want to delete a fingerprint.

The five switches under the fingerprints allow you to use Touch ID to unlock your Mac, use Apple Pay, make purchases from the iTunes Store, Mac App Store, and Apple Books, autofill your password, and use your fingerprint for fast user switching between users. Flip the switches on for the features you want to use with Touch ID.

Apple Pay

If you did not set up Apple Pay when first setting up your MacBook Pro or if you need to make changes, open System Settings, scroll down and select **Wallet & Apple Pay** from the sidebar.

To add a new credit card to Apple Pay, click the **Add Card...** button. If you have multiple credit cards, select the default card from the pop-up menu next to **Default Card** under **Payment Details**. If can also change your shipping address, email, or phone number in the payment details.

To delete an existing credit card, click on the card and select the **Remove Card...** button in the next window.

Customize the Touch Bar

By default, the Control Strip is collapsed to the right side of the Touch Bar. If you tap the left expand arrow, the Control Strip is replaced by the Expanded Control Strip, as shown in the images below.

Touch Bar with the Control Strip:

Touch Bar, after tapping the left expand arrow to reveal the Expanded Control Strip:

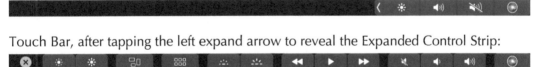

macOS allows you to change what the Touch Bar displays, offering 5 different displays configured in the Keyboard settings. You can configure your Touch Bar to display App Controls, the Expanded Control Strip, F1, F2, etc. Keys, Quick Actions, or Spaces.

When configured for App Controls, the Touch Bar shows commonly used actions available in the active application. The Expanded Control Strip mirrors the macOS system tools located on the top row of physical function keys on a MacBook Pro without a Touch Bar or on an Apple Magic Keyboard. When set to **F1, F2, etc. Keys**, the Touch Bar displays the function keys. If you have created quick action workflows in Automator, the Touch

Bar displays them when set to Quick Actions. Finally, the Touch Bar can be configured to show your Spaces.

To change the Touch Bar display, open System Settings, scroll down and select **Keyboard** in the sidebar. Click the **Touch Bar Settings…** button to reveal a configuration sheet.

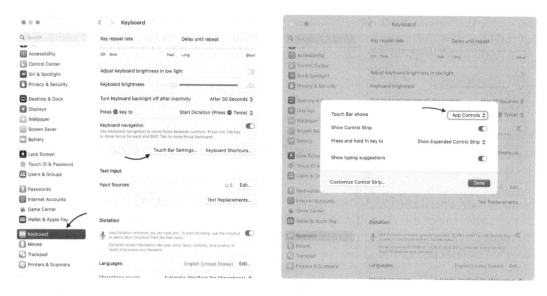

Using the pop-up menu next to **Touch Bar Shows**, select whether you want your Touch Bar to display App Controls, the Expanded Control Strip, F Keys, Quick Actions, or Spaces.

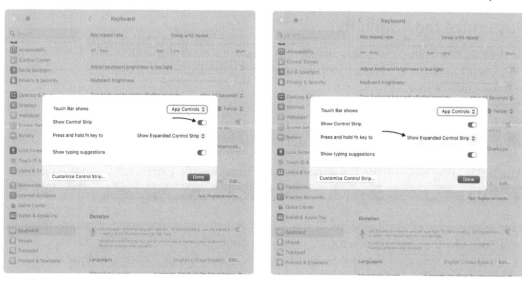

Decide whether you want your Touch Bar to show the Control Strip, the set of four icons at the right of the Touch Bar. The switch next to **Show Control Strip** toggles the Control Strip on and off. By default, your Touch Bar will offer typing suggestions. Press the suggestion in the Touch Bar to enter it into your document.

Next, select whether you want your Touch Bar to display App Controls, the Expanded Control Strip, F Keys, Quick Actions, or Spaces when you press and hold the **fn** ⊕ (function/globe) key using the pop-up menu next to **Press and hold fn key to**.

The Control Strip is available with App Controls, Quick Actions, and Spaces. Each of these options can also be configured without the Control Strip. If you select the Expanded Control Strip or F Keys options, the switch next to **Show Control Strip** toggles to off. The following set of images depicts your Touch Bar choices.

App Controls (the app is Microsoft Word) with the Control Strip:

App Controls (the app is Microsoft Word) without the Control Strip:

Expanded Control Strip (no Control Strip option):

F1, F2, etc. Keys (no Control Strip option):

Quick Actions with the Control Strip:

Quick Actions without the Control Strip:

Spaces with the Control Strip:

Spaces without the Control Strip:

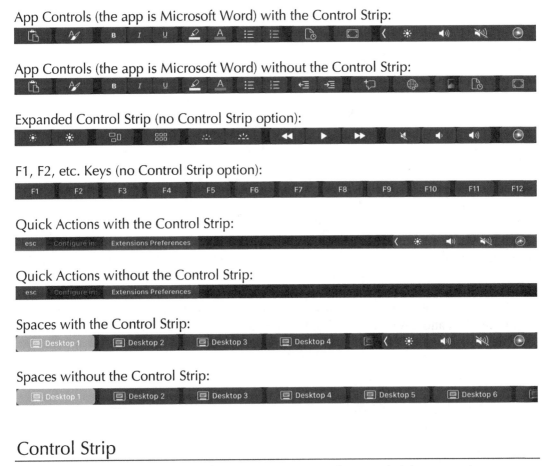

Control Strip

By default, the Control Strip displays 4 icons to control screen brightness, volume, mute, and Siri as shown in the image below.

You don't have to settle for the default toolset. macOS lets you customize the Control Strip to meet your needs. Putting the icons for the actions you use most often at your fingertips will greatly increase your productivity.

To add, remove, or rearrange the Control Strip tools, open System Settings, scroll down and select **Keyboard** in the sidebar. Click the **Touch Bar Settings...** button to reveal a configuration sheet. Click the **Customize Control Strip...** button to reveal a palette of icons at the bottom of your desktop. Remember that the Control Strip is only available when the Touch Bar shows App Controls, Quick Actions, or Spaces and the **Show Control Strip** switch is on.

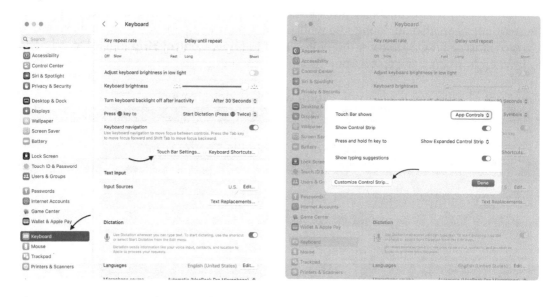

The icons on your Touch Bar will jiggle slightly like the icons on an iPhone or iPad jiggle when editing. The next part is going to seem a bit weird. To add a tool to the Control Strip, drag a tool from the tool palette to the Control Strip. This means you will drag the tool to the bottom of your screen and continue dragging past the bottom of your screen until the icon appears on your Touch Bar. Once on the Touch Bar, the icon will be highlighted. Drag it left or right. Other icons move out of the way. When the tool is in your desired location, release your hold. If you are replacing an existing tool, position it over the icon you want to replace and release your hold.

Removing a tool from the Touch Bar is equally weird the first time you try it. Move your pointer through the bottom of your desktop and continue until an icon on the Touch Bar is highlighted. Move left or right to highlight the desired tool. Drag the tool from the Touch Bar and back onto the tool palette and release.

To rearrange the tools on your Touch Bar, move your pointer through the bottom of your desktop and continue until a tool on the Touch Bar is highlighted. Move left or right until the icon you want to move is highlighted. Drag it to your desired location.

The Control Strip supports a maximum of four tools. macOS lets you configure less, supporting one to four tools.

When finished, click the **Done** button on the tool palette. Then click **Done** on the Touch Bar configuration sheet and close System Settings.

To revert to the default set of tools, drag the set of tools called the **Default Set** to the Control Strip and click the **Done** button. Then click **Done** on the Touch Bar configuration sheet and close System Settings.

Expanded Control Strip

The default set of tools on the Expanded Control Strip may look familiar if you have an Apple Magic Keyboard or have upgraded from a non-Touch Bar MacBook Pro. The toolset is the same set of tools in the same order on a keyboard with physical keys.

Like the Control Strip, macOS lets you customize the Expanded Control Strip. Placing your most frequently used tools on the Expanded Control Strip will increase your productivity. Another reason to customize the Expanded Control Strip is that two tools have trackpad gestures to invoke them – Mission Control and Launchpad – and Siri is available in the Menu Bar, as a keyboard shortcut, and by saying, "Hey Siri." Replacing these tools frees up three spaces on your Touch Bar's Expanded Control Strip.

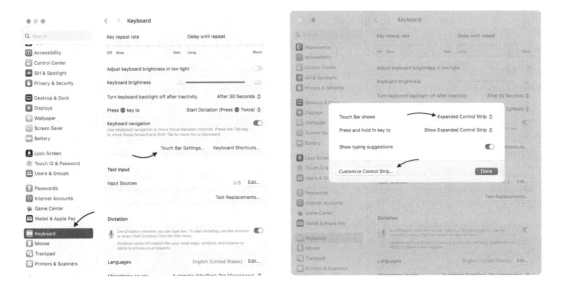

To add, remove, or rearrange the tools on your Expanded Control Strip, open System Settings, scroll down and select **Keyboard** in the sidebar. Click the **Touch Bar Settings...** button to reveal a configuration sheet. Select **Expanded Control Strip** next to **Touch Bar** shows. Then click the **Customize Control Strip...** button to reveal a palette of icons at the bottom of your desktop.

The icons on your Touch Bar will jiggle. To add a tool to the Expanded Control Strip, drag a tool from the palette through the bottom of your desktop and onto the Touch Bar. Once on the Touch Bar, the tool's icon will be highlighted. Drag it left or right, and other icons will move out of the way. When the tool is in your desired location, release your hold. If you are replacing an existing tool, position it over the tool you want to replace and release.

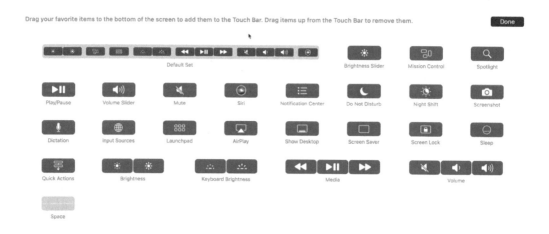

To remove a tool from the Touch Bar, move your pointer through the bottom of your desktop and continue until a tool on the Touch Bar is highlighted. Move left or right to highlight the desired tool. Drag the tool from the Touch Bar back onto the tool palette.

To rearrange the tools on your Touch Bar, move your pointer to the bottom of your desktop and keep going until a tool on the Touch Bar is highlighted. Move left or right until the tool you want to move is highlighted. Drag the icon to your desired location.

The Expanded Control Strip has 13 spaces, enough room for a maximum of 13 single-button tools. Older MacBook Pro laptops only support 12 spaces. Four tools take up two or three spaces on your Touch Bar – Brightness, Keyboard Brightness, Media, and Volume. To save space, you can replace the Brightness control with the Brightness Slider, which only takes one space. Similarly, the Volume control can be replaced with the Volume Slider to save two spaces. You can replace the Media control with the Play/Pause tool, saving two spaces but at the expense of the skip forward and back controls. There isn't a smaller control to adjust the keyboard brightness.

To revert to the default set of tools, drag the set of tools called the **Default Set** to the Expanded Control Strip and click **Done** on the tool palette.

When finished customizing your Expanded Control Strip, click the **Done** button on the tool palette, click **Done** on the Touch Bar configuration sheet, and close the System Settings application.

App Controls

If you configured your Touch Bar to show App Controls, you'll see application-specific tools in your Touch Bar if the application offers Touch Bar support. The App Controls area will be blank if an application doesn't support the Touch Bar.

While many applications populate the App Controls with a set of commonly used controls, most do not let you customize the tools on your Touch Bar. I'll show you how to create a custom Touch Bar to overcome this limitation later in this chapter. First, let's cover Safari and Mail, which allow you to customize their App Controls.

To check if an application lets you customize App Controls, check the application's **View** menu to see if it has a **Customize Touch Bar...** option. If this option is present, the app offers support to add, change, delete, and rearrange the App Controls. If this option is not present, the application does not support Touch Bar customization.

If you find the **Customize Touch Bar...** option grayed out, you do not have the Touch Bar configured to show App Controls. Open System Settings, scroll down and select **Keyboard** in the sidebar. Click the **Touch Bar Settings...** button to reveal a configuration sheet. Select **App Controls** from the pop-up menu next to **Touch Bar shows**.

Safari App Controls

The default Safari App Controls are shown in the image below with the Control Strip in its usual spot on the Touch Bar's right side. I have customized my Control Strip with the Screen Lock and Launchpad replacing the Mute and Siri icons.

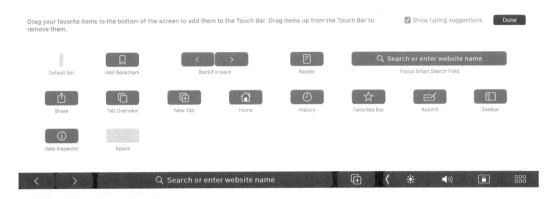

To customize the Safari tools on the Touch Bar, launch Safari and select **View > Customize Touch Bar...** to reveal the Safari tool palette.

To add a tool, drag it from the Safari tool palette to the App Controls section of your Touch Bar. Once on the Touch Bar, the icon for the tool will be highlighted. Drag the icon left or right until it is in your desired location and release your hold. Note that you cannot drag an application tool to the Control Strip.

To remove a tool from the Touch Bar, move your pointer through the bottom of your desktop until an icon on the Touch Bar is highlighted. Move left or right until the tool you want to remove is highlighted. Drag the tool from the Touch Bar onto the Safari tool palette and release.

To rearrange the tools, move your pointer through the bottom of your desktop until an icon on the Touch Bar is highlighted. Move left or right until the tool you want to move is highlighted. Drag the tool to your desired location and release.

To revert to the default Safari App Controls, drag and drop the **Default Set** from the Safari tool palette onto the Touch Bar.

Tap **Done** on the Safari tool palette when finished.

The image below shows my Touch Bar after I customized it with the tools I use most often. From left to right, the tools in my Safari App Controls are Sidebar, Bookmark, New Tab, Tab Overview, Back/Forward, History, and Share.

Mail App Controls

The Apple Mail App Controls are shown in the image below with the Control Strip in its usual spot on the Touch Bar's right side. I have customized my Control Strip with the Screen Lock and Launchpad replacing the Mute and Siri icons.

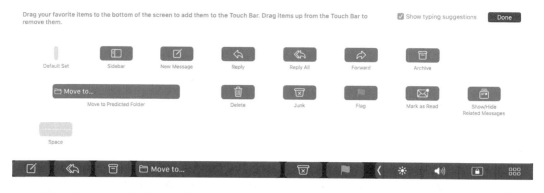

To customize the Mail tools on the Touch Bar, launch Mail and select **View > Customize Touch Bar...** to reveal the Mail tool palette.

Customizing the Mail App Controls is the same process as customizing the Safari App Controls. To add a tool to the App Controls, drag it from the tool palette to the Touch Bar. Drag left or right until the tool is in your desired location then release. Note that you cannot drag an application tool to the Control Strip on the right of the Touch Bar.

To remove a tool from the Touch Bar, move your pointer through the bottom of your desktop and keep going until an icon on the Touch Bar is highlighted. Move left or right until the tool you want to remove is highlighted. Drag the tool from the Touch Bar back onto the tool palette.

To rearrange the tools, move your pointer through the bottom of your desktop until a tool on the Touch Bar is highlighted. Move left or right until the tool you want to move is highlighted. Drag the tool to your desired location.

To revert to the default Mail Touch Bar, drag and drop the **Default Set** from the Mail tool palette onto the Touch Bar.

Tap **Done** in the Mail tool palette when finished.

The image below shows my Touch Bar after customization with the tools I use most often. From left to right, the tools in my Mail App Controls are: New Message, Reply, Reply All, Forward, Mark as Read, Flag, Junk, and Delete.

Show F Keys in an App

If you have an application that utilizes the **F** (function) keys, macOS lets you configure the Touch Bar to display the function keys when that application is active. This is a handy feature that eliminates the need to configure the Touch Bar to toggle **F** keys when you press the **fn** ⊕ (function/globe) key.

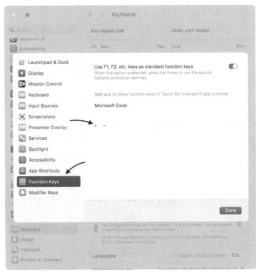

An application that comes immediately to mind is Microsoft Excel, which uses the F keys to perform various functions. Let's configure the Touch Bar to show the F keys when Excel is the active app.

To configure the Touch Bar to show the F keys in a specific application, open the System Settings app, scroll down, and select **Keyboard** in the sidebar. Click the **Keyboard Shortcuts...** button to reveal a configuration sheet.

To add an application, click the **+** (add) button, which will open your Applications folder. Select the application and click the **Open** button. In this example, the app I chose was Microsoft Excel. Repeat to add another application. Click **Done** and close System Settings to finish.

To delete an app, highlight it and click the **–** (delete) button. Click **Done** to finish.

Touch Bar Zoom

If you are having difficulties seeing the Touch Bar tools, you can enable Touch Bar zoom. This feature displays a larger version of the Touch Bar at the bottom of your desktop.

To enable Touch Bar Zoom, open the System Settings app and select **Accessibility** from the sidebar. Next, click **Zoom** in the **Vision** section to configure the Zoom settings. Flip the switch next to **Enable Touch Bar Zoom** on.

To zoom, place and hold a finger on the Touch Bar without tapping. A larger version of your Touch Bar with a circle appears at the bottom of your desktop. Without leaving the Touch Bar, slide your finger left or right to highlight your desired button. When the circle changes color indicating the icon is selected, you can lift your finger off the Touch Bar to activate the control.

The image above shows the Touch Bar zoomed on the desktop with the circle between the Skip Forward icon and the Mute icon.

Custom Touch Bars

Now that you are familiar with the out-of-the-box macOS Touch Bar let's learn how to create a custom Touch Bar. We'll use an application I introduced in Chapter 2, BetterTouchTool, which lets you create a custom Touch Bar filled with buttons that execute over 200 predefined actions or keyboard shortcuts.

BetterTouchTool is available for $10 for a standard license or $22 for a lifetime license at the time of this writing. You can download a 45-day free trial to test BetterTouchTool before purchasing a license. BetterTouchTool is available at https://folivora.ai/.

Please refer to Chapter 2 to set the security and privacy settings and to configure basic and user interface settings. If you have already set up BetterTouchTool, let's start with some settings that are specific to the Touch Bar.

Touch Bar Specific Settings

BetterTouchTool has some additional configuration settings that are specific to the Touch Bar. Open the BetterTouchTool configuration window by selecting **Configuration** from the BetterTouchTool Menu Extra in your Menu Bar.

Select **Touch Bar** from the pop-up menu at the top of the configuration window. Next, click the **Touch Bar Settings** button next to the pop-up menu or click the ellipsis in the upper-right corner to open the BetterTouchTool settings window.

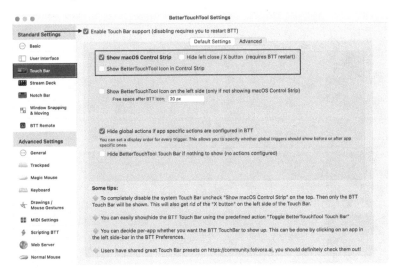

Touch Bar should be highlighted in the sidebar under **Standard Settings**. To enable the BetterTouchTool Touch Bar, ensure that the checkbox next to **Enable Touch Bar support** is checked. Unchecking this checkbox disables the BetterTouchTool Touch Bar and may require you to restart BetterTouchTool to take effect.

You have the option of displaying the macOS Control Strip along with your custom Touch Bar. First, ensure that the Control Strip is enabled in the Touch Bar settings in the System Settings app. Then check the checkbox next to **Show macOS Control Strip**. Unchecking this checkbox will remove the macOS Control Strip from your Touch Bar even if it is enabled in the **Keyboard** settings.

If you would like to see the BetterTouchTool icon in your Touch Bar's Control Strip, check the checkbox next to **Show BetterTouchTool Icon in Control Strip**. This icon will allow you to toggle between your custom Touch Bar and the macOS App Controls.

Creating a Custom Touch Bar

Let's create your first button for your custom Touch Bar. Creating a Touch Bar button consists of selecting whether it works in all apps or only in a specific app, selecting a trigger, customizing the Touch Bar button, and assigning an action.

The left sidebar contains the **App List**. A Touch Bar button can be created for a specific application or **All Apps**. A button created for a specific application will work only when that application is active. A button created for **All Apps** works in all applications.

By default, you will see 2 items listed in the App List, **All Apps**, and **Finder**. You can add other applications by clicking the **+** (add) button at the lower-left corner of the window

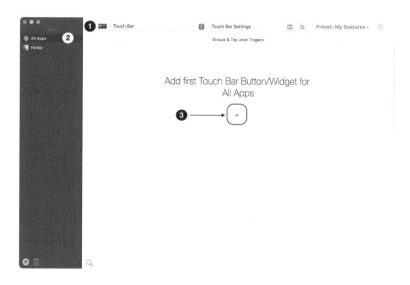

and selecting an app from your Applications folder or one that is currently running. You can also drag an application from your Applications folder into the App List.

In this example, I'll create a custom Touch Bar button to empty the trash that will work in all applications. First, select **Touch Bar** from the toolbar's pop-up menu at the top of the BetterTouchTool configuration window. Next, click on **All Apps** in the left sidebar. Click the blue **+** (add) button under **Add first Touch Bar Button/Widget for All Apps**.

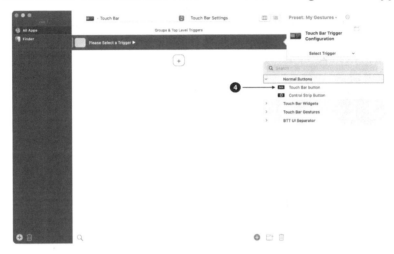

This reveals the **Touch Bar Trigger Configuration** panel and opens the **Select Trigger** pop-up menu where you will select your trigger. The triggers under **Normal Buttons** will open, offering the choice of a Touch Bar button or a Control Strip Button. You also have the choice to add a Touch Bar widget or gesture. We'll cover widgets later. For this example, I chose the Touch Bar button.

In the Touch Bar Trigger Configuration panel, you will enter the title for the button in the field under **Button Title**. In this example, since I am creating a button to empty the trash, I entered "Empty Trash" in this field.

The default color for buttons is black. To change it, click the black square to the right of the **Button Background Color** to open a predefined set of 30 colors from which to choose. I chose red for my empty trash button. You also have the option of launching a color picker by clicking on the color picker button to the right of the black square next to the **Button Background Color**.

In the **Font** section, you can select the font color, size, and alignment. For this example, I left the defaults of white, 15 points, and left alignment.

Next, click on the white box to the right of the **Select Button Icon** in the Touch Bar Trigger Configuration panel to reveal a huge palette of icons. You can browse through the icons or search for a "trash" icon. Click on an icon to select it.

The button title appears on your button by default. If you don't like it, you can remove the title by checking the checkbox next to **Show only icon, no text** to remove it.

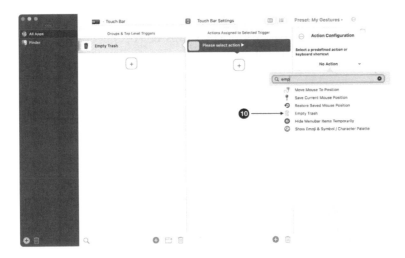

Next, click the **+** (add) button under **Assign First Action to Selected Trigger** to reveal the **Action Configuration** panel. Like creating a custom gesture, you can select a predefined action or enter a keyboard shortcut from the pop-up menu.

In this example, I entered "emp" in the search field to find the Empty Trash action to avoid browsing through the huge list of actions BetterTouchTool supports. Had I browsed through BetterTouchTool's extensive list of available actions, I would have found empty trash under **System Actions**.

Here is what the empty trash button looks like on my Touch Bar:

The button title appears on your button by default and can be removed by checking the checkbox next to **Show only icon, no text** (step 8).

We have finished our first Touch Bar button. If you were following along, give it a try. Tap your newly created button and watch as the empty trash warning appears on your desktop.

That empty trash button looks rather lonely. Continue to add more buttons to fill out your custom Touch Bar using the same process. Don't worry if you can't display all the buttons you create. You can access any buttons hidden under your Control Strip by sliding your finger left along the Touch Bar.

Touch Bar Widgets

BetterTouchTool includes many handy widgets to display the weather, date, time, calendar, the song playing in the Music app, reminders, a clipboard manager, an app switcher, shortcuts, and brightness and volume sliders.

To add a widget to your custom Touch Bar, click the blue **+** (add) button underneath the Empty Trash button we just created in the **Groups & Top Level Triggers** panel. Select **Tough Bar Widgets** to display the list of available widgets. For this example, I'll select the Weather Widget.

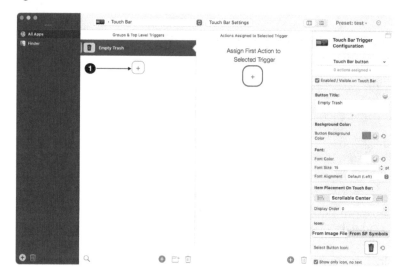

The Weather Widget offers a few customization options. It automatically determines your location when the checkbox next to **Automatically get location** is checked. You can change the display format from the default by entering variables in the text field under **Optional Display Format**. Supported variables are listed below the text field. You can also customize the icons for weather conditions. The widget offers the choice of the current weather, today's weather forecast, or a forecast up to 7 days in the future.

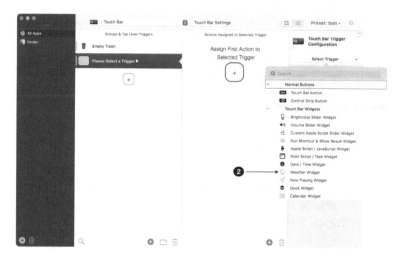

Let's look at our Touch Bar with our Empty Trash button and Weather Widget.

You can continue to add buttons and widgets to your custom Touch Bar until it is fully populated. Let's look at my custom Touch Bar. From left to right, I have the following buttons and widgets on my Touch Bar – an application switcher, Notification Center, System Settings, weather widget, date & time widget, battery widget, and a now playing widget.

But wait! It looks like there are more buttons under the Control Strip. Sliding my finger to the left along the Touch Bar reveals additional buttons to toggle light and dark mode, move a window to the next Space to the left, move a window to the next Space to the right, hide all apps, Mission Control, empty trash, and a sleep button.

Multiple-Action Buttons

You can assign multiple actions to a button. A multiple-action button is a perfect way to accomplish multiple tasks with a single tap on your Touch Bar. The only limit to multiple action buttons is your imagination. Let's create a multiple action button by adding another action to an existing button.

For this example, I'll add a second action to an existing button I created that moves a window one Space to the right. First, I selected the **Move Window to the right** button in the **Groups & Top Level Triggers** panel. Next, I clicked the **+** (add) button under the existing Move Window One Space/Desktop Right action in the **Actions Assigned to Selected Trigger** panel.

The existing button moves a window one Space to the right. It also moves the desktop one Space to the right. For second action, I wanted my desktop to move back one Space to the left, to the original desktop from which I moved the window. I entered "Space" into the search field in the **Action Configuration** panel and chose **Move left a Space**. Had

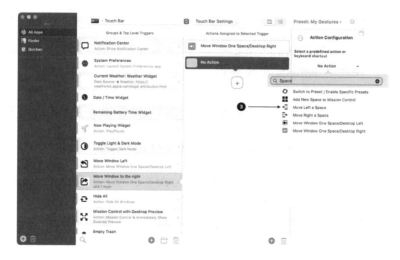

If I browsed through BetterTouchTool's list of available actions, I would have found this action under **Navigating Spaces / Desktops**.

The resulting button allows me to push a window from the Space in which I am working to the Space to the right and returns to the original Space, so I can continue working.

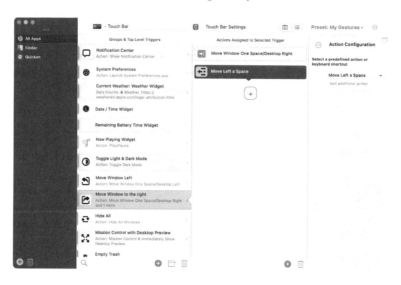

Modifier Keys

A nice feature of BetterTouchTool is that it supports modifier keys to control buttons and widget visibility in your Touch Bar. This feature allows you to display certain buttons and widgets only while pressing one or more of the modifier keys. This feature can be effectively used to create multiple Touch Bars accessible by pressing their assigned modifier key(s).

Modifier keys are added to a button or widget in the Touch Bar Trigger Configuration panel by selecting a choice from the pop-up menu under **Modifier based visibility**. The available choices in the pop-up menu consist of: Only show while all these modifiers are pressed, Show if some modifier keys are pressed, but NONE of these, Show if NO modify key is pressed OR if NONE of these are pressed, and Show always (don't care about modifiers at all). If you haven't configured modifier keys, the default is to always display the button regardless of whether modifier keys are pressed or not, essentially the last choice in the pop-up menu.

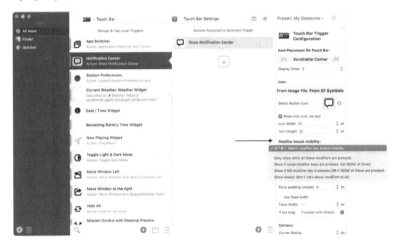

Once you have made your selection from the pop-up menu, select the modifier key(s) you wish to use by checking the checkbox(es) above them. Supported modifier keys include the ⇧ fn ⌃ ⌥ ⌘ (shift, function, control, option, and command) keys.

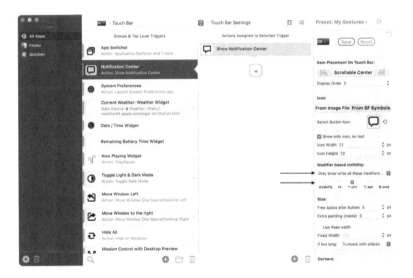

Rearrange Custom Touch Bar Buttons & Widgets

The buttons on your custom Touch Bar are easily rearranged. To move a button or widget, open the BetterTouchTool configuration window. Click and drag a button or widget to a new location in the Groups & Top Level Triggers panel. A button or widget at the top of the list appears first, at the far left of your Touch Bar, with the remaining items appearing in order, top to bottom, left to right across your Touch Bar.

Modify a Custom Touch Bar Button or Widget

You can modify the Touch Bar button's appearance, or the action assigned to it, in the BetterTouchTool configuration window. To modify the button appearance, choose the app from the App List in the sidebar, then click on the button you want to modify in the Groups & Top Level Triggers panel.

The button's appearance is modified in the Touch Bar Trigger Configuration panel. You can change the button name, background color, icon, modifier key(s), size, and whether the button displays its title.

To modify the action assigned to a button, click on the button you want to change in the Groups & Top Level Triggers panel. Next, click the action under Actions Assigned to Selected Trigger panel. This reveals the Action Configuration panel, where you can change the assigned action.

Delete a Custom Touch Bar Button

BetterTouchTool offers three deletion options. You can delete the action associated with a button. You can delete the button (the trigger) or delete an application and its custom Touch Bar.

If you want to delete an application and its Touch Bar, highlight the application in the App List and click the Trash Can icon at the bottom of the sidebar. BetterTouchTool will not let you delete **All Apps** and **Finder**.

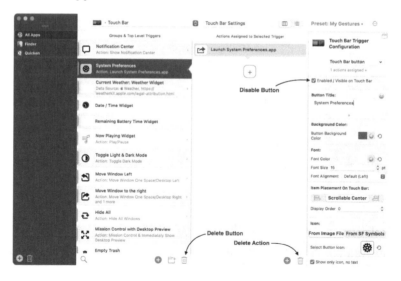

To delete a button, highlight the button you wish to delete in the Groups & Top Level Triggers panel and click the Trash Can icon. To delete an action associated with a button, highlight the action in the Actions Assigned to Selected Trigger panel and click on the Trash Can icon.

Disable a Custom Touch Bar Button

If you prefer to disable a button rather than deleting it, you can do so by unchecking the checkbox next to **Enabled / Visible on Touch Bar** in the Touch Bar Trigger Configuration panel. Disabling a button makes it essentially invisible, allowing you to enable it later.

Import and Export your Custom Touch Bar

If you want to share your Touch Bar with friends or want to create a backup, you can export your BetterTouchTool configuration to a file. BetterTouchTool's **Preset** feature lets you import and export your gestures.

Click **Preset** in the upper-right corner of the BetterTouchTool configuration window to reveal the Preset configuration sheet. Select the **Name** from the list and then click **Export Highlighted**. Name your file, choose the save location, and press **Save**.

To import a file, click **Preset** and then click **Import** from the configuration sheet. Browse to the file, select it, and click **Open**.

5

Desktop

Like other macOS releases, the macOS Sonoma Desktop consists of three major components – the **Menu Bar** along the top of your display, the **Dock** along the bottom, and the macOS Desktop itself. We'll learn how to customize each of these components in separate chapters. First, let's start with the new features of the macOS Sonoma Desktop.

What's the first thing you noticed in the image of my Desktop? **Widgets!** Apple released Widgets from the purgatory of Notification Center in macOS Sonoma. No longer hidden off the right side of your screen, Widgets now take their rightful place front and center on your Desktop.

Desktop Widgets

Widgets first appeared in macOS Big Sur as a component of Notification Center, the hidden panel at the right edge of your desktop, which gathers notifications and alerts you may have missed. In macOS Sonoma, you now have the option of placing widgets anywhere your desktop or in Notification Center. You don't have to settle on either the desktop or Notification Center, macOS Sonoma lets you have widgets in both locations.

What is great about Desktop Widgets is that they are interactive. News, Stocks, and Weather update throughout the day. You can play or pause media in podcasts, take notes, check off to-dos in the Reminders app, see your calendar, and control your smart home devices in the Home widget. Using Apple's Continuity feature, you can even bring your iOS widgets onto your desktop when your iPhone is connected to the same Wi-Fi network or near your Mac. Click on a Widget and its associated app launches.

To avoid cluttering up your desktop and distracting you, Widgets fade into your desktop background, adapting to the color of your wallpaper, when you have an app open. Want to check out the current temperature in the Weather widget when working in an app? Click anywhere on your desktop to execute the Show Desktop command and clear your desktop of app windows. No need to set up a Hot Corner or use the **fnF11** keyboard shortcut to clear your desktop.

To get started, secondary click anywhere on your desktop and select **Edit Widgets...** to reveal the widget browser at the bottom of your desktop. An animation shows you how to move widgets to your desktop. It couldn't be simpler. Drag a widget from the widget browser onto your desktop. You can also hover over a widget with your pointer until a green **+** (add) button appears. Click the **+** button to add the widget to your desktop.

Apps with widgets are listed in the widget browser's sidebar. Scroll down the sidebar to find your favorite apps or choose a widget from a selection of suggested widgets. You can also search for a widget using the search field. Depending on the app, small, medium, and large widget versions will be available.

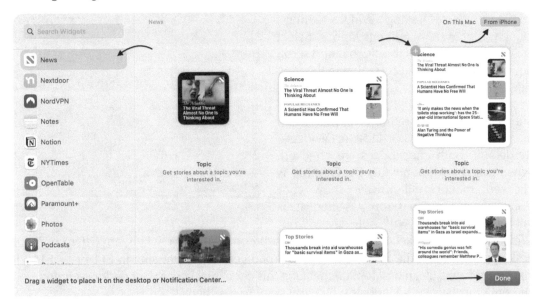

Apple's Continuity feature allows you to add widgets from you iPhone. If an iPhone widget is available for the app selected in the sidebar, you'll see **On This Mac** and **From iPhone** buttons in the upper right corner of the widget browser. Click on **From iPhone** to add a widget from your iPhone or **On This Mac** to add the macOS version.

When the widget browser is open, a – (delete) button will appear in the upper left corner of any widgets on your desktop. Click the – (delete) button to remove a widget from your desktop.

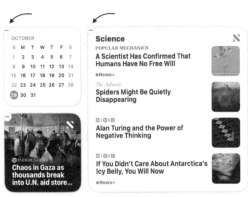

You can also remove a widget by secondary clicking on the widget to reveal the edit widget contextual menu. Select **Remove Widget**. Widgets can be rearranged on your desktop by dragging them into place.

The edit widget contextual menu also allows you to change the size of a widget by selecting **Small**, **Medium**, or **Large**. Select **Edit Widgets** to open the edit widgets panel at the bottom of your desktop.

If you have a favorite widget in Notification Center, you can drag it directly from Notification Center to your desktop.

Widget Settings

macOS lets you configure when to display Desktop Widgets, change their style, and whether you want to use iPhone widgets. To configure your Desktop Widget settings, launch the System Settings app. Select **Desktop & Dock** from the sidebar and scroll down to find the **Widgets** section in the right side of the window.

The **Show Widgets** setting controls when macOS will display your Desktop Widgets. By default, both checkboxes are checked. When the checkbox next to **On Desktop** is checked, macOS will always show your Widgets on your desktop. When it is unchecked, macOS will only show your Widgets when you execute the Show Desktop command by clicking anywhere on your desktop, performing the Show Desktop trackpad gesture, or pressing **fn F11** or ⊕ **F11**. If you appreciate a clean desktop, unchecking this checkbox keeps your desktop uncluttered and only displays your Widgets when you want to see them.

When the checkbox next to **In Stage Manager** is checked, your Desktop Widgets will be displayed only when you are using Stage Manager, a feature that controls window sprawl and minimizes distractions caused by multiple windows. Read more about Stage Manager in the chapter on Managing Windows.

The pop-up menu next to **Widget Style** allows you to change the style from the default of **Automatic** to **Monochrome** or **Full-color**. When Automatic is selected, your widgets will display in full color when you show your desktop but will fade into the background with a monochrome style when an app is active. Selecting **Monochrome** configures your Desktop Widgets to always display in monochrome, even when no apps are running. When **Full-Color** is selected, your Widgets will always display in full color and never fade into the background when an app is open.

The switch next to **Use iPhone widgets** enables and disables the ability to have iPhone widgets display on your macOS desktop. By default, this feature is enabled. If you do not want to utilize the iPhone widgets feature, flip the switch off to disable.

Wallpaper

Apple significantly upped its Wallpaper game in macOS Sonoma, introducing a stunning set of aerial wallpapers from around the world. The new wallpaper can now double as slow-motion screen savers like the aerial screen savers, which play in tvOS on an Apple TV. Not only can you change your Wallpaper to any of the aerial wallpapers Apple provided, but you also now have the option of making your wallpaper your screen saver.

Apple provided a nice selection of over 100 images from around the world, categorized by **Landscape**, **Cityscape**, **Underwater**, and **Earth** as well as the usual set of Dynamic Wallpapers. You have the option of choosing from scenes from across the globe, captured with drones, underwater cameras, and from the International Space Station. Your wallpaper not only doubles as your aerial screen saver, but it will also play on your lock screen. And if you can't decide which aerial wallpaper to use, Apple included a **Shuffle Aerials** option that will shuffle each category or all the aerial wallpapers.

As in other macOS releases, you have the option to change your Wallpaper to any image you chose, as you can see from the image at the start of this chapter. The wallpaper in that image is a picture I captured of Weaver's Needle, a 1,000-foot high eroded spire of fused volcanic ash, as seen from Freemont Saddle, off the Peralta Trail in the Superstition Mountains east of Phoenix, Arizona.

Dynamic Wallpapers

Under the **Dynamic Wallpapers** category, you can choose from 10 dynamic wallpapers. First introduced in 2018 with the release of macOS Mojave, Dynamic Desktop wallpaper automatically changes the lighting conditions of your wallpaper throughout the day based on the time in your location. As the sun moves across the sky, the lighting and shadows change until a nighttime version eventually appears. This effect is accomplished by utilizing 16 variations of the same image that are saved in a compressed High Efficiency Image Format (HEIF) container.

Similarly, 21 different Light & Dark wallpapers, also listed in the Dynamic Wallpapers category, change with the time of day, with the light image displayed during the day and the dark image at night. Some wallpapers offer only light and dark versions. The image below compares the Sonoma wallpaper in light (left) and dark (right).

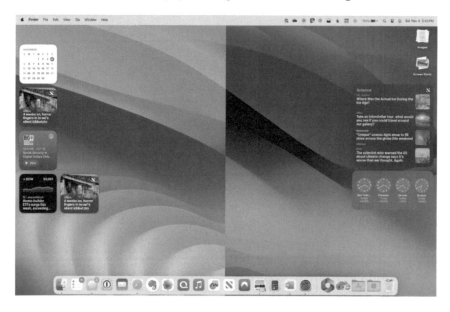

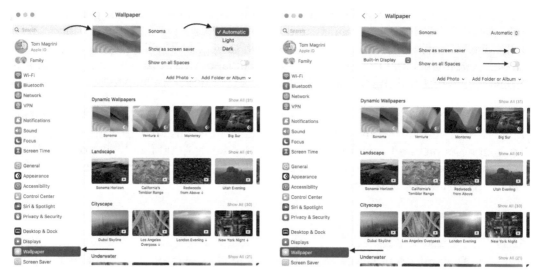

To select or change your desktop wallpaper, open the System Settings app and choose **Wallpaper** from the sidebar. You may have to scroll down the sidebar to find the Wallpaper settings.

The thumbnail image at the top of the Wallpaper settings window shows the current wallpaper. In the left image on the previous page, the current wallpaper is the **Sonoma** image, its name shown to the right of the thumbnail. Since this image supports light and dark options, a pop-up menu next to the name lets you choose **Light**, **Dark**, or **Automatic**, which changes between from light during the day to dark at night.

macOS Sonoma added the capability for your desktop wallpaper to do double duty as your screen saver. If you'd like to enable the screen saver that matches your desktop wallpaper, flip the switch next to **Show as screen saver** on, as shown in the right image on the previous page. Only the Sonoma wallpaper offers the **Show as screen saver** option. To set the Ventura or Monterey desktop wallpaper as your screen saver, you'll have to open the Screen Saver settings window and select them from the macOS category.

Another new feature in macOS Sonoma is the ability to set the same desktop wallpaper on all Spaces with the flip of a switch. If you'd like the same wallpaper on all your Spaces, flip the switch next to **Show on all Spaces** on. If you enabled the screen saver for your wallpaper, all Spaces will use the same screen saver. I will cover the Spaces feature in depth in the Mission Control chapter.

Aerial Wallpaper

The new **Aerial Wallpapers** in macOS Sonoma are truly gorgeous. These wallpapers are so amazing, it's worth upgrading to Sonoma simply to add this feature.

The Aerial wallpapers are organized into four categories – **Landscape**, **Cityscape**, **Underwater**, and **Earth**. There are 61 choices in the Landscape category, 30 in Cityscape, 21 in Underwater, and 22 options in the Earth category. The default is Sonoma Horizon, which is the first of 61 options under Landscape.

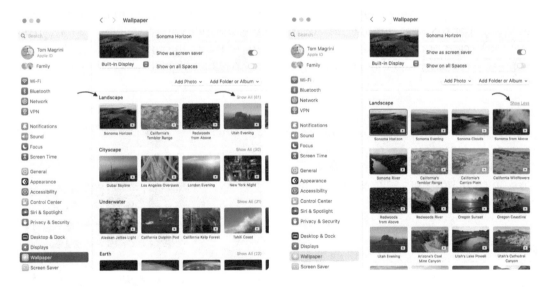

To see all the available wallpaper options in a category, place your point over one of the images and scroll left and right. Or click **Show All** for the category you wish to see and it will expand and allow you to scroll up and down through the wallpaper options. Click on your desired wallpaper, choose whether you want to use it as your screen saver, and if you want to show it on all Spaces. If you want a different wallpaper on each Space, move the System Settings app to each Space to select a unique wallpaper and screen saver for each. Click **Show Less** to close the category.

If you see a down arrow next to the name, it indicates the image and screen saver needs to be downloaded. Clicking on an Aerial Wallpaper will download it.

Shuffling Aerial Wallpaper

You don't have to settle for a single Aerial Wallpaper. Apple anticipated that its customers would like to see all the Aerial Wallpapers and added a shuffle feature that allows you to rotate through all the Aerial Wallpapers or just those in one category.

To shuffle through the Aerial Wallpapers, open the System Settings app and select Wallpaper from the sidebar. When the Wallpaper settings window opens, scroll down until you see **Shuffle Aerials**. Click **Show All** to see the five choices – Shuffle All, Shuffle Landscape, Shuffle Cityscape, Shuffle Underwater, and Shuffle Earth. Click on your desired shuffle option.

Once you have made your selection, it will appear in the thumbnail image at the top of the Wallpaper settings window. By default, the wallpaper will change every day. You have the option of changing how often you want to rotate through the images by using the pop-up menu next to the name of the shuffle. You can choose every 12 hours, every day, every 2 days, every week, every month, or continuously.

If you want to use the same wallpaper on all Spaces, flip the switch next to **Show on all Spaces** on. Note that you don't have to use the same wallpaper on every Space, you have the option of setting a different wallpaper for each Space.

Pictures

Apple provided 17 images of abstract art called Hello Metallic, Radial, Pro Black, Light Stream, and Studio Color in the **Pictures** category. You'll also find static images from previous releases of macOS including 9 images of Big Sur and 7 of Catalina Island. Click **Show All** to open the category to see your 33 available choices.

If you choose one of these images, you will not see the option to show as a screen saver since these images are static and do not offer slow-motion video. You can choose to show the same wallpaper image on all Spaces. Click **Show Less** to close the category.

Colors

If you prefer a simple color background, Apple provided a set of 19 solid colors in the **Colors** category. Scroll down in the Wallpaper settings window to find the Colors section. Place your pointer over one of the colored circles and scroll left or right to see your options. You can also click **Show All** to expand the category. Click **Show Less** to close the category.

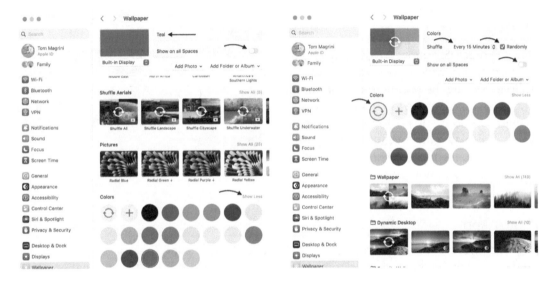

Like Pictures, you will not have the option to show as a screen saver. You can show the same color on all Spaces by flipping the switch next to **Show on all Spaces**.

If you don't see a color you like, you can select your own color by clicking the **+** (add) button to open a color picker window. Click the icons at the top of the window to change the type of color window from a wheel, sliders, spectrum, Apple colors, and colored pencils as shown left to right.

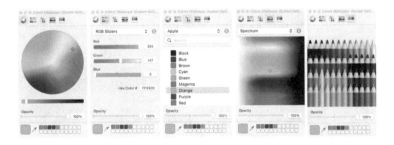

You don't have to settle for a single color as Apple provided a shuffle option. Select how frequently you want your colors to change using the pop-up menu next to **Shuffle**. You have the option of changing every 5 seconds, 1, 5, 15, or 30 minutes, every hour, daily, or on login or wakeup. You can shuffle the colors in order or randomly by checking the checkbox next to **Randomly**.

Multiple Displays

If you have multiple displays, a new feature in macOS Sonoma lets you set the wallpaper for each display from the Wallpaper settings window. In previous releases, you would have to launch System Settings, select Wallpaper, and then move the app to each display on which you wanted to set the wallpaper.

Now in macOS Sonoma, you can choose the display on which you want to set the wallpaper using the pop-up menu under the thumbnail image at the top of the Wallpaper settings window. It no longer matters on which display the Wallpaper settings window is open. If you do not have multiple displays, you will not see this option.

Photos App

Now that we know how to change the default wallpaper using the images provided by Apple, let's personalize your desktop by using images from your Photos application. You can use an image of your choice as your wallpaper, setting it directly from the Photos app.

Open the Photos app, find your desired picture and click on it. A blue border will appear around the image. Click the **Share** button located at the top of the Photos window and select **Set Wallpaper** from the pop-up menu. You can also use secondary click on your photo to reveal a contextual menu. Select **Share... > Set Wallpaper**. Alternatively, you can select **File > Share... > Set Wallpaper**.

You can select an image from your Photos app directly from the Wallpaper settings window. Launch the System Settings app and select **Wallpaper** from the sidebar. Click the **Add Photo** button to reveal a pop-up menu. Select **From Photos...** from the pop-up menu to open a window where you can access images stored in your Photos app. Use the sidebar to scroll through favorites, albums, and events. Find your desired image and click on it to set it as your wallpaper. Your image will appear in the top row above the Dynamic Wallpapers.

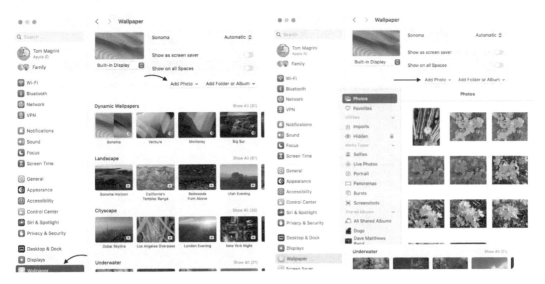

You can add as many images as you like. Repeat the process above until you have selected all your desired images. Each image will be added to the row above the Dynamic Wallpapers. macOS will automatically create a shuffle option for your photos. Select how frequently your wallpaper will change and whether to cycle through your photos in order or randomly. You can show your photos on all Spaces by flipping the **Show on all Spaces** switch on.

To remove an image, hover your pointer over the image and click the **X** (delete) button in the upper left corner.

Photo Albums

If you organized your photos into albums in the Photos app, you could add an entire album as your wallpaper. Click the **Add Folder or Album** button and select your album from the pop-up menu. Your album will appear below the Colors row in the Wallpaper settings window.

You can select a single image as your wallpaper or choose the shuffle option. Set the frequency you want your wallpaper to change and whether your photos will appear in order or randomly. You can show your photos on all Spaces by flipping the **Show on all Spaces** switch on.

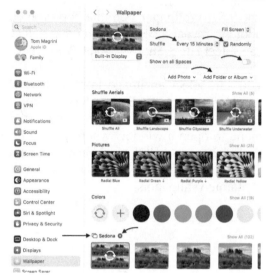

To remove an album, click the **X** (delete) button next to the name of the album. In the example, the name of my album is Sedona.

Image Folders

Another option for your wallpaper is to utilize a folder containing images. I like to collect wallpaper from the internet, usually landscape scenes. I have hundreds of pictures in a folder called Wallpaper located in the Pictures folder in my Home directory.

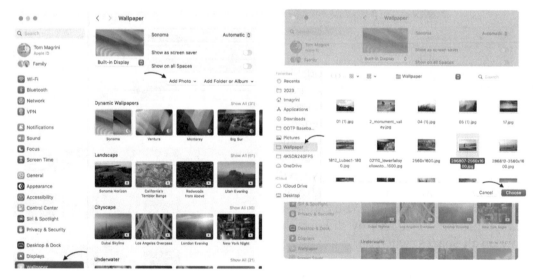

macOS Sonoma lets you select an image from an image folder as your desktop wallpaper or you can select the entire folder and shuffle through the images. To select a single image from a folder, open the Wallpaper settings window and click the **Add Photo** button. Select **Choose…** from the pop-up menu, which opens a Finder window. Navigate to your image folder and select the image you want as your desktop wallpaper. Click the **Choose** button to set the image as your desktop wallpaper. Your image will appear in the top row above the Dynamic Wallpapers.

You can add as many images as you like. Repeat the process above until you have selected all your desired images. Each image will be added to the row of images above the Dynamic Wallpapers. macOS will create a shuffle option for your images. Set how frequently you want your wallpaper to change and whether to cycle through your images in order or randomly. You can show your images on all Spaces by flipping the **Show on all Spaces** switch on.

If you want to remove an image, hover your pointer over the image and click the **X** (delete) button in the upper left corner.

To select a folder containing multiple images, open the Wallpaper settings window and click the **Add Folder or Album** button. Select **Choose Folder...** from the pop-up menu to open a Finder window. Navigate to your image folder and click the **Choose** button.

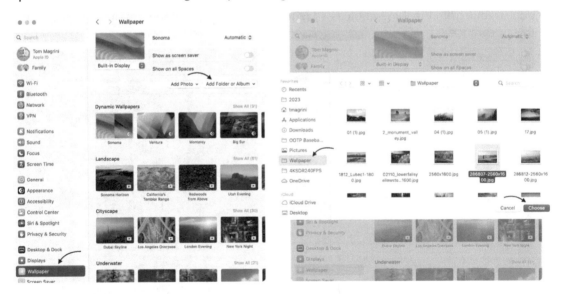

Your image folder will appear at the bottom of the Wallpaper settings. In the example, I chose an image folder I creatively named "Wallpaper."

Set the shuffle options for your image folder. Select how often you want to rotate through your images by using the pop-up menu next to **Shuffle**. You can choose every 5 seconds,

1, 5, 15, or 30 minutes, every hour, daily, or on login or wakeup. You can rotate through your images in order or randomly by checking the checkbox next to **Randomly**. Lastly, choose whether to **Show on all Spaces** using its switch.

To remove an image folder, hover your pointer over the name of the image folder and click the **X** (delete) button.

One of the advantages of using a folder as the source for your wallpaper is that macOS Sonoma automatically uses any new images you add to the folder without any further configuration on your part. You can create multiple folders with themes (i.e., landscapes, animals, space, people) and use a different theme for each of your Spaces. We'll cover Spaces the chapter on Mission Control.

Appearance

If you chose a Light or Dark wallpaper, you may want to configure the buttons, menus, and windows to match your wallpaper. To change the appearance of macOS Sonoma, open System Settings, choose **Appearance** in the sidebar, and select your desired appearance from the three choices – **Light**, **Dark**, or **Auto** – at the top of the settings next to Appearance.

Light was the default on all versions of macOS before Mojave, which first introduced a true Dark mode. Light sets the background of the Menu Bar, Dock, and windows to a light gray color. Dark changes the backgrounds of these onscreen elements to black, and the fonts and Menu Bar icons switch to white. Many users prefer the Dark appearance because content appears to stand out better against other onscreen elements. **Auto** automatically adjusts the appearance of macOS from light during the day to dark at night. Select **Auto** if you choose **Automatic** for your Dynamic Desktop wallpaper setting.

The image above compares the light Sonoma wallpaper with a Light appearance (left) with the dark Sonoma wallpaper with a Dark appearance (right). Note the change in the Menu Bar and Dock.

Accent Color

The **Accent color** is used for buttons, pop-up menus, and other macOS user interface controls. The default color is blue. macOS allows you to set your accent color to blue, purple, pink, red, orange, yellow, green, graphite, or multicolor.

To change the accent color used by macOS, open System Settings, select **Appearance** in the sidebar, and choose your desired accent color from the nine choices next to **Accent color**. The highlight color, which is used when selecting text in an application, will change to match your Accent color. It does not have to match the accent color. You can change the highlight color using the pop-up

menu next to **Highlight color**. The same nine choices are available along with an **Other** option, which opens a color picker for you to select a custom color.

Wallpaper Tinting

Wallpaper Tinting is enabled by default and allows colors from the wallpaper to subtly tint windows, toolbars, the Menu Bar, and Dock. If you do not like the tinting, flip the switch next to **Allow wallpaper tinting in windows** off.

Aerial Screen Savers

If you own an Apple TV, you have seen the breathtaking, high-resolution video screen savers of daytime and nighttime flyover footage from around the world. Now you can experience these stunning screen savers on your Mac. The new **Aerial Screen Savers** in macOS Sonoma are so amazing, it's worth upgrading to Sonoma just to add this new feature. Aerial Screen Savers can also double as your desktop wallpaper.

One of the coolest features is how an Aerial Screen Saver seamlessly transitions, cruising to a smooth stop, to become your desktop wallpaper when you wake or log into your Mac. Because the wallpaper image is taken from the video, it's not static. You get a different view of your wallpaper each time you log in or wake your Mac. Since the Aerial Screen Saver also plays on your lock screen, the effect flows seamlessly from your screen saver to your lock screen and to your desktop wallpaper.

Like the macOS Sonoma Aerial Wallpaper, the Aerial Screen Savers are organized into four categories – **Landscape**, **Cityscape**, **Underwater**, and **Earth**. There are 61 choices in the Landscape category, 30 in Cityscape, 21 in Underwater, and 22 options in the Earth category.

The default screen saver is Sonoma Horizon, the first of 61 screen saver options in the Landscape category. To select another Aerial Screen Saver, open System Settings, and select **Screen Saver** in the sidebar. You may have to scroll down the sidebar to find the Screen Saver settings.

The thumbnail image at the top of the Screen Saver settings window shows the current screen saver. In the images below, the current screen saver is **Oregon Sunset**, its name shown to the right of the thumbnail.

macOS Sonoma added the capability for your screen saver to do double duty as your desktop wallpaper. If you'd like to enable the wallpaper that matches your screen saver, flip the switch next to **Show as wallpaper** on.

Also new in macOS Sonoma is the ability to set the same screen saver on all Spaces with the flip of a switch. If you'd like the same screen saver on all your Spaces, flip the switch next to **Show on all Spaces** on. I will cover the Spaces feature in depth in the Mission Control chapter.

To see all the available screen saver options in a category, place your pointer over one of the images and scroll left and right. Or click **Show All** for the category you wish to see, and it will expand and allow you to scroll up and down through the screen saver options. Click **Show Less** to close the category.

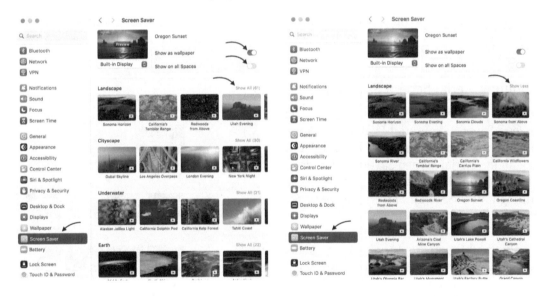

Click on your desired screen saver. You can preview a screen saver by hovering your pointer over the thumbnail at the top of the settings window and clicking the **Preview** button to launch a full-screen preview. Move your pointer to end the preview and return to the Screen Saver settings window.

If you see a down arrow next to the name of a screen saver, it indicates the video needs to be downloaded. Clicking a screen saver to download it. Aerial Screen Savers download on demand to save storage space.

Storage space the one downside to the Aerial Screen Savers. They take up a lot of storage. After you have picked your favorites, you may want to clean up the folder where the videos are stored, deleting the ones you don't like to reclaim storage space.

To clean up the Aerial Screen Saver video folder, open Finder and enter ⇧⌘G (shift+command+G) to open the **Go to the folder** dialog box. Enter the following path:

`/Library/Application Support/com.apple.idleassetsd/Customer/`

The Aerial Screen Savers are stored in the **4KSDR240FPS** folder as QuickTime videos. If you'd like to play a video, double click on it to open QuickTime. Otherwise, you can drag the videos you do not want to the trash. Enter your password when prompted. Note that the Wallpaper settings window will not update until you have restarted your Mac or have logged out and logged back in.

Shuffling Aerial Screen Savers

You don't have to settle for a single Aerial Screen Saver. Like Aerial Wallpaper, Apple anticipated that its customers would like to see all the Aerial Screen Savers and added a shuffle feature that allows you to rotate through all the Aerial Screen Savers or just those in one category.

To shuffle through the Aerial Screen Savers, open the System Settings app and select Screen Saver from the sidebar. When the Screen Saver settings window opens, scroll down until you see **Shuffle Aerials**. Click **Show All** to see the five choices – Shuffle All, Shuffle Landscape, Shuffle Cityscape, Shuffle Underwater, and Shuffle Earth. Click on your desired shuffle option.

Once you have made your selection, it will appear in the thumbnail image at the top of the Screen Saver settings window. By default, the Screen Saver will change every day. You have the option of changing how often you want to rotate through the screen savers by using the pop-up menu next to the name of the shuffle. You can choose every 12 hours, every day, every 2 days, every week, every month, or continuously. Don't forget to enable the wallpaper by flipping the switch next to **Show as wallpaper** and choose whether to **Show on all Spaces** using its switch.

macOS Themed Screen Savers

Apple included macOS themed screen savers for each of the last 3 macOS releases – Sonoma, Ventura, and Monterey. Only the Sonoma screen saver offers light, dark, or automatic options from a pop-up menu. You can set Sonoma as your wallpaper from the Screen Saver settings window by flipping the switch next to **Show as wallpaper** on. You can also use the Sonoma screen saver on all Spaces by flipping the switch next to **Show on all Spaces** on.

The Ventura and Monterey screen savers do not offer light, dark, and automatic options nor do they allow you to set their wallpaper in the Screen Saver settings window. If you want the Ventura or Monterey wallpapers, you'll have to select them from the Wallpaper settings window. These two wallpapers feature a Dynamic option that automatically changes the lighting conditions of your wallpaper throughout the day based on the time in your location. As the sun moves across the sky, the lighting and shadows change until a nighttime version eventually appears. Both Ventura and Monterey also offer light and dark versions.

Legacy Screen Savers

If you haven't fallen in love with macOS Sonoma's Aerial Screens Savers and still prefer the screen saver options from previous releases, Apple included the 10 screen saver options from which to choose. These legacy screen savers from previous macOS releases are located at the bottom of the Screen Saver settings window under a heading called **Other**.

These legacy screen savers include **Photos**, which can use a folder of images or a photo album as a source. Click the **Options...** button to reveal a configuration sheet that lets you choose a folder or a photo album from your Photos app using a pop-up menu. If you prefer solid colors, the pop-up menu offers a colors option. When the checkbox next to **Shuffle slide order** is checked, your images will appear randomly instead of being displayed sequentially. A pop-menu next to **Style** in the Screen Saver settings window lets you choose from among several screen saver styles. You also have the option of using the same screen saver on all Spaces by flipping the switch next to **Show on all Spaces** on.

Other screen savers such as Hello, Drift, Flurry, Album Artwork, and Word of the Day have configurable options accessible by clicking the **Options…** button in the Screen Saver settings. The Message screen saver lets you enter a message that will be shown when the screen saver is running. Selecting Random randomizes the screen saver, playing a different one each time.

Starting the Screen Saver

Now that you have configured your desired screen saver, you need to select how long your Mac will be inactive for before your screen saver starts. To configure the inactivity timer, open System Settings, scroll down the sidebar and select Lock Screen. Select an inactivity time from the pop-up menu next to **Start Screen Saver when inactive**. You can select 1, 2, 3, 5, 10, 20, or 30 minutes, 1, 1½, 2, 2½, and 3 hours of inactivity.

Disable your Screen Saver

If you do not want to use a screensaver, macOS allows you to permanently disable the screen saver functionality. To disable the screen saver, open System Settings, scroll down and select **Lock Screen** in the sidebar. Select **Never** from the pop-up menu next to **Start Screen Saver when inactive**.

Display Sleep

Another option if you do not want to use a screensaver is to put your display to sleep after a period of inactivity. The benefit of this feature is that it saves electricity or battery power.

To configure the display sleep timer, open System Settings, scroll down, and select **Lock Screen** from the sidebar. If you have an Apple laptop, the display sleep timer is configured separately for when your Mac is on battery and AC power.

To set the display sleep timer for when your MacBook is on battery power, use the pop-up menu next to **Turn display off on battery when inactive**. Select from 1, 2, 3, 5, 10, 20, or 30 minutes, 1, 1½, 2, 2½, and 3 hours of inactivity. Never is also an option.

To set the display sleep timer for when your Mac is plugged in, use the pop-up menu next to **Turn display off on power adapter when inactive**. Select from 1, 2, 3, 5, 10, 20, or 30 minutes, 1, 1½, 2, 2½, and 3 hours of inactivity. Never is also an option.

Locking Your Mac

Locking your Mac helps protect your data and files from prying eyes and deters others from accessing your Mac. To configure your Mac to require a password, open the System Settings app. Scroll down the sidebar and select **Lock Screen**. Select an amount of time for your Mac to lock from the pop-up menu next to **Require password after screen saver**

begins or display is turned off. I recommend you select **Immediately** from the pop-up menu. This will protect the data on your Mac from prying eyes if you happen to walk away from your Mac without locking it. The pop-up menu offers options of immediately, 5 seconds, 1, 5, or 15 minutes, 1, 2, 4, or 8 hours, or never.

However, note that if your screen saver starts after 10 minutes of inactivity, your Mac will be unlocked and accessible to others for the 10 minutes until your screen saver starts. I recommend you set the screen saver inactivity timer to its lowest setting of 1 minute.

macOS lets you quickly lock your Mac. To lock your Mac immediately, use the keyboard shortcut ^⌘Q (control+command+Q) or select ⌘ > **Lock Screen** from the Apple Menu. Another option is to configure a Hot Corner to lock your Mac. You can also add a Screen Lock button to the Control Strip, as shown in the image below. The Screen Lock button is the third from the right.

You can also lock your Mac using the keyboard shortcut ⇧^**power** (shift+control+power). On an older Mac, the shortcut is ⇧^**eject** (shift+control+eject).

Lock Screen

macOS Sonoma features a completely redesigned lock screen with a large digital clock with the date and day of the week. Apple moved your photo and log in to the bottom of the screen. If you configured a lock screen message, it is found directly above your photo.

If you don't like the digital clock, macOS Sonoma allows you to remove it. You also have the option of showing the clock on both the screen saver and lock screen, or on just the lock screen. By default, macOS will only show the digital clock on the lock screen. To configure your lock screen, open the System Settings app, and scroll down the sidebar to select **Lock Screen**. To configure the clock, select your choice from the pop-up menu next to **Show large clock**. Your options include **on Screen Saver and Lock Screen**, **on Lock Screen**, and **Never**.

If you want to show your username and photo on your lock screen, flip the switch next to **Show user name and photo** on.

If you set up a password hint, you have the option of showing your password hint on the lock screen. Your password hint will be shown if you enter your password incorrectly 3 times.

To set a password hint, open System Settings, scroll down the sidebar, and select **Users & Groups**. Click the **i** (info) button next to your name to open a configuration sheet. Click the **Change...** button. Enter your old and new passwords in the appropriate fields, then enter your password hint. Click **Change Password** to finish. Although Apple recommends it, you are not required to create a password hint.

Lock Screen Message

macOS lets you configure your Mac to show a message when the screen is locked. It is a good idea to provide contact information on the lock screen in case your lost Mac is found by an honest person.

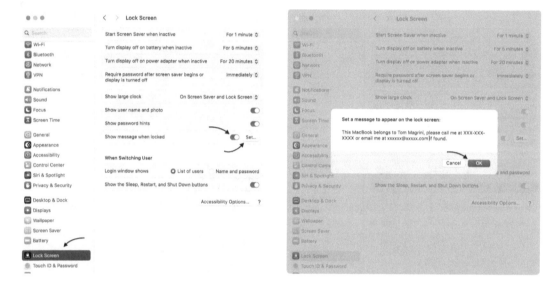

To set a lock screen message, open the System Settings app. Scroll down the sidebar and select **Lock Screen**. Flip the switch next to **Show message when locked** on. Next, click the **Set...** button to reveal a configuration sheet where you can enter your lock screen message in a text box. Click **OK** when finished.

Log Out Inactivity Timer

macOS can automatically log you out after a period of inactivity. This is a great feature if you walk away and forget to log out, lock your Mac, or put your display or Mac to sleep.

To set the log out inactivity timer, open the System Settings app and select **Privacy & Security** from the sidebar. Scroll to the bottom of the Privacy & Security settings window. Click the **Advanced...** button at the bottom of the window to reveal a configuration sheet. Flip the switch next to **Log out automatically after inactivity** on and enter the number of minutes in the pop-up menu next to **Log out after**. Click **Done** when finished.

Show Desktop

Do you have widgets, drives, folders, or files on your desktop that you need to access but they are covered by window clutter? Have you ever wanted to take a moment to look at a beautiful desktop wallpaper image and imagine for a moment you were there instead of waiting for the next hellish round of video conferences? macOS offers several methods to quickly clear the clutter from your desktop and put it back when done.

A new feature in macOS Sonoma offers the quickest method to clear your desktop. Click anywhere on your desktop wallpaper, and all windows will be pushed to the edge of your desktop. Click again to restore the windows.

If you don't like this new feature, you can change it so clicking the desktop will perform like it did in macOS Ventura. Open System Settings and select **Desktop & Dock** from the sidebar. Scroll down in the Desktop & Dock settings window to find the **Desktop & Stage Manager** section. By default, the pop-up menu next to **Click wallpaper to reveal desktop** is set to **Always**. Select **Only in Stage Manager**. Now clicking on the desktop will work exactly as it did in macOS Ventura, clearing the desktop only when you are in Stage Manager. We'll cover Stage Manager in Chapter 16.

Other methods from previous releases of macOS remain the same. If you configured the **Show Desktop** trackpad gesture, you could clear the desktop by spreading your thumb and three fingers on your trackpad. All windows will be pushed to the edge of your desktop. Reverse the gesture to restore the windows. You could also use the keyboard shortcut **fn F11** or ⊕ **F11**. Press **fn F11** or ⊕ **F11** again to restore the windows.

Hide Apps

Having too many windows open on your desktop can be distracting, especially if you are trying to concentrate on a particular window. Of course, you could always minimize or close all the windows or quit the applications entirely to clean up the clutter. But that takes time, and you may not want to quit all applications because you want to leave them open for later use. In that case, quitting or closing windows are not viable options. You could minimize each window; however, that could take a lot of time if you have lots of windows open. And minimized windows clutter the right side of the Dock, making each icon smaller and more difficult to differentiate as the Dock expands.

A handy feature is to hide all the other applications except for the one you are working in. Hiding an application will cause all its windows to disappear without crowding the Dock. Because macOS remembers where the windows were located before you hid them, the windows will return to their original positions when unhidden. If you have lots of applications open and want to hide all but the active application, enter ⌥⌘H (option+command+H). You can also choose to **Hide Others** from the Application Menu.

To hide the current running application, enter ⌘H (command+H), or select the **Hide** option from the Application Menu.

To unhide any application, simply click on its icon in the Dock, and macOS immediately restores the application's windows to their original locations. You can use the **App Exposé** feature to see the windows of any application, whether hidden or not.

How do you know which applications are hidden and which are not? By default, the macOS Dock does not differentiate between hidden applications and those that are not. A tweak I will show you in the chapter on the Dock will differentiate between hidden and unhidden applications.

Remove Devices from your Desktop

macOS displays icons of external hard drives or optical drives on your desktop when you connect them to your Mac. These icons represent more desktop clutter. There is no need to display external devices on your desktop as they are available under **Locations** in the Finder sidebar. macOS allows you to stop external devices from appearing on your desktop. Additionally, turning off the display of external devices is particularly useful when you are using a Volumes Stack, which displays your internal and external drives as a single

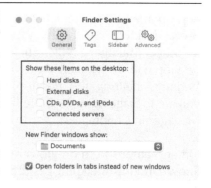

stack in the Dock. See the chapter on Stacks to see how to create one.

To disable the display of external devices on your desktop, open **Finder** and select **Preferences...** from the Finder menu or by using the keyboard shortcut ⌘, (command+comma). By default, macOS displays icons for hard disk drives, external disks, CDs, DVDs, iPods, and connected servers. To disable this feature, uncheck the checkboxes next to each of these items. Changes take effect immediately, and any device icons on your desktop will disappear. Don't worry. Your devices have not been removed. They have been hidden and can be accessed from the Finder sidebar.

Desktop Stacks

For many users, their desktop quickly turns out to be the catch-all location for documents and other files they're working on. Screenshots are saved to the desktop by default, and many applications save items there too. Desktop clutter can become overwhelming and detract from your ability to get work done. Not only does the mess make your desktop look unsightly, CPU and memory resources are stolen because each icon must be rendered, and its contents previewed. If your desktop has more icons than wallpaper, you have inadvertently made your Mac slower by forcing macOS to dedicate resources to render the clutter.

Items saved to your desktop aren't actually saved on your desktop. They are saved to the Desktop folder located in your Home directory either on your Mac or in iCloud if you enabled iCloud Drive. The Desktop folder is easily accessible from the Finder sidebar, a Desktop stack in the Dock, or by using Desktop Stacks.

Desktop Stacks is one of my favorite features of macOS. Desktop Stacks remove clutter by organizing and grouping the files on your desktop into stacks. Desktop Stacks can instantly take a desktop with a cluttered, unsightly, and disorganized mess of files and organize them into a neat stack of files.

To enable Desktop Stacks, secondary click anywhere on your desktop to reveal a contextual menu. Select **Use Stacks**. Next, select **Group Stacks by** to choose your desired file grouping. You can group your files by kind, shared by, date last opened, date added, date modified, date created, or tags.

Desktop Stacks can instantly organize an unsightly mess on your desktop into an organized set of tidy desktop stacks based on your grouping choice. Click on a Desktop Stack to expand it and display its contents. Click again to close. You can navigate through the thumbnails in a Desktop Stack by swiping left or right with your mouse or trackpad.

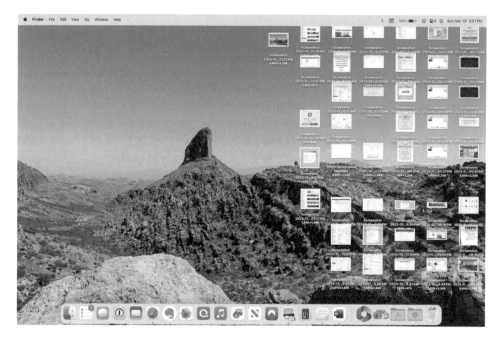

The Desktop Stacks feature ensures your macOS desktop is clean and organized as you can see in this comparison of a desktop without stacks (top) and a desktop with stacks enabled (bottom).

Pristine Desktop

If you want a super clean desktop, this tweak will give you a pristine desktop utterly free of clutter. This tweak turns off desktop icons, preventing them from being displayed. It also prevents you from dragging icons onto your desktop and disables the ability to secondary click on the desktop to create new folders, Get Info, or change the desktop wallpaper. This tweak also disables Desktop Stacks and the new macOS Sonoma feature of clicking the desktop to execute the Show Desktop command. However, each of these features is easily accessible via other means. This is a handy tweak if you are about to give an important presentation and are embarrassed by your lack of desktop cleanliness.

Launch Terminal and enter the following commands.

```
defaults write com.apple.finder CreateDesktop -bool false
```

```
killall Finder
```

Any icons that normally would have appeared on your desktop are safely tucked away in the Desktop folder in your Home directory.

To return to the macOS default, enter the following commands.

```
defaults write com.apple.finder CreateDesktop -bool true
```

```
killall Finder
```

Desktop Icons

If you prefer to see icons for devices and files on your desktop, macOS gives you the option of changing the icon size.

To change how icons are displayed, click anywhere on your desktop, and enter ⌘J (command+J). This launches the Desktop view options panel. Note that the pristine desktop hack must be disabled for ⌘J to work.

The top two options are pop-up menus that control the stacking and sorting of items on your desktop. Selecting None in the stacking pop-up menu disables Desktop Stacks. Available stacking options include kind, shared by, date last opened, date added, date modified, date created, and tags. Available sort options are name, kind, shared by, last modified by, date last opened, date added, date modified, date created, size, or tags.

Use the **Icon size** slider to change the size of icons. Drag the slider to the left to make them smaller or drag the slider to the right to increase the icon size. Changes take effect immediately. The default size is 64 x 64.

The next slider controls the tightness of the grid separating the icons. For tighter spacing, drag the slider to the left. For more open spacing, drag the slider to the right.

The next section controls the size and location of the text label. macOS places the text label underneath an icon using a 12-point font. You can choose any text size between 10 and 16 points. The text label can be located at the bottom, which is the default, or to the right of the icon by selecting the radio button next to **Right**.

By default, **Show item info** is disabled. Enabling item info displays the number of items in the Desktop Stacks.

By default, the **Show icon preview** checkbox is checked. Unchecking this box disables the macOS preview function. Only default icons indicating the application in which the file was created will be displayed.

Display Brightness

There are a couple of ways to adjust the display brightness of your Mac. First, you can use the **F1** and **F2** keys to adjust the brightness manually. Pressing **F1** reduces screen brightness, while **F2** increases brightness. If you own a MacBook Pro with a Touch Bar, you can adjust your screen brightness by tapping on the brightness icon and using the slider.

Another option is to adjust the display brightness in the **Displays** settings in System Settings. Move the slider to the right to make the display brighter and to the left to make it darker.

Automatic Brightness

If your MacBook has an ambient light sensor, it will automatically adjust the brightness of your display based on current lighting conditions. This feature is enabled by default. If you would like to disable it so that brightness can only be manually adjusted, open System Settings, select **Displays** in the sidebar and flip the switch next to **Automatically adjust brightness** off.

Apple's True Tone technology makes the images on your display appear more natural. If your Mac has a True Tone display, it will automatically adjust the color and intensity of your display and Touch Bar to match the ambient lighting conditions. True Tone is enabled by default. If you want to disable this feature, open System Settings, select **Displays** in the sidebar and flip the switch next to **True Tone** off.

Precisely Adjust Display Brightness

Sometimes it seems you never can get the display brightness adjusted to your liking. One segment more is too much. One less is too little. Wouldn't it be awesome if you could adjust the display brightness in smaller increments? macOS has the solution!

Holding down the ⇧ ⌥ (shift+option) keys while pressing the **F1** or **F2** allows you to adjust the brightness in quarter-segment increments. This tweak also works if you have a MacBook Pro with a Touch Bar. Hold down the ⇧ ⌥ (shift+option) keys while tapping the display brightness control on the Touch Bar.

Night Shift

The blue light emitted from your Mac's display mimics daylight, which can disrupt your body's sleep cycle. If you work on your Mac at night, your display's blue light tricks your brain into thinking it is still daytime, causing your brain to not produce melatonin, making it harder for you to fall asleep.

Night Shift is a feature that adjusts your display's color temperature based on the time of day. macOS will adjust your display's color temperature to provide warmer light during nighttime hours to help you sleep better.

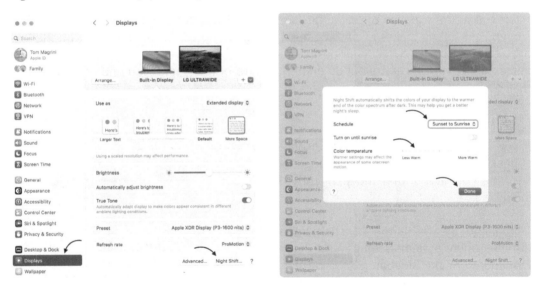

To enable Night Shift, open System Settings, select **Displays** in the sidebar, and click the **Night Shift** button in the lower right corner to reveal a configuration sheet. Choose **Custom** or **Sunset to Sunrise** from the pop-up menu next to **Schedule**. If you select **Custom**, **From** and **to** fields appear for you to set the start and end times to enable and disable Night Shift.

Choosing **Sunset to Sunrise** enables Night Shift based on when the sun sets and rises in your location. This is a handy feature if you travel with your Mac. If you want to enable Night Shift immediately, flip the switch next to **Turn on until sunrise** on. Use the slider next to **Color temperature** to select how warm you want your display when Night Shift is active. To disable Night Shift, choose **Off** from the pop-up menu next to **Schedule**.

Built-in Display Resolution

MacBook laptops and desktop computers with built-in displays allow you to adjust their display resolution to provide larger, more easily readable text or more usable screen real estate.

To change the display resolution, open System Settings and select **Displays** from the sidebar. Depending on your display, you have a few options from which to choose.

My MacBook Pro's built-in display is shown in the image at the right. The current setting is enclosed by a blue border. If you prefer more screen real estate, click **More Space**, which provides the most usable screen real

estate but at the expense of readability as windows and fonts will appear smaller. The **Larger Text** setting makes everything appear bigger and easier to read, but with the loss of screen real estate. Select your desired resolution by clicking on it. Changes take place immediately, so you can try out different screen resolutions until you find one you like.

External Display Resolution

If you have one or more external displays connected to your Mac, you can change the resolution of each display independently of the others.

To change the resolution of an external display, open System Settings and select **Displays** from the sidebar. Your displays appear at top of the Display settings window. By default, external displays always run at native resolution. Available resolutions will be listed under the default. Flipping the switch on next to **Show all resolutions** provides more options from which to choose. Select your desired resolution by clicking on it. Changes take place immediately.

Extended and Mirrored Displays

If you have multiple displays, you can set them up as your main display, extended display, or as a mirrored display. The main display option configures the selected display as the main display for your Mac. An extended display creates one large continuous desktop across all your displays, allowing you to drag a window from one display to another. Another option is to mirror the displays. Mirroring displays the same image on all displays.

To configure displays, open System Settings and select **Displays** from the sidebar. Choose a display from those shown at the top of the Displays settings window. Using the pop-up menu next to **Use as**, choose whether to use the display as the Main display, an Extended display, or a Mirror. The **Use as** pop-up menu will only appear if you have external displays connected to your Mac.

Arranging Displays

When you have two or more displays, macOS assumes where they are in reference to each other. To change the arrangement of your displays, open System Settings, select **Displays** in the sidebar, and click the **Arrange...** button to reveal a configuration sheet. Drag your displays to your desired positions.

If you hold down the ⌥ (option) key while dragging one display on top of another display, they will become mirrored. Separate the displays to break the mirror.

You can relocate the Menu Bar, which appears as a translucent bar at the top of one of the displays in the configuration sheet, by dragging it to another display.

If your display supports rotation, use the pop-up menu next to **Rotation** to select 90°, 180°, or 270° of rotation.

Sidecar

Sidecar is a macOS feature that lets you use your iPad as an external display, allowing you to drag windows to your iPad and interact with them using your Mac's keyboard, trackpad, mouse, or Apple Pencil. Unlike a monitor, you don't have to connect your iPad to your Mac with a cable. The magic happens wirelessly!

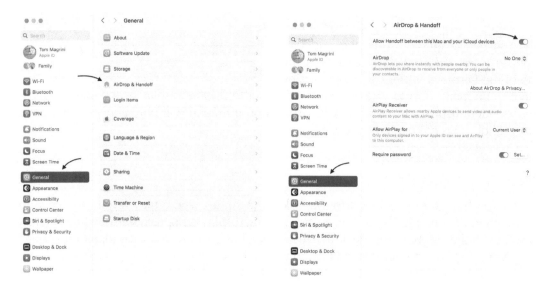

First, ensure Wi-Fi and Bluetooth are enabled on both devices and that you are signed into iCloud with the same Apple ID. Handoff must be enabled on both your iPad and Mac. On your iPad, go to **Settings > General > Airplay & Handoff**. Flip the switch next to **Handoff** on to enable. On your Mac, open System Settings and select **General** from the sidebar. Next, click on Airdrop & Handoff. On the next window, flip the switch next to **Allow Handoff between this Mac and your iCloud devices** on.

To add your iPad as an external display, open System Settings and select **Displays** from the sidebar. Select your iPad from the **+** (add) pop-up menu at the top of the Displays settings window. If you own an AppleTV, you'll also see it listed as an external display option.

The image below shows my iPad Air 4 configured as an external display. Note the black bar on the right side of the screen. This is the Sidebar, which contains commonly used macOS controls. Starting at the top of the Sidebar, the controls are show and hide the Menu Bar, show and hide the Dock, macOS modifier keys ⌘ ⌥ ^ ⇧ (command, option, control, and shift), undo the last action, show and hide the iPad keyboard, and disconnect your iPad from your Mac. The black strip at the bottom of my iPad should look familiar if you have a MacBook Pro with a Touch Bar and use Microsoft Word. It will only appear when you are running an app that supports the Touch Bar.

You have the option of displaying either or both the Sidebar and Touch Bar on your iPad when it is used as an external display.

To configure your iPad display options, open System Settings, select **Displays** from the sidebar and then click on the thumbnail of your iPad at the top of the settings window. Use the pop-up menu next to **Use as** to configure your iPad as an extended or mirrored display.

The Sidebar can be displayed on the left, right, or disabled by selecting your desired option from the pop-up menu next to **Show Sidebar**.

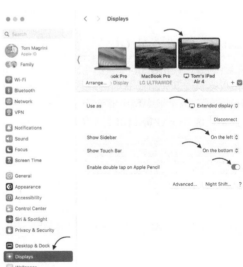

The Touch Bar can be displayed on the bottom, top, or disabled by selecting your desired option from the pop-up menu next to **Show Touch Bar**.

If your iPad supports the Apple Pencil, you can use it to point, click, select, draw, edit photos, and manipulate objects on your iPad when it is configured as an extended or mirrored display. Flip the switch next to **Enable double tap on Apple Pencil** to enable double tap support for applications that support this feature, which allows you to switch drawing tools and perform custom actions within certain apps.

Like any display, you can change your iPad's position by clicking on the **Arrange...** button at the top of the Display settings window to reveal a configuration sheet that allows you to rearrange your displays.

You can disconnect your iPad using the **Disconnect** button in the Displays settings, pressing the disconnect button in your iPad's Sidebar, or from Control Center, which we will cover in a later chapter.

The iPad external display feature is supported on the following Mac models and iPads running iPadOS 13 or higher.

Macs		iPads
2016 or later MacBook Pro	2016 or later MacBook	iPad Pro
2017 or later iMac	2019 or later Mac Pro	iPad Air (3rd Gen or later)
2018 or later Mac mini	iMac Pro	iPad (6th Gen or later)
2018 or later MacBook Air	Mac Studio	iPad mini (5th Gen or later)

Universal Control

Universal Control lets you connect to three devices (Macs and iPads) seamlessly and wirelessly, allowing you to control them with a single keyboard and mouse or trackpad. Universal Control requires macOS 12.3 or later and iPadOS 15.4 or later. Universal Control is supported on the following devices.

Macs		iPads
2016 or later MacBook Pro	2016 or later MacBook	iPad Pro
2017 or later iMac	2019 or later Mac Pro	iPad Air (3rd Gen or later)
2018 or later Mac mini	iMac Pro	iPad (6th Gen or later)
2018 or later MacBook Air	Mac Studio	iPad mini (5th Gen or later)

To use Universal Control, ensure that Wi-Fi, Bluetooth, and Handoff are enabled and that you are signed into iCloud with the same Apple ID with two-factor authentication on all your devices. Universal Control is enabled by default, so all that is required is to bring your Mac(s) and iPad(s) close to each other. All devices must be logged into the same iCloud account, awake, unlocked, and close together.

To engage Universal Control, move your pointer to the right or left edge of your Mac's display toward the side where your iPad or another Mac is located. When a border appears at the edge, move your pointer through the edge of your Mac's display until your pointer appears on your other device. That's it. Universal Control is that simple.

The direction that you moved your pointer when establishing the connection between your devices determines which side of your Mac you will use to connect to your devices. You can change the arrangement in the Display settings by clicking on the **Arrange...** button.

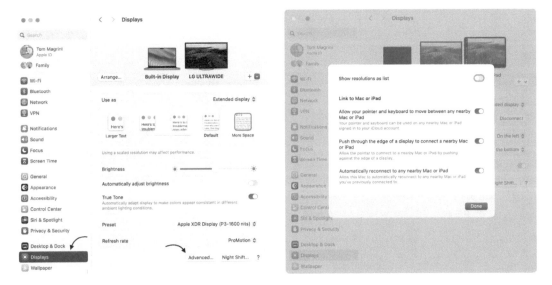

Universal Control settings can be found by opening System Settings, selecting **Displays** in the sidebar, and clicking the **Advanced...** button to reveal a configuration sheet. By default, the three switches under **Link to Mac or iPad** will be enabled.

The switch next to **Allow your pointer and keyboard to move between any nearby Mac or iPad** enables and disables Universal Control.

The switch next to **Push through the edge of a display to connect a nearby Mac or iPad** allows you to connect to a nearby Mac or iPad by moving your pointer through the edge of your display toward the device.

When the switch next to **Automatically reconnect to any nearby Mac or iPad** is on, your Mac will automatically reconnect to any device you have previously connected to using Universal Control.

6

Mission Control

Mission Control provides a view of everything on your Mac – windows, Full screen and Split View apps, and Spaces. It allows you to jump to another Space, Full Screen or Split View app, and any app running in another Space. Mission Control lets you move windows to other Spaces and create, rearrange, and delete Spaces.

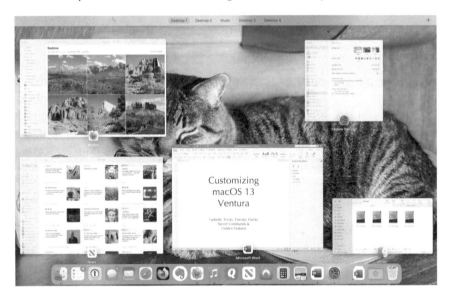

To open Mission Control, use the trackpad gesture (swipe up with either 3 or 4 fingers), launch it from Launchpad or Spotlight, press the **F3** key, enter **^up** (control+up arrow), or tap its icon on the Touch Bar's Expanded Control Strip.

The bar at the top of Mission Control is called the Spaces Bar and it lists the Spaces, full screen apps, and Split View apps. You can expand the Spaces Bar by moving your pointer into it. This allows you to view the Spaces, full screen apps, and Split Viewapps as thumbnails, as shown in the image on the next page. Clicking on any of the Spaces or apps immediately switches to that Space or app.

| Desktop 1 | Desktop 2 | Music | Desktop 3 | Desktop 4 |

In the above image above, there are four Spaces and one full screen app displayed in the Spaces Bar. The Spaces are numbered Desktop 1 to 4 from left to right, and Music, located between Desktops 2 and 3, is running as a full screen app. Each Space is a virtual desktop onto which you can open apps or move application windows. Apple's Spaces feature is a nifty way of increasing desktop real estate to accommodate more windows and declutter your desktop. Did you notice anything about the Spaces? Each Space can have a different wallpaper.

You can rearrange the order of the desktops by dragging them. Any desktop, full screen application, or Split View app can be rearranged. macOS renumbers the desktops accordingly as you rearrange them. Desktops are always numbered from left to right, starting from Desktop 1 at the left. Full screen and Split View apps are labeled by their application names.

Once you have opened Mission Control, you can navigate between the Spaces, full screen apps, and Split View apps by swiping with either three or four fingers to the left or right on the trackpad. If you are using a Magic Mouse, swipe left or right with either one or two fingers. You can also hold down the ^ (control) key and press the left or right arrow to navigate. Clicking on any thumbnail in the Spaces Bar makes that Space or application active.

The Dock appears at the bottom of Mission Control, letting you launch applications onto the active Space, highlighted by a blue border in the Spaces Bar. If you try to launch an application from the Dock while a full screen app is active, it opens in Desktop 1.

Spaces

Desktop clutter can be a real productivity killer. If you have ever opened lots of applications and windows, you know how hard it is to sift through all the windows looking for a particular one. If you only had more desktop space, your desktop would not be so cluttered, and life would be so much easier. macOS Sonoma granted your wish. You can add more desktop space with a macOS feature called Spaces.

Spaces lets you create virtual desktops. Using Spaces, you can create additional desktops, each containing a single app or set of apps. Spaces remove clutter by allowing you to assign windows to desktops instead of piling all the windows onto a single desktop. For example, let's say you were writing a book on customizing macOS using Microsoft Word, you can run Word on Desktop 1, and create separate Spaces for Music, Mail, and Safari – effectively quadrupling your desktop real estate! Spaces are so flexible that windows from the same application can even be split between different Spaces.

Mission Control is the command center for Spaces, allowing you to create and manage desktops, and see which windows are assigned to each Space. To create a new Space, open Mission Control and move your pointer to the top of your screen to expand the Spaces Bar. If you haven't yet created a Space, the Spaces Bar at the top of Mission Control will show a single virtual desktop, called Desktop 1.

To create a new Space, move your pointer to the **+** (add) button at the far-right edge of the Spaces Bar to reveal a partial Space containing a **+** (add) button in a gray circle. Click the **+** (add) button to create a new Space. macOS allows you to create up to 16 Spaces, numbered sequentially from left to right, starting with Desktop 1.

Remove a Space

To remove a Space, hover your pointer over the Space you want to remove in the Spaces Bar. Click the **X** (delete button) in the upper left corner of the Spaces' thumbnail. Any windows located in the deleted Space will be reassigned to the desktop in the foreground. Full screen and Split View apps can also be removed using this method.

Another method to remove a Space is to move your pointer to the Spaces Bar and hold down the ⌥ (option) key. An **X** (delete) button will appear in the upper left corner of every Space. Remove Spaces by clicking on the delete button while keeping the ⌥ (option) key depressed. Full screen and Split View apps display an exit button, denoted by two arrows pointing to each other. Release the ⌥ (option) key when finished.

Full Screen Apps

You can take an app full screen in Mission Control using the Spaces Bar. Activate Mission Control and navigate to the Space with the app you want to take full screen. Drag the app's window onto the Spaces Bar between two Spaces or after the last Space. A new Space will appear with a **+** (add) button in it, as shown in the images below. Drop the app onto this Space to take it full screen.

You can also take any window to Full screen by clicking the green button in the upper left corner of the window's Title Bar. If you click and hold the green button, a pop-up menu will appear where you choose between Enter Full Screen, Tile Window to the Left of Screen, or Tile Window to the Right of Screen. The latter two commands evoke a feature called Split View, which I cover in the next section.

To take an app out of full screen, hover your pointer over a full screen app in the Spaces Bar. An exit button will appear, which is denoted by two arrows in the upper left corner of the app's thumbnail. Click the exit button.

You can also drag the full screen app's thumbnail from the Spaces Bar onto your desktop to take it out of full screen. Another method is to make the app active and move your pointer to the top of your screen to reveal the Menu Bar and Title Bar controls. Click on the green button in the Title Bar's upper left corner to exit full screen mode and restore the window to its original size. Clicking and holding the green control button offers an Exit Full Screen option in a pop-up menu. The keyboard shortcut 🌐**F** (globe+F) will toggle full screen on and off.

Split View Apps

Two applications can be placed side by side in the same Space using feature called Split View. Split View is a great feature when you need to compare two documents or move data from one document to another. If neither application is running in full screen or Split View, open Mission Control and navigate to the Space with the first application. Drag and it onto the Spaces Bar to put it into full screen.

Desktop 1   Desktop 2   Desktop 3   Microsoft Word   Desktop 4

Next, navigate to the Space with the second application window and drag and drop it onto the app you just took full screen in the Spaces Bar. Note that the full screen app will blur and move to the left or right half of the Space. The other half will display a **+** (add) symbol. Drop the app on the **+** (add) symbol to put the two apps into Split View.

Desktop 1   Desktop 2   Desktop 3   Microsoft Word   Desktop 4

 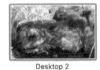

Desktop 1   Desktop 2   Desktop 3   Microsoft Word & Safari   Desktop 4

You can control which half each application occupies by moving the second app to the full screen app's left or right side before releasing your hold.

You can also take two applications into Split View using the green button in the Title Bar of each application window. First, ensure both app windows are in the same Space. Click and hold the green button in the first app's Title Bar to reveal a pop-up menu. Choose from Tile Window to Left of Screen or Tile Window to Right of Screen. Next, click on the thumbnail of the second app that will occupy the other half of the Split View to snap it into place.

You can use the Spaces Bar to take apps out of split view. Hover your pointer over a set of Split View apps in the Spaces Bar. An exit button will appear, which is denoted by two arrows in the upper left corner of the thumbnail. Click the exit button to take both apps out of split view.

Desktop 1   Desktop 2   Microsoft Word & Safari   Desktop 3   Desktop 4

You can also drag the Split View apps' thumbnail from the Spaces Bar onto your desktop to take both apps out of split view.

Another method is to unhide the Menu Bar and Title Bar controls of one of the apps in split view. Click on the green button in the Title Bar's upper-left corner and choose from Replace Tiled Window, Move Window to Desktop, or Make Window Full Screen. Selecting Replace Tiled Window will reveal your desktop, allowing you to select from the available applications.

Resize Windows in Split View

Once your two apps are running side by side in Split View, you can adjust how much space each occupies. To resize an application window running in split view, place your pointer on the black vertical separator between the two apps. A double-headed black arrow appears. Drag the arrow to the right or left to resize.

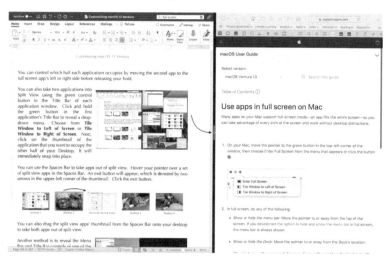

Automatic Space Rearrangement

After working with Spaces for a while, you may notice they rearrange themselves. By default, macOS rearranges Spaces based on their most recent use. Desktop 4 can work its way up to become Desktop 1 if the apps on Desktop 4 are used more recently than the apps on the other three desktops. This gives you quicker access to the desktops you use the most. However, if you find this behavior confusing, you can disable it.

Open System Settings, select **Desktop & Dock** from the sidebar. Scroll down to the Mission Control section of the Desktop & Dock settings window. Flip the switch next to **Automatically rearrange Spaces based on most recent use** off.

You can also stop macOS from automatically rearranging your Spaces by entering the following commands in Terminal.

```
defaults write com.apple.dock mru-spaces -bool false

killall Dock
```

To return to the macOS default where Spaces are rearranged by their most recent use, enter the following commands in the Terminal application.

```
defaults delete com.apple.dock mru-spaces

killall Dock
```

Switch to Space by Application

macOS can automatically switch to a Space with open windows for an application you select. For example, if you are working in Pages on Desktop 1 and click on the Numbers icon in the Dock, macOS will automatically switch to Space which has a Numbers' windows open.

To configure macOS to automatically switch Spaces when you switch apps, open System Settings, select **Desktop & Dock** from the sidebar. Scroll down to the Mission

Control section of the Desktop & Dock settings window. Flip the switch next to **When switching to an application, switch to a Space with open windows for the application** on.

Separate Spaces on other Displays

macOS allows you to have a separate set of Spaces on each display in your system. In a dual-monitor setup, you can have up to 32 Spaces! Enabling this feature also allows you to drag Spaces between your main and extended display.

If you wish to enable this feature, open System Settings, and select **Desktop & Dock** in the sidebar. Scroll down to the Mission Control section in the Desktop & Dock settings window. Flip the switch next to **Displays have separate spaces** on. You must log out and log back in for this change to take effect.

Navigating Spaces

You don't have to be in Mission Control to navigate between Spaces. Swipe left or right with either three or four fingers on the trackpad. If you are using a Magic Mouse, swiping left or right with either one or two fingers navigates between your Spaces. You can also hold down the ^ (control) key and press the left or right arrow to move left or right through your Spaces.

Keyboard Shortcuts

A handy method to quickly jump between Spaces is to set up keyboard shortcuts for each Space to navigate between them without swiping or using Mission Control. Keyboard shortcuts are the quickest way to jump between Spaces because you can jump directly from Desktop 1 to Desktop 4.

To enable the Mission Control keyboard shortcuts, open the System Settings app, scroll down, and select **Keyboard** from the sidebar. Next, click on the **Keyboard Shortcuts...** button to reveal a configuration sheet. Select **Mission Control** from the configuration sheet's sidebar and then expand the Mission Control keyboard shortcuts in the window.

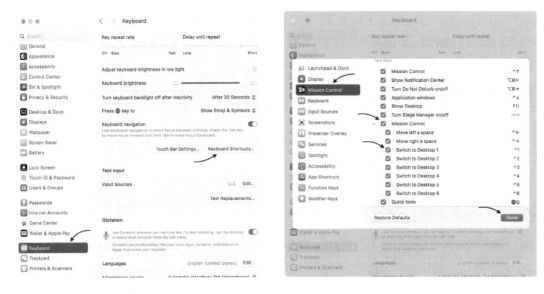

Two shortcuts are enabled by default, ^**left** (control+left arrow) and ^**right** (control+right arrow), which will move left or right a Space. The other **Switch to Desktop** shortcuts are disabled by default. Check the checkboxes to enable each shortcut. Once enabled, simply type the number of the Space you want to go to while holding down the ^ (control) key. macOS immediately jumps to that Space.

If you add new Space, you will have to return to the Keyboard settings to enable the shortcut for any newly created Space.

Switch Spaces with the Touch Bar

If you own a MacBook Pro with a Touch Bar, you can configure it to allow you to quickly jump between Spaces with just a tap. You can configure your Touch Bar to display the

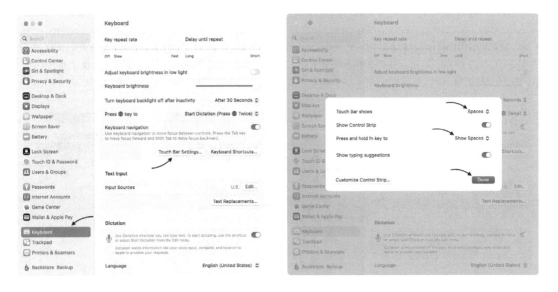

Spaces with or without the Control Strip. Another option is to configure your Touch Bar to show your Spaces when you hold down the **fn** ⊕ (function/globe) key. This second option allows you to display App Controls, the Expanded Control Strip, or **F** keys on the main Touch Bar.

To configure the Touch Bar to display your Spaces, open System Settings, scroll down the sidebar and select **Keyboard**. Click on the **Touch Bar...** button in the Keyboard settings to reveal the Touch Bar configuration sheet. You can configure your Touch Bar to display buttons for your Spaces with or without the Control Strip using the switch next to **Show Control Strip**. The following images show the Touch Bar configured for Spaces with and without the Control Strip. Note that the currently active Space is highlighted.

The Touch Bar can only display a maximum of 4 Spaces with the Control Strip enabled and 6 without the Control Strip. If you have more Spaces, slide your finger left or right along your Touch Bar to see them.

You can also configure your Touch Bar to display Desktop Spaces only when you are holding down the **fn** ⊕ (function/globe) key. From the Touch Bar configuration sheet, select **Show Spaces** from the pop-up menu next to **Press and hold fn key to**.

When this option is configured, the Touch Bar will show 6 of your Spaces when you hold down the **fn** ⊕ (function/globe) key. If you have more Spaces, slide your finger left or right along your Touch Bar while keeping the **fn** ⊕ (function/globe) key depressed.

Move a Window to Another Space

A window can be moved from one Space to another in Mission Control by dragging it. Find the window you want to move on your desktop and drag it up to the top of your desktop and push it up to open Mission Control and the Spaces Bar. Drag your window to your destination Space in the Spaces Bar and release your hold to complete the move.

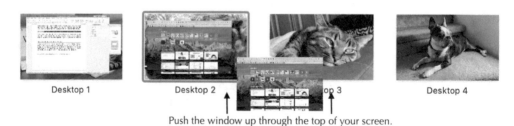

Desktop 1   Desktop 2   op 3   Desktop 4

Push the window up through the top of your screen.

Another method is to first open Mission Control. Hover your pointer over the window you want to move. It will become highlighted by a blue border. Next, drag and drop the window to your desired destination in the Mission Control Spaces Bar. Note that macOS allows you to split Windows from the same app across multiple Spaces.

Group Windows by App

You can move all the windows of an app to another Space by grouping windows by application. Open System Settings, select **Desktop & Dock** from the sidebar. Scroll down to the Mission Control section of the Desktop & Dock settings window. Flip the switch next to **Group windows by application** on. All windows of an app will now be grouped in Mission Control.

To move all the windows of an app, open Mission Control. Next, click and hold the app's icon at the bottom of the top window. Drag the group to the destination Space in the Spaces Bar. All the app's windows will move as a group.

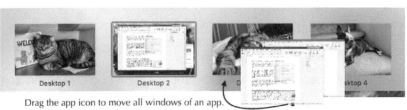

Drag the app icon to move all windows of an app.

147

Move a Window & Create a Space

You can move a window and simultaneously create a new Space for it. Launch Mission Control and hover your pointer over the window you intend to move. The window will be highlighted by a blue border. Drag the window to the upper-right corner of the Mission Control Spaces Bar and onto the + (add) button to create a new Space and for the window.

Drag a Window to Another Space

There are several methods to move an application window to another Space. You could use any of the methods described earlier to move a window in Mission Control. Another method is to simply drag the window to the left or right edge of your screen until the pointer reaches the edge and can no longer move any further. macOS will move the window to the neighboring Space after a short delay.

Note that if you have multiple displays set up as an Extended Desktops, moving a window to the right or left edge of your screen moves the window to the other display. Depending on how you arranged your displays in the Display settings determines whether your second display is to the left or right of your main display.

Drag Delay Between Spaces

If you move a window between Spaces by dragging it to the left or right edge, you will notice a slight delay before macOS moves the window to the neighboring Space. You can remove this delay by entering the following commands in Terminal.

```
defaults write com.apple.dock workspaces-edge-delay -float 0

killall Dock
```

Now you can move a window to the neighboring Space without a delay. However, I've found that without a delay, a window will fly across all the Spaces before I have a chance to drop it. The delay we just eliminated was useful, albeit longer than necessary. The following commands configure a ½ second delay, just long enough to prevent a window from flying out of control but shorter and more responsive than the default.

```
defaults write com.apple.dock workspaces-edge-delay -float 0.5

killall Dock
```

Feel free to play with the decimal number after -float to adjust the delay to your personal preference.

To revert to the default macOS behavior, enter the following commands in Terminal.

```
defaults delete com.apple.dock workspaces-edge-delay

killall Dock
```

Assign an App to a Space

macOS allows you to permanently assign an app to a specific Space. By assigning apps to Spaces, you ensure they always open in the Space of your choice.

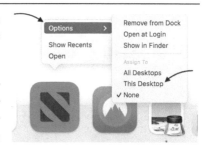

You can use this feature to create a themed Space. For example, you can have one Space for all your productivity applications, another Space for your browsers, and another for social media, etc. How you organize your apps is up to you.

To assign an app to a Space, navigate to the Space to which you want to assign the app. If you need to create a new Space, first launch Mission Control and add the new Space. Find the app in the Dock. If it is not in the Dock, launch the app to make it appear in the Dock. Secondary click on the application icon in the Dock to reveal the **Options** menu. By default, the None option is checked, which allows the application to be run on any Space. To assign the app to the current Space, select **This Desktop** from the menu.

If you have multiple displays, you can assign an app to a Space on a specific display. The **Options** menu offers will list each of your displays. Assigning an application to a display does not prevent you from moving that application to another display later. Once an application has been assigned to a Space, it always appears on its assigned Space regardless of how it was launched.

Assign an App to Every Space

macOS offers an option to assign an application to every Space. This is a handy feature if you have an app you use frequently and always want immediate access to it. For example, I'm always looking for the Calculator, and it's never on the Space I need it to be on. Now, I assign Calculator to all desktops to ensure it is available when I need it.

Find the application in the Dock. If the app is not in the Dock, launch it first. Secondary click on the application icon in the Dock to reveal the **Options** submenu. To assign the app to every Space, select **All Desktops**.

Quick Look

When windows are grouped in Mission Control, it is sometimes difficult to differentiate between them because they are grouped on top of each other. The solution is the macOS Quick Look feature, which is especially useful when you have windows grouped by app.

To see the contents of any window in Mission Control, hover over it with your pointer. When a border appears around the window, press the **spacebar**. Mission Control zooms in to the highlighted window. In the image above, Quick Look is enabled for the Preview application. To toggle the zoom off, press the spacebar again and the window shrinks back to its original size.

Keyboard Shortcut

The default keyboard shortcut to launch Mission Control is **^up** (control+up arrow). macOS allows you to change this shortcut to utilize any F key from **F1** to **F13**, the left or right ⇧ ^ ⌥ ⌘ (shift, control, option, or command) keys, or the **fn** ⊕ (function/globe) key.

To change the keyboard shortcut, open the System Settings and select **Desktop & Dock** in the sidebar. Scroll to the bottom of the Desktop & Dock settings window. Click the **Shortcuts...** button found at the bottom of the window to reveal a configuration sheet.

Select your desired keyboard shortcut from the pop-up menu next to **Mission Control**. You can also use the following keys as modifiers: ⇧ ⌘ ^ ⌥ (shift, command, control, or option), alone or in any combination.

The Mission Control settings also lets you change the keyboard shortcuts for **Application windows** (App Exposé) and **Show Desktop**. Choose your desired shortcuts from the pop-up menus next to these options.

App Exposé removes desktop clutter to reveal all the windows of a selected application. To launch App Exposé, select an application and enter ^**down** (control+down arrow). You can then select the desired window by clicking on it to make it active. App Exposé can also be executed with a trackpad gesture by swiping three or four fingers down, depending on how you configured the gesture in the Trackpad settings.

The **Show Desktop** command clears your desktop of all open windows by pushing them off the edge of the screen. Its default keyboard shortcut is **fn F11** or ⊕ **F11**.

To turn off any of the shortcuts, select the – (delete) option from the pop-up menus.

Hot Corners

The macOS Hot Corners feature allows you to assign a specific action to any or all four corners of your desktop. The associated command is executed by moving your pointer to the corner assigned to the action you wish to perform. The supported commands include starting or disabling the screen saver; opening Mission Control or Windows (App Exposé); Show the Desktop, Notification Center, or Launchpad; creating a Quick Note in the Notes app; starting or disabling the screen saver; putting the display to sleep; and locking the screen.

To configure Hot Corners, open System Settings, and select **Desktop & Dock** in the sidebar. Scroll to the bottom of the window and click the **Hot Corners...** button in the lower right to reveal a configuration sheet. Assign an action to any or all four corners using the pop-up menu associated with each corner. Click **Done** when finished.

To execute the command assigned to a hot corner, move your pointer to the appropriate corner.

While hot corners are very handy, sometimes moving your pointer close to the corner of your desktop accidentally triggers the hot corner. Sometimes moving the pointer to the menu can accidentally trigger the command assigned to the upper-left hot corner.

To avoid accidentally triggering a hot corner, you can configure it to trigger only when you are pressing a modifier key. In the image above, the ⌘ (command) key must be held down for the screen saver to start when the pointer is moved to the lower right hot corner. By using a modifier key, you can eliminate the possibility of accidentally triggering a hot corner.

To add a modifier key, hold down the desired modifier key(s) when selecting an action from the pop-up menu. Any of the following modifier keys are supported: ⇧ ⌘ ^ ⌥ (shift, command, control, or option), alone or in any combination.

To disable a hot corner, select – (delete) from the pop-up menu on the hot corner configuration sheet for each corner you want to disable.

Configuring Hot Corners in Terminal

macOS Sonoma also offers the option of configuring Hot Corners using the Terminal app. For example, I could have configured the Hot Corners shown in the image on the previous section in Terminal with the following commands:

```
defaults write com.apple.dock wvous-tl-corner -int 11
defaults write com.apple.dock wvous-bl-corner -int 13
defaults write com.apple.dock wvous-br-corner -int 5
defaults write com.apple.dock wvous-tr-corner -int 0

defaults write com.apple.dock wvous-tl-modifier -int 1048576
defaults write com.apple.dock wvous-bl-modifier -int 0
defaults write com.apple.dock wvous-br-modifier -int 1048576
```

```
defaults write com.apple.dock wvous-tr-modifier -int 0

killall Dock
```

Let's break these commands down. The first 4 commands assign an action to each corner. The corners are identified as **tl-corner** for top left, **bl-corner** for bottom left, **br-corner** for bottom right, and **tr-corner** for top right. The number after **-int** indicates the action.

0	Do Nothing	6	Disable Screen Saver
2	Mission Control	10	Display Sleep
3	App Exposé	11	Launchpad
4	Show Desktop	12	Notification Center
5	Start Screen Saver	13	Lock Screen

The next set of 4 commands assign a modifier key to each corner. The modifier keys are assigned to each corner as follows: **tl-modifier** for top left, **bl-modifier** for bottom left, **br-modifier** for bottom right, and **tr-modifier** for top right. The number after **-int** indicates the modifier assigned to the corner.

0	No Modifier	524288	Show Desktop
131072	Shift	1048576	Start Screen Saver
262144	Control		

The final command, **killall Dock**, resets the Dock.

To see your Hot Corner configuration, open System Settings, and select **Desktop & Dock** in the sidebar. Scroll to the bottom of the window and click the **Hot Corners...** button.

7

Menu Bar

macOS offers several customizations for the Menu Bar to change the Status Menus and Control Center. Recall from Chapter 5 that there are two halves to the Menu Bar. The left half contains the Apple and the App menus, as shown in the image below. The name of active app is shown in bold next to the Apple Menu. In the image below, Finder is the active app its menu is called the Finder Menu.

The right half, shown in the image below, contains the Status Menus. If you upgraded from a previous version of macOS and customized your Status Menus (as I did), your Status Menus will look different than what is shown in the image below.

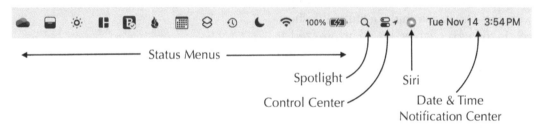

The Status Menus display the status of and quick access to various macOS features and third-party applications via small icons called Status Menus. Status Menus are also sometimes called menulets, menu items, or Menu Extras. At the far right of the Status Menus are icons to launch Spotlight, Control Center, Siri, and Notification Center, which is launched by clicking on the date and time. We will cover Spotlight, Siri, and Notification Center in later chapters.

Status Menus

Status Menus are generally displayed in the order in which they started. If you launch a new third-party application that provides a Status Menu icon, it will appear at the left end of the Status Menus. By default, native macOS Status Menus are located on the right side of the Status Menus, while third-party Status Menus appear on the left. macOS lets you rearrange them.

To move a Status Menu icon, hold down the ⌘ (command) key while dragging its icon to a new location. The Status Menu icon will turn gray while you are dragging it, and other Status Menus move out of the way to make room.

Note that you can only reorder the Status Menus within the Status Menu Bar. You cannot relocate a Status Menu icon to the Menu Bar's left side as it is reserved for the Apple and the App Menus. If you try to move a Status Menu item to the App Menu, it bounces back to its original location. Except for Control Center and Siri, you can rearrange any of the Status Menus by holding down the ⌘ (command) key and dragging them.

If you don't need a particular Status Menu, macOS allows you to remove it by holding down the ⌘ (command) key while dragging it off the Menu Bar. Once off the Menu Bar an **X** (delete) will appear next to the Status Menu icon. Release and poof, the Status Menu disappears. Note that you cannot remove the Control Center and Siri using the ⌘ (command) key. Third-party app Status Menus generally cannot be removed using this method; however, they often provide the ability to hide their icon in their settings.

Hide the Menu Bar

macOS allows you to hide the Menu Bar when not in use. Hiding the Menu Bar off-screen provides more desktop real estate and fewer distractions. When combined with the Dock auto-hide feature I'll show you in the next chapter, you'll be amazed at the amount of clean, uncluttered desktop space these two features provide.

Menu Bar auto-hiding is disabled by default. To change the auto-hiding configuration, open System Settings and select **Control Center** in the sidebar. Scroll to the bottom of the window and use the pop-up menu next to **Automatically hide and show the menu bar** to select an auto-hiding setting. You have 4 options – always, on desktop only, in full screen only, and never.

Always does what you would expect it to do – it always hides the Menu Bar. In full screen only hides the Menu Bar when you are using an app in full screen. On Desktop Only hides the Menu Bar when you are not using an app in full screen. Never disables the Menu Bar hiding feature.

When the Menu Bar hiding is enabled, you can unhide the Menu Bar by moving your pointer to the top of your screen and leaving it there momentarily. The Menu Bar will automatically reappear. It will disappear when no longer needed.

Recent Items

To save you the trouble of looking for a recently opened application, document, or server, macOS keeps a list of Recent Items in your Menu Bar under the (Apple) Menu. Select **> Recent Items** to display a list of the last 10 applications, documents, and servers. While 10 is the default, you can change the number of recent items in System Settings.

To change the number of recent items, open the System Settings app and select Control Center from the sidebar. Scroll to the bottom of the Control Center settings window to the **Menu Bar Only** section. Select none, 5, 10, 15, 20, 30, or 50 items using the pop-up menu next to **Recent documents, applications, and servers**.

If you want to clear the recent items, select **> Recent Items > Clear Menu**. If you have many recent items, you will have to scroll down to access the **Clear Menu** command at the very bottom.

Menu Bar Text Size

If you find that the Menu Bar's default text size to be too small, making it difficult to read, macOS allows you to increase the font size.

To make the Menu Bar text larger, open the System Settings app and select **Accessibility** from the sidebar. Click **Display** in the Accessibility settings window. Scroll down to the **Text** section in the Display settings windos. Click the **Large** radio button next to **Menu bar size**. You must log out and log back in for the change to take effect.

To revert to the macOS default Menu Bar, click the **Default** radio button next to **Menu bar size**. Log out and log back in for the change to take effect.

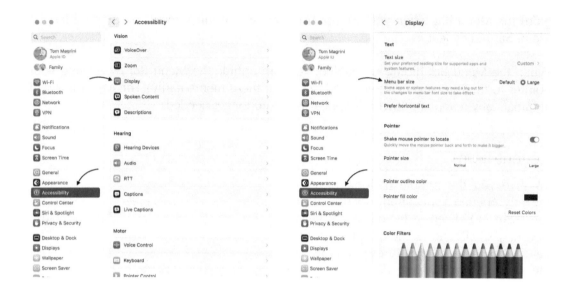

Control Center

Apple took one of the best features of iOS and iPadOS, Control Center, and incorporated it into macOS. Control Center groups several Status Menus, called Modules, into a single, intuitive panel, giving you direct control over some of the most used macOS features.

Control Center is accessed by clicking its Status Menu in the Menu Bar. By default, Control Center is configured with modules for Wi-Fi, Bluetooth, AirDrop, Focus, Stage Manager, Screen Mirroring, Display Brightness, Sound Volume and Output, and Now Playing. Controls consist of circular icons to toggle features on and off, sliders to adjust display brightness and volume, and clickable panels that allow access to granular controls.

Like most macOS features, Control Center offers customization options, allowing you to add more modules. To customize Control Center, open the System Settings app and select **Control Center** from the sidebar. The Control Center settings window is divided into 3 sections: **Control Center Modules**, **Other Modules**, and **Menu Bar Only**.

The modules listed in the Control Center Modules section are always shown in Control Center. They include Wi-Fi, Bluetooth, AirDrop, Focus, Stage Manager, Screen Mirroring, Display, Sound, and Now Playing. The only configurable option for these modules is to choose whether they should be displayed in the Menu Bar. Adding them to your Menu Bar makes the Status Menus for these modules accessible from both the Menu Bar and Control Center.

You can add up to 5 additional modules to Control Center. These modules are listed in the **Other Modules** section of the Control Center settings window. You can add Accessibility Shortcuts, Battery, Hearing, Fast User Switching, and Keyboard Brightness. To add these modules to Control Center, flip the switch next to **Show in Control Center** on. When enabled, the Other Control Center Modules will appear at the bottom of Control Center.

Adding Modules to the Menu Bar

You can add any of the modules in the Control Center settings window to your Menu Bar for quicker access to the ones you use most often. Open System Settings and select **Control Center** from the sidebar. In the **Control Center Modules** section, use the pop-up menu next to each item to select **Show in Menu Bar** or **Don't Show in Menu Bar**. The Focus, Screen Mirroring, Display, Sound, and Now Playing modules offer the additional option of **Show when Active**, which only displays the status icon in your Menu Bar when those features are active.

Similarly, the modules in the Other Modules section of the Control Center settings window can be added to your Menu Bar by flipping the switch next to **Show in Menu Bar** on. **Fast User Switching** uses a pop-up menu instead of a switch. The pop-up menu offers 4 options: show the full name, account name, or icon or don't show in the Menu Bar. The Battery Module adds an option to show the battery percentage by flipping the switch next to **Show Percentage** on.

Date & Time

By default, the Date & Time Menu Extra displays the day of the week, date, and the current time. To customize the date and time display in your Menu Bar, open System Settings, and select **Control Center** in the sidebar. Scroll to the bottom of the window to see the **Menu Bar Only** options. Click the **Clock Options...** button to reveal a configuration sheet.

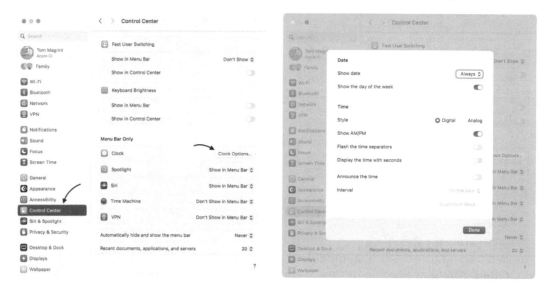

You cannot completely remove the time from your Menu Bar. Since clicking on the date and time reveals Notification Center from under the right edge of your screen, the time is mandatory. However, you can remove the day of the week, date, and AM/PM or show the time using a 24-hour clock. You can forego digital in favor of an analog clock, which offers the most minimalist version of the Date & Time. The radio buttons next to **Style** allow you to switch between a digital or analog clock. When the clock is configured as analog, all options, including the day of the week and date options, are grayed out, and a tiny analog clock is displayed in the Menu Bar.

If you select Digital, you have additional configuration options. The time can be displayed with or without seconds. The colons separating hours, minutes, and seconds can be set to flash on and off. And you have the option of displaying a 12-hour or 24-hour clock. If you select the 12-hour option, you can choose whether to show AM and PM.

The options under **Date** allow you to show the date and the day of the week. A pop-up menu next to **Show Date** offers choices of always, never, and when space allows. When the latter option is selected, macOS will remove the date when the Status Menu becomes too full to show the date. If you are in this boat, I'll show you a neat app that will solve the problem of Status Menu overcrowding.

You can configure macOS to announce the time by flipping the switch on next to **Announce the time**. Choose how often you want the time announced from the pop-up menu. The default is hourly with options for the quarter and half hour.

Click **Customize Voice...** button to access the voice configuration sheet. Select the voice you wish to use from the choices in the pop-up menu next to **Voice**. You can click the **Play** button to hear a sample of the voice you selected. Selecting **Manage Voices...** from the pop-up menu reveals another configuration sheet where you can select from nearly 4 dozen languages, many of which offer multiple male and female speaker options.

You can adjust voice volume by checking the checkbox next to **Use custom volume** and adjusting the slider. If you want to change the speed, either slowing it down or speeding it up, check the checkbox next to **Use custom rate** and adjust the slider.

Location Services

Location Services is an essential feature of macOS that allows you to get the local weather, restaurant recommendations, location-based reminders, and a host of other features that require knowledge of your current location. Many apps rely on your location to provide relevant information. Maps, Siri, Weather, Calendar, Photos, Find My and Reminders are a few examples. When an application accesses your location, the Location Services icon will appear to the right of the Control Center icon in your Menu Bar. Open Control Center to see the last app that accessed your location data.

To control which apps can access your location, open the System Settings app, and select **Privacy & Security** from the sidebar. Next, click **Location Services** at the top of the Privacy & Security settings window.

A small location services icon to the right of an application will identify that the app has accessed your location in the past 24 hours. To the right of each application is a switch to enable or disable the app's ability to access your location. The switches allow you to pick which apps are allowed to access your location data and which are not.

Scroll to the bottom of the Locations Services settings window and click the **Details...** button next to **System Services** to reveal a configuration sheet. You can allow System Services to use your location for various services, including location-based alerts, suggestions, time zone, system customization, Find My Mac, HomeKit, networking and wireless, Mac analytics, networking, Wi-Fi calling, and significant locations.

By default, the switch next to **Show location icon in Control Center when System Services requests your location** is on. You will see a tiny Locations Services icon appear in your Menu Bar to the right of the Control Center icon when System Services accesses your location data. Location data is so integral to macOS that you'll constantly see the Location Services icon, so often it that provides little value. If you don't care to see the Location Service icon, you can flip this switch off.

Don't flip the switch off next to **Location Services** at the top of the Location Services settings window unless you want to disable Location Services entirely. While this stops apps from accessing your location, it also prevents you from locating your Mac with the **Find My** app and eliminates the ability of macOS to provide localized content.

Clicking the **Details...** button next to **Significant Locations** will reveal a window showing a list of locations that your Apple devices have collected as you traveled around town. The detail of the location data may shock you. Apple states that location data is only used to provide useful location-related information and this data is encrypted and cannot be read by Apple. You must decide if the convenience of location data outweighs the risk to your privacy. If the level of detail surprises you or if this invasion of privacy creeps you out, you can disable this feature. Click the **Done** button to go back to the previous configuration sheet and flip the switch next to **Significant Locations** to toggle it off.

8

Dock

Whether you are starting your Mac for the first or the thousandth time, the most iconic and recognizable feature of macOS is the Dock. It is also one of the most customizable features of macOS. Appearing as a strip of icons at the bottom of your desktop, the Dock serves a twofold purpose. It combines the functions of an application launcher to open applications with an application switcher to jump between running applications. The Dock is an ingenious feature of macOS that provides a convenient and speedy method to launch applications, open documents, open folders, or switch between applications with a single click of your trackpad or mouse.

The Dock is organized into three distinct sections by a pair of translucent vertical Separators. Application icons are located on the left side of the Dock. The three most recently opened apps are located between the two Dock Separators in the Recent Apps section, even if they are not currently running. A tiny black dot beneath an app's icon called the open app indicator denotes that the app is running. Minimized windows, folders, stacks, and the Trash can are located to the right of the right-most Dock Separator.

Rearranging Apps

The first order of business in customizing your Dock is to put the app icons in the order you want to see them. This is easily accomplished by moving your pointer to the application icon you wish to move, clicking, holding, and dragging it horizontally, left, or right, along the Dock to its new location. While you are moving the icon, other icons politely move out of the way. Once in its desired location, release your hold. If you click and hold too long without moving the icon, a contextual menu appears, and you won't be able to move the icon. In this case, click anywhere on your desktop and try again.

Removing Apps

Once you have your application icons in the proper order, the next step is to remove apps that you don't want in your Dock. Note that you are not removing an application from your Mac when you remove it from the Dock. You only remove its alias. The app remains safely tucked away in your Applications folder.

There are often multiple ways of doing things in macOS. It is your personal choice which method you prefer. You can click and hold the icon you wish to remove until a contextual menu appears. You can also make this menu appear using a secondary click, holding the control key down while clicking, or using the two-finger tap gesture. Select **Options > Remove from Dock**.

An application that is running behaves differently when you try to remove it. Remember, an app that is currently running has an app indicator beneath its icon. You can click and hold the icon or use a secondary click to access its contextual menu. Select **Options**, and a submenu appears. Note the lack of the Remove from Dock option. Since the app is running, you will not be allowed to remove it until you quit the app. Since the Dock functions as an application switcher, running apps must appear in the Dock.

By far, the fastest and easiest way to remove an app icon from the Dock is to drag it up past the middle of your desktop. About a quarter way up the screen, the app icon dims and **Remove** appears above its icon. Release your hold to remove it. If the app icon jumps back to the Dock, it means one of two things. Perhaps you didn't move it far enough away from the Dock. Be sure to move it far enough from the Dock until **Remove** appears above the app's icon. The other possibility is that the app is currently running. If the app is running, it won't

disappear from the Dock until you quit. Running apps must appear in the Dock due to the Dock's function as an application switcher.

Oops! Everyone panics the first time they accidentally remove the wrong application icon from the Dock, and it disappears. Don't worry. There's an easy fix. Simply add the application back onto the Dock. We'll cover how to do that next.

Adding Apps

Adding an application to the Dock is even easier than removing one. Of course, there are multiple ways to do so. The simplest method is to launch the application, and once it appears in the Dock, drag it to the left to your desired location. The simple act of moving an app icon to the left along the Dock is a signal to macOS that you want to keep the app in the Dock. Another method is to secondary click to reveal the contextual menu. Select **Options > Keep in Dock**.

Another method to add an application to the Dock is to open the Applications folder in Finder, find the application icon, and drag it to the Dock. Note that you are not moving the app. You are creating an alias. You can also add an application to the Dock using a keyboard shortcut. Find the app in the Applications folder, click on it to highlight it, and then enter the keyboard shortcut ⇧^⌘T (shift+control+command+T).

Automatically Opening Apps

The **Options** contextual menu controls how an application behaves. Checking **Open at Login** opens the app immediately when you log in. This is handy if you have an app or set of apps you open every time you start your Mac. For example, if you always open Safari, Mail, and Music, setting these apps to open at login saves you from having to launch each one individually.

Secondary click to make the **Options** menu appear and select **Open at Login**. A checkmark indicates the application launches when you log in or start your Mac. If you no longer want an application to open when you log in, select **Options > Open at Login** to remove the checkmark.

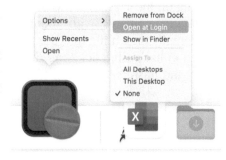

If you want to see the folder where the application is in Finder, choose **Show in Finder**. This command opens the Applications folder with the app highlighted. Occasionally applications are mistakenly installed in other folders. This is a handy way to find them.

The **Assign To > This Desktop** feature allows you to assign an application to appear on a specific desktop Space. This feature is handy if you prefer certain applications to always appear on specific desktop Spaces.

It is quite common to have more than one window open for the same application. As your desktop becomes crowded with windows from multiple applications, it becomes increasingly difficult to find a specific window. This is especially true if you moved a window or two to another desktop. The **Show All Windows** command executes a feature called **App Exposé**, which removes the clutter to reveal all the windows of the chosen application. You can then select a window by clicking to make it active.

App Exposé can also be executed with a trackpad gesture. Click on any open window of the application you are interested in seeing, and then swipe down with three or four fingers, depending on how you set up the gesture in the Trackpad settings.

Separator

The Dock's vertical Separator segregates applications from Stacks, minimized windows, documents, and the Trash. The icon at the end of the Dock that looks like a white trash can is the Trash, a temporary holding area for files you want to delete. You can move files to the Trash by dragging them onto its icon. Another option is to secondary click on a file in Finder to reveal a contextual menu and select **Move to Trash**. You can also click on a file in Finder to highlight it and use the keyboard shortcut ⌘**delete** (command+delete) to send it to the Trash.

Once items are in the Trash, the icon changes to display a full trash can. Secondary clicking on the Trash icon when there are items in it, offers the option to **Empty Trash** or display its contents with the **Open** command. The latter feature is handy if you accidentally drag a file into the trash and need to restore it. To restore a file accidentally placed in the trash, click, and drag it back to its original location. Select **Empty Trash** to empty the trash. A warning dialog will appear to confirm that you want to empty the trash.

Size

The Dock automatically resizes itself based on the number of icons it contains. As you squeeze more icons into your Dock, it stretches across the bottom or the left or right edge of your desktop. The size of the screen limits your Dock's maximum size. macOS does not allow you to make the Dock so big that it won't fit on screen, although the left- and right-most icons will slide off the screen when magnified.

Once the Dock reaches the maximum size allowed by the screen, you can continue to add icons. However, each icon becomes smaller to allow all icons to fit. If your Dock has become overcrowded with app icons, check out the next chapter where I show you a nifty method to group apps into stacks and use them as application launchers.

To resize your Dock, open the System Settings app and select **Desktop & Dock** from the sidebar. At the top of the pane is the **Size** slider, which controls your Dock's size. When you make the Dock smaller, it takes up less space on your desktop. Sometimes it seems that sliding the slider towards large does not change the size of your Dock. This is because macOS scales the Dock to the maximum size horizontally (or vertically if positioned along the left or right edge) to fit within your desktop. When you resize the Dock, macOS changes the size of each icon to fit within your newly resized Dock.

You can utilize Terminal to size the icons more precisely. Try out the following commands. They make your Dock small. Don't worry, you can resize it.

```
defaults write com.apple.dock tilesize -int 32
```

```
killall Dock
```

macOS allows you to replace the 32 in the first command with an integer from 1 to 256. The smaller the number, the smaller the Dock. Try using the integer 1.

```
defaults write com.apple.dock tilesize -int 1
```

```
killall Dock
```

Don't worry. Your Dock is still there. It's that tiny blob where it used to be. A Dock this small is not useable even with magnification. Let's change it to a more reasonable size.

```
defaults write com.apple.dock tilesize -int 64
```

```
killall Dock
```

There, that's better. You can try other integers between 1 and 256. If you were hoping for a super-sized Dock, you're out of luck. The size of the Dock is limited to the maximum size that fits on your screen.

Sometimes getting the Dock sized is like adjusting the driver's seat in your car. It's never quite right. If you want to return the Dock to its default size and start over, open Terminal and enter these commands.

```
defaults delete com.apple.dock tilesize
```

```
killall Dock
```

Magnification

Magnification is a handy feature that allows you to conserve desktop real estate by keeping your Dock small and magnifying icons as you move your pointer over them. Magnification is handy if you prefer a small Dock or your Dock is crowded with many icons. With magnification enabled, the icons in your Dock grow bigger as you move your pointer over them.

To enable Dock Magnification, open System Settings and select **Desktop & Dock** from the sidebar. Using the slider beneath **Magnification**, select your desired level of magnification from "Min" to "Max," which is 128 pixels. If you want to disable Dock Magnification, slide the slider to off.

You can also access the **Desktop & Dock** settings from the Dock. Position your pointer over the Dock Separator. When the pointer turns into a two-headed vertical white arrow, use a secondary click to open the Dock contextual menu. Select **Dock Settings...** to go directly to the Desktop and Dock settings. You can also enable and disable magnification and hiding and change the Dock's position and minimization effect from this contextual menu.

Holding down the ⇧^ keys (shift+control) while moving your pointer across your Dock temporarily toggles magnification on or off. If you have Dock magnification disabled, holding the ⇧^ (shift+control) keys while moving your pointer across the Dock temporarily enables magnification. Conversely, if you have Dock magnification enabled, holding the ⇧^ (shift+control) keys while moving your pointer across the Dock temporarily disables magnification.

If you want more magnification than what is configurable in the Desktop & Dock settings, you can set magnification levels up to a ridiculously large 512 pixels. Open Terminal and enter the following commands. The 256 at the end of the first command doubles the default maximum magnification of 128 accessible from the slider in the Desktop & Dock settings.

```
defaults write com.apple.dock largesize -float 256
```

```
killall Dock
```

Why not go all the way and double the magnification level again? Now that's ridiculously large! You can enter an integer between 1 and 512. Enter the following commands to revert to the default maximum magnification level.

```
defaults write com.apple.dock largesize -float 128
```

```
killall Dock
```

Position

The default position of the Dock is at the bottom of your desktop. macOS allows you to relocate the Dock to the left or right edges of your desktop. The image below shows you what the Dock looks like in all the three positions.

To relocate your Dock, open System Settings and select **Desktop & Dock** in the sidebar. Select the **Left**, **Bottom**, or **Right** from the pop-up menu next to **Position on screen**.

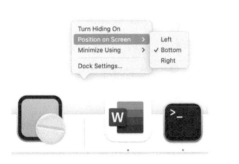

You can relocate the Dock by positioning your pointer over a Separator. When the pointer turns into a two-headed vertical white arrow, secondary click to open the Dock

171

contextual menu. Select **Position on Screen** and then choose left, bottom, or right. The current setting is denoted by a checkmark.

You can also change the position of the Dock using the Terminal application. To change the Dock's position so it is on the left side of your desktop, enter the following commands.

```
defaults write com.apple.dock orientation -string left
```

```
killall Dock
```

Replacing left in the first command with right, moves your Dock to the right side of your desktop.

```
defaults write com.apple.dock orientation -string right
```

```
killall Dock
```

To return the Dock to its default position at the bottom of your desktop, enter the following commands in Terminal.

```
defaults delete com.apple.dock orientation
```

```
killall Dock
```

Minimizing Windows

macOS features two standard animation effects when windows are minimized or maximized. The default is the **Genie effect**, in which windows minimize or maximize like a genie entering or exiting a magic lamp. The second option is the **Scale effect**, where a window scales smaller and smaller until it finally disappears into the Dock. When maximizing, the window scales larger as it restores itself to its original size.

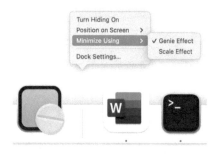

To change how windows minimize, open the System Settings app, and select **Desktop & Dock** from the sidebar. Choose Genie effect or Scale effect from the pop-up menu next to **Minimize windows using**.

You can also change how windows are minimized from the Dock. Position your pointer over the Dock Separator. When your pointer turns into a two-headed vertical white arrow, secondary click to open the Dock contextual menu. Select **Minimize Using** and choose Genie effect or Scale effect. The current setting is denoted by a checkmark.

Hidden Suck Effect

macOS offers one more animation, the **Suck** effect, which is not available in the Desktop & Dock settings window. As the name suggests, a minimized window appears as if it is being sucked into the Dock by a powerful vacuum cleaner. Maximizing a window reverses the effect, with the window shooting back to its original position, as if pushed by a powerful leaf blower.

To enable the Suck effect, open Terminal, and enter the following commands. Be sure to press the **return** key after each line. The change takes place immediately. Minimize a window and check it out.

```
defaults write com.apple.dock mineffect -string suck
```

```
killall Dock
```

Once you have configured the suck effect, the Desktop & Dock settings will no longer show the minimization effect. Note the lack of a selection next to **Minimize windows using** in the image to the right.

You could have also replaced **suck** with either **genie** or **scale** in the above write command to configure either window animation directly in Terminal.

To revert to the default Genie animation, enter the following commands in Terminal.

```
defaults delete com.apple.dock mineffect
```

```
killall Dock
```

Double-Click to Minimize or Zoom

You can configure macOS so that double-clicking a window's Title Bar minimizes it, zooms it, or does nothing, which essentially disables this macOS feature. Double-clicking behavior is configured in the Desktop & Dock settings. Open System Settings and select **Desktop & Dock** from the sidebar. Make your selection from the pop-up menu next to **Double-click a window's title bar to**. You can disable this feature by selecting Do Nothing from the pop-up menu.

When set to minimize, double-clicking the Title Bar does the same thing as clicking a window's yellow control button. When set to zoom, double-clicking expands the window vertically to cover available desktop space between the Menu Bar and the Dock. Double-clicking again returns the window to its previous size.

If you have chosen to hide both the Menu Bar and Dock when not in use, double-clicking to zoom expands the window vertically to cover the desktop. While this sounds like full screen, it is not. Mission Control does not recognize zoomed windows as full screen. You can still take an app to full screen when zoomed by clicking the green button in its Title Bar.

Minimize Windows into App Icon

By default, macOS minimizes windows to the right side of your Dock, placing a tiny app icon on each minimized window. This can become problematic if you minimize many windows. As you minimize more windows, your Dock expands. Once your Dock reaches its maximum size, each successive window minimization causes the icons in your Dock to become smaller as macOS crowds more minimized window icons into the right side of the Dock. Eventually, overcrowding causes the Dock icons to become difficult to differentiate, especially the minimized windows.

Instead of minimizing windows into the Dock, you can configure macOS to minimize windows into their application icon. This reduces the overcrowding and clutter on the right side of the Dock and avoids the Dock having to increase its size.

Minimized Windows

Open the System Settings app and select **Desktop & Dock** from the sidebar. Flip the switch next to **Minimize windows into application icon** on. When this option is enabled, macOS minimizes windows into their app icon, saving a great deal of Dock real estate.

When you want to see all the windows of an application, use **App Exposé** on the app icon. App Exposé is activated by hovering your pointer over an application icon in the Dock and swiping down with either three or four fingers on the trackpad, depending on how you configured it in the Trackpad preferences.

You can also invoke App Exposé by secondary clicking on an app icon in your Dock and selecting **Show All Windows**.

Hide the Dock

Although the Dock is a handy feature of macOS, it takes up a significant amount of real estate at the bottom of your desktop. This can sometimes be problematic when moving your pointer to the bottom of a window as it sometimes inadvertently interacts with the Dock. macOS gives you the option of hiding the Dock when not in use. When combined with the Menu Bar auto-hide feature I showed you in the last chapter, you'll be amazed at the amount of clean, uncluttered desktop real estate these two features provide.

To enable Dock hiding, open the System Settings app and select **Desktop & Dock** from the sidebar. Flip the switch next to **Automatically hide and show the Dock** on. You'll see the change take effect immediately as the Dock hides itself.

One enabled, the Dock slips beneath the bottom of your desktop when not in use. To make the Dock reappear, move your pointer to the bottom of your desktop and pause momentarily. The Dock will unhide itself. You can also use the keyboard shortcut ⌥⌘D (option+command+D) to make the Dock reappear.

You can also enable the Dock Hiding feature directly from the Dock. Position your pointer over a Dock Separator. When the pointer turns into a two-headed vertical white arrow, secondary click to open the Dock contextual menu. Select **Turn Hiding On**. To disable, secondary click the Dock Separator and select **Turn Hiding Off**.

Lastly, if you want to use Terminal commands to enable or disable this feature, open Terminal, and enter the following commands to enable the Dock's auto-hiding feature.

```
defaults write com.apple.dock autohide –bool true
```

```
killall Dock
```

To return to the macOS default where the Dock does not auto-hide, enter the following commands.

```
defaults delete com.apple.dock autohide
```

```
killall Dock
```

You can also use a keyboard shortcut the keyboard shortcut ⌥⌘D (option+command+D) to make the Dock disappear and reappear on demand.

Animate Opening Apps

Application icons in the Dock bounce when you launch them or if the application requires your attention. The latter event typically occurs when a dialog box opens with a warning, needs your input, or the application wants to tell you a task has been completed.

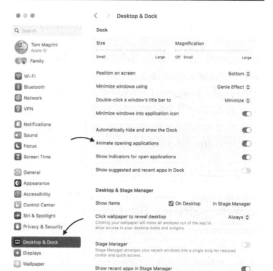

Animation is enabled by default. If you do not like this feature, you can disable it. To disable app animation, open the System Settings app and select **Desktop & Dock** from the sidebar. Flip the switch next to **Animate opening apps** off.

Some applications bounce their icon continuously until you respond by clicking the bouncing icon. The incessant bouncing can be irritating if you are busy doing something else and are not at a convenient breakpoint. Stopping icons from bouncing in response to a warning or when the app needs your attention requires configuration using the Terminal application.

To disable bouncing apps, launch Terminal and enter the following commands.

```
defaults write com.apple.dock no–bouncing –bool true
```

```
killall Dock
```

To turn bouncing back on for warnings, enter the following commands.

```
defaults delete com.apple.dock no-bouncing

killall Dock
```

App Indicators

By default, macOS puts a tiny black indicator dot underneath the app icon of open applications. If you move the Dock to the left or right edge of your desktop, the indicator will be on the left or right, respectively. If you don't care to know which applications are open, you can disable this feature.

To remove open app indicators, open the System Settings app and select **Desktop & Dock** from the sidebar. Flip the switch next to **Show indicators for open applications** off.

You can also turn off application indicators using Terminal. Launch Terminal and enter the following commands.

```
defaults write com.apple.dock show-process-indicators -bool false

killall Dock
```

Enter the following commands to turn the indicator lights back on.

```
defaults write com.apple.dock show-process-indicators -bool true

killall Dock
```

Recent Apps

macOS displays the icons of recently used apps, in a special section of the Dock. If you don't want to see your recent apps, macOS allows you to hide this section of the Dock, reclaiming the space for more app icons.

Recent Apps

Open the System Settings app and select **Desktop & Dock** from the sidebar. Flip the switch next to **Show recent applications in Dock** off.

You can also enter the following commands in Terminal to disable the recent apps from being displayed in your Dock.

```
defaults write com.apple.dock
show-recents -bool false
```

```
killall Dock
```

To reset macOS to its default of displaying the recent apps in the Dock, enter the following commands in Terminal.

```
defaults delete com.apple.dock
show-recents
```

```
killall Dock
```

If you disabled recent apps in your Dock, you can find your recently opened apps by selecting > **Recent Items**. This menu also displays your recently opened documents.

Add a Space

Appl icons are equally spaced next to each other in the Dock. Grouping icons together can help you better organize your apps. macOS allows you to add a blank space to the Dock, which can be used to separate application groups.

To add a blank space to your Dock, launch Terminal, and enter the following commands. The first two lines are a single command. **Do not** hit the **return** key until you have entered both lines.

```
defaults write com.apple.dock persistent-apps -array-add '{tile-
data={};tile-type="spacer-tile";}'
```

```
killall Dock
```

A blank space appears at the end of the app icons. Drag the blank space to your desired location or move the other app icons to reposition the blank space. Repeat the Terminal commands if you want to add another space.

If you have the Dock configured to show recent apps, the blank space will appear to the left of the first Dock Separator.

Removing a blank space is rather interesting. You drag it off your Dock to remove it like any other icon. What makes this interesting is it appears as if you are dragging nothing because the blank space is invisible! If that is too weird for you, secondary click on the blank space to display the **Remove from Dock** option.

Space Out Your Trash Can

The Trash is the very last icon in the Dock. This command adds a blank space to the left of the Trash to separate it from the other icons located on the right side of your Dock.

Open Terminal and enter the following commands. The first two lines are a single command. Do not hit the **return** key until you have entered both lines.

```
defaults write com.apple.dock persistent-others -array-add '{tile-
data={};tile-type="spacer-tile";}'
```

```
killall Dock
```

A blank space appears to the left of the Trash. Drag the space to your desired location. Repeat the commands if you want to add more spaces.

Remove the space by dragging it off the Dock past the middle of your Desktop and release. Remember, the blank space is invisible, so it appears that you are dragging nothing. If you prefer, secondary click on the blank space and select **Remove from Dock** as shown in the image.

Dim Hidden Apps

How do you know which applications are hidden? An indicator light under the icon denotes a running app, but the Dock provides no feedback to tell you which applications are hidden versus the ones that are not. You can customize the Dock to dim the icon of a hidden application, allowing you to immediately spot the apps you have hidden.

Note the difference between the icons for Safari, Firefox, and Music compared to Evernote and Photos. Both Evernote and Photos are hidden, and their icons appear dimmed.

To enable this feature, open Terminal and enter the following commands.

```
defaults write com.apple.dock showhidden -bool true
```

```
killall Dock
```

If you hid applications before entering the commands above, you'll notice no change to the icons. Click on the hidden apps to open them, then hide them again to see them dim.

Use the following commands to change the Dock back to its default behavior.

```
defaults write com.apple.dock showhidden -bool false
```

```
killall Dock
```

Taskbar Mode

The Dock serves a twofold purpose, combining the functions of an application launcher and an application switcher to switch between running apps. macOS lets you change the Dock's behavior so that it operates solely as a taskbar, displaying only the running apps.

Enter the following commands into Terminal to switch the Dock to taskbar mode.

```
defaults write com.apple.dock static-only -bool true
```

```
killall Dock
```

Once the Dock is operating in taskbar mode, you may want to turn off the indicator lights for the running applications. Since your Dock now only shows running apps, the indicator lights are superfluous. You can disable indicator lights in the Desktop and Dock settings by flipping the switch next to **Show indicators for open applications** off.

With no apps open, your Dock will display only the icons for Finder and the Trash.

Running the Dock in taskbar mode is particularly useful if you don't want to use the Dock to launch applications. It is common to want to put all the applications you routinely use in your Dock. The problem is the Dock's maximum size is limited, and once reached, each app icon becomes smaller and more difficult to differentiate from the others. macOS offers several alternative methods to launch applications. Launchpad offers a quick and easy method to launch your applications. Alternatively, if there is a particular set of applications you use regularly, you can set them to launch when you start your Mac. Another option is to use the keyboard shortcut **⌘space** (command+space) to activate Spotlight and use it as an application launcher. You can also hold down the **⌘space** (command+space) keys to activate Siri and use it to launch your applications.

To change the Dock back to its default behavior, enter the following commands.

```
defaults write com.apple.dock static-only -bool false

killall Dock
```

App Exposé Two-Finger Swipe

App Exposé can only be accessed using a three- or four-finger swipe down on a trackpad, so you are out of luck if you use a Magic Mouse unless you activate this tweak. This tweak allows you to open App Exposé using a swipe up gesture on an app icon in the Dock. Swipe up with one or two fingers on an Apple Magic Mouse or two fingers on a trackpad. Swipe in the opposite direction with the same number of fingers to close App Exposé.

Open Terminal and enter the following commands to activate this feature.

```
defaults write com.apple.dock scroll-to-open -bool true

killall Dock
```

If you configured your trackpad to launch App Exposé with a three- or four-finger swipe down, you may wonder why you should configure this tweak. The benefit is this tweak also allows you to open and close a stack by swiping up or down, respectively.

Enter the following commands in Terminal to deactivate this feature.

```
defaults delete com.apple.dock scroll-to-open

killall Dock
```

Single App Mode

Hiding applications is a handy technique to keep your desktop free of clutter and distractions to help you stay focused. A Dock shortcut allows you to simultaneously accomplish two commands – launching an application while hiding all other apps.

Hold down the ⌥⌘ (option+command) keys while clicking on an application icon in the Dock. The app launches and open windows from other running applications are instantly hidden. You can use this shortcut even if the application is already open.

If you like this behavior, you can make it permanent by configuring the Dock to operate in single application mode. Anytime you open a new application from the Dock or switch applications, all other apps are hidden. Note that this tweak does not affect applications launched from Launchpad, Spotlight, or the Applications folder.

Enter the following commands in Terminal to turn on single application mode.

```
defaults write com.apple.dock single-app -bool true
```

```
killall Dock
```

To turn off single application mode and return the Dock to its default behavior, enter the following commands.

```
defaults delete com.apple.dock single-app
```

```
killall Dock
```

Autohide Animation

If you like to keep your Dock hidden, you'll notice that macOS animates the Dock's disappearance and reappearance to and from underneath the desktop. macOS allows you to eliminate this animation, making the Dock hide and unhide instantly.

Enter the following commands in Terminal to eliminate the Dock animation.

```
defaults write com.apple.dock autohide-time-modifier -float 0
```

```
killall Dock
```

macOS also lets you increase the animation's length. Setting the animation to a larger number slows it down. Using a smaller number speeds it up. The following commands set the animation to 4 seconds so you can watch the Dock animation in slow motion.

```
defaults write com.apple.dock autohide-time-modifier -float 4
```

```
killall Dock
```

You can replace the 4 in the above command with another number or a decimal, like 0.15 or 0.5, to tune the length of the animation to your liking.

To restore the Dock to its default animation, enter the following commands.

```
defaults delete com.apple.dock autohide-time-modifier
```

```
killall Dock
```

Autohide Delay

To make your Dock reappear when it is hidden, you must move your pointer to the bottom of your desktop and leave it there momentarily. By default, the macOS Dock autohide delay is set to ½ second. You can remove the Dock autohide delay, so the Dock reappears instantly when you move your pointer to the bottom of your desktop.

To remove the autohide delay, enter the following commands in Terminal.

```
defaults write com.apple.dock autohide-delay - float 0
```

```
killall Dock
```

macOS also lets you increase the Dock autohide delay. Setting the animation to a larger number will require you to keep your pointer at the bottom of your desktop longer before the Dock reappears. You can even use decimals like 0.15 and 0.75 to tune the autohide delay to your liking.

To restore the Dock autohide delay to its default, enter the following commands.

```
defaults delete com.apple.dock autohide-delay
```

```
killall Dock
```

Find an App's Location

A handy trick is to hold down the ⌘ (command) key while clicking on an app icon in the Dock. This shortcut takes you to the app's location in Finder and highlights it.

Lock Your Dock

You spent a significant amount of time customizing your Dock. However, it is very easy to accidentally reorder or remove icons or resize or reposition the Dock. One bad click could ruin your customization. You can prevent this from happening by locking your Dock. macOS allows you to individually lock the Dock's contents size, position, magnification, and autohide settings. By default, your Dock's settings are unlocked. Be sure that the System Settings app is closed before executing any of the commands in the following sections.

Contents

To prevent unintentional changes to your Dock's contents, launch Terminal and enter the following commands. Hit the **return** key after each line.

```
defaults write com.apple.dock contents-immutable -bool true
```

```
killall Dock
```

To unlock your Dock contents so you can make changes to its content or the order of the icons, enter the following commands in Terminal.

```
defaults delete com.apple.dock contents-immutable
```

```
killall Dock
```

Size

The following commands prevent accidental changes to the size of your Dock. After running these commands, you'll notice the **Size** slider in the Desktop & Dock settings will be grayed out. This command also disables the double-headed white arrow, which will no longer appear when you hover your pointer over one of the Dock Separators.

Launch Terminal and enter the following commands. Hit the **return** key after each line.

```
defaults write com.apple.dock size-immutable -bool true
```

```
killall Dock
```

To unlock your Dock so you can change its size, enter the following commands in the Terminal app.

```
defaults delete com.apple.dock size-immutable
```

```
killall Dock
```

Position

To lock your Dock's position on the desktop, enter the following commands in Terminal. After running these commands, you'll notice the **Position on screen** choices in the Desktop & Dock settings will be grayed out.

```
defaults write com.apple.dock position-immutable -bool true
```

```
killall Dock
```

To unlock your Dock's position on the desktop, enter the following commands in the Terminal application.

```
defaults delete com.apple.dock position-immutable
```

```
killall Dock
```

Magnification

To prevent changes to your Dock's magnification setting, enter the following commands in the Terminal app. After running these commands, you'll notice the **Magnification** slider in the Desktop & Dock settings will be grayed out.

```
defaults write com.apple.dock magnify-immutable -bool true
```

```
killall Dock
```

To unlock Dock magnification, enter the following commands in Terminal.

```
defaults delete com.apple.dock magnify-immutable
```

```
killall Dock
```

Autohide

To lock your Dock's autohide feature, enter the following commands in the Terminal application. After running these commands, you'll notice the **Automatically hide and show dock** option in the Desktop & Dock settings will be grayed out.

```
defaults write com.apple.dock autohide-immutable -bool true
```

```
killall Dock
```

Although you have locked the Dock autohide feature, you can still use the ⌥⌘D (option+command+D) keyboard shortcut to make the Dock disappear and reappear on demand.

To unlock your Dock's autohide feature, enter the following commands in Terminal.

```
defaults delete com.apple.dock autohide-immutable
```

```
killall Dock
```

Reset Your Dock

Do you need to start all over again? macOS lets your reset your Dock to its default by entering the following commands in Terminal. Note that this command will delete your Desktop & Dock settings and return all of them to their macOS defaults.

```
defaults delete com.apple.dock
```

```
killall Dock
```

9

Stacks

Stacks are another cool feature of macOS, offering quick access to frequently used items directly from the Dock. Stacks are located to the right of the Dock Separator, the thin vertical line separating applications and recent apps from stacks, minimized windows, and the Trash can.

Unless you upgraded from a previous version of macOS where you customized the Dock, macOS gets you started with one stack, an alias pointing to your Downloads folder. The Downloads stack is the same Downloads folder you see under Favorites in the Finder sidebar. Anything downloaded using Safari, Mail, Messages, or AirDrop is saved to this folder. Holding down the ⌥⌘ (option+command) keys while clicking on the Downloads stack in your Dock opens the Downloads folder in Finder.

When you click on the Downloads stack, its contents spring from the Dock in a fan. Clicking on any item in a stack opens it. At the very top of the fan is a link to open the Downloads folder in Finder. You can change this setting and view the contents as a Fan, Grid, or List. An Automatic option lets macOS select the most appropriate view depending on the number of items in the stack. You can access a contextual menu to configure how the stack is displayed and how its contents are viewed and sorted by secondary clicking on the Downloads stack.

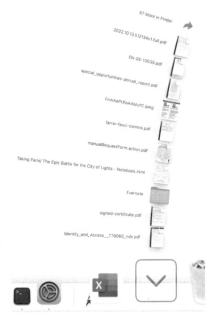

macOS offers four options to view stack contents. Automatic is the default, automatically switching between Fan and Grid, depending on the number of items in the stack. Choosing Fan always displays the contents as a fan; however, only the first ten items are shown. macOS shows you how many more items are available in Finder at the top of the fan. Clicking this circular icon opens a Finder window so you can see the other items.

As their names imply, Grid displays stack contents as a grid and List as a list. Both the Grid and List options behave differently than the Fan view. Clicking on a folder in a Fan stack opens the folder in Finder. Clicking on a folder in a Grid or List stack opens the sub-folder directly in the Grid or List view, allowing you to navigate through your folder hierarchy to your intended destination. If you don't want to navigate further in the grid or list, holding down the ⌥⌘ (option+command) keys while clicking a folder opens it in Finder. In addition to changing how you want the contents to display, the stack contextual menu allows you to change the stack icon to a folder icon.

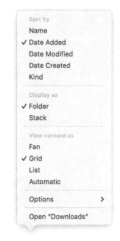

macOS offers five sorting options. A stack's contents can be sorted by Name, Date Added, Date Modified, Date Created, or Kind. The default is to sort by Name. In a Fan, the closest icon to the Dock is based on the sort selected. For example, if a Fan is sorted by name, the closest item to the Dock is the first item alphabetically. Similarly, when the Fan is sorted by date added, the item with the most recent date appears closest to the Dock.

Adding Stacks

You can customize the right side of the Dock by adding stacks for frequently accessed folders or devices. Adding a frequently accessed folder to the Dock as a stack is more efficient than navigating in Finder. The image below shows stacks for my Microsoft Office 365 Apps and my Applications, iCloud Documents, and Downloads folders.

To add a folder stack to your Dock, locate the folder you want to add in Finder and drag it to the Dock. It's that easy. If the folder is in the Finder sidebar, secondary click on it to open a contextual menu. Choose **Add to Dock**. Any item in the Finder sidebar can be added to the Dock as a stack except for AirDrop. Folders located in iCloud can be added to the Dock as stacks too. macOS allows you to create as many stacks as you want or can fit in your Dock.

To add a disk drive, look under **Locations** in the Finder sidebar. Secondary click the device and select **Add to Dock**.

You can even drag individual documents into the Dock, although technically, a document is not a stack; it is an alias to a document. Adding a document to the Dock is particularly useful if you need to access it frequently.

Once your stacks are in the Dock, you can rearrange them. Rearrange stacks by dragging them left or right. Remember, you cannot drag a stack to the left of the first vertical Dock Separator as that side is reserved for applications.

To open a stack in Finder, secondary click on the stack, select **Options** from the contextual menu, and choose **Show in Finder** or hold down the ⌥⌘ (option+command) keys while clicking on the stack. If you want to see where a stack's folder is in Finder, hold the ⌘ (command) key down while clicking on it.

You can remove a stack by dragging it off the Dock until **Remove** appears above its icon, release, and the stack disappears. Another method is to secondary click on the stack, select **Options** from the contextual menu, and choose **Remove**.

You can drag and drop items contained in a stack to move them to another folder, stack, onto the Dock, to the desktop, into the Trash, to an external disk drive, or any other location.

This happens all the time. You think you are dragging a file from the Downloads stack, but you accidentally dragged the entire Downloads stack off the Dock and poof, it's gone! Doh! Don't panic. Open Finder, navigate to the Downloads folder, and drag it back onto the Dock. If the Downloads folder is in the Finder sidebar, secondary click on it and select **Add to Dock**. To avoid accidentally removing or rearranging items in the Dock, lock it.

Highlight Grid Stack Items

macOS offers a feature that highlights an item in a grid Stack as you hover over it with your pointer. In the image to the right, the Mail app is highlighted.

To enable highlighting, open Terminal, and enter the following commands. Don't hit the **return** key until you have entered the first two lines as it is a single command.

```
defaults write com.apple.dock mouse-over-
hilite-stack -bool true
```

```
killall Dock
```

To turn off highlighting and go back to the macOS default, enter the following commands.

```
defaults delete com.apple.dock mouse-over-hilite-stack
```

```
killall Dock
```

If you don't want to permanently enable highlighting of grid stack items, macOS lets you turn highlighting temporarily. Click and hold the Stack icon. Do not remove your finger from the trackpad or mouse as the Grid Stack expands. With your finger still pressing down on the trackpad or mouse, move up the Grid Stack. The item your pointer is hovering over will be highlighted. Continue to hold the trackpad or mouse until you hover over the item you want to open and release. The highlighted item will immediately open.

Another option is to click and hold the stack icon, then immediately release it after the stack expands. Now type the first few letters of the desired item's name. macOS highlights items as you type. Once the desired item is highlighted, press the **return** key to open it.

App Stacks

If your Dock is crowded with applications, making it difficult to quickly find an app, a solution to the overcrowding is to organize your apps into App Stacks. You can organize your apps by any method imaginable – by application type like productivity, social media, utilities, or browsers, or by how often you use them. This feature is particularly useful if you like a neat and tidy Dock or if you switched the Dock to taskbar mode, where it only shows the running applications.

Follow these steps to create an App Stack:
1. Open Finder and navigate to your Home directory.
2. Create a new folder using ⇧⌘N or **File > New Folder** and name it "Stacks."
3. Open your new Stacks folder.
4. Create and name a new folder for your App Stack.
5. Open a new Finder Window using ⌘N or **File > New Finder Window**. Click on the Applications folder in the Sidebar.
6. Select an application you wish to add to your App Stack folder from the Applications folder, hold down the ⌥⌘ (option+command) keys, and drag the app into your App Stack folder. Holding down ⌥⌘ creates an alias.
7. Repeat step 6 for each application you want to add to your App Stack.
8. Drag and drop your App Stack folder onto the right side of the Dock.
9. Repeat starting at step 4 to create another App Stack, if desired.

Dragging a folder from the Stacks folder to the Dock creates the App Stack. By default, the contents of an App Stack are sorted by Name, displayed as a Stack, and content viewed as Automatic. Secondary click on the App Stack to set the sort, display, and view options.

The images on below show the contents of my Microsoft Office 365 App Stack folder in Finder (left) and how the App Stack appears in the Dock (right).

Adding a new application to an existing App Stack is a snap. Open the Applications folder and select the application you want to add to your App Stack. Hold down the ⌥⌘ (option+command) keys and drag the app into your App Stack folder.

Removing an app from your App Stack is just as easy. Open the App Stack in the Dock and drag the app's alias to the Trash. To remove an App Stack, drag it off the Dock until **Remove** appears above its icon and release.

Document Stacks

If you have a particular set of documents that you access frequently, the quickest and easiest method to access them is to create a Document Stack. A Document Stack can be created for any folder in Finder, including your Home and Documents folders.

To create a Document Stack, locate the desired folder or create a new one in Finder, then drag it to the right side of the Dock. By default, the contents of a Document Stack are sorted by Name, displayed as a Stack, and content viewed as Automatic. Secondary click on the Document Stack to set the Sort by, Display as, and View content as options.

To remove a Document Stack, drag it off the Dock until **Remove** appears above its icon, release, and poof; the stack disappears. Another option is to secondary click on the stack, select **Options** from the contextual menu, and choose **Remove**.

Desktop Folder Stack

If you like a clean and clutter-free desktop, you probably configured the macOS pristine desktop tweak. However, a lot of items are saved to the Desktop folder by default. If they no longer appear on the Desktop, where do they go? MacOS doesn't save these items to your Desktop. They are saved in a folder in your Home directory called Desktop. You can access this folder in Finder, but because so many items get saved to the Desktop folder by default, you may want to add a Desktop Stack to your Dock for quicker access.

To create a Desktop Stack, open Finder. If the Desktop folder is in the Finder sidebar, drag it to the right side of the Dock or secondary click on it and select **Add to Dock**. If the Desktop folder is not in the Finder sidebar, locate it in your Home directory. Drag it to the right side of the Dock. You may want to drag the Desktop Folder to the Finder sidebar to provide another method to quickly access it.

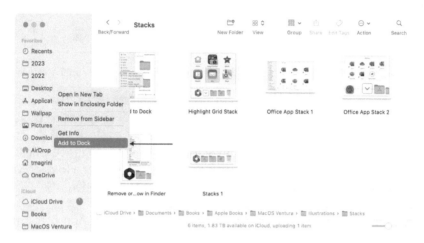

By default, the contents of a Desktop Stack are sorted by Name, displayed as a Stack, and content viewed as Automatic. Secondary click on the Desktop Stack to set the sort, display, and options.

To remove a Desktop Stack, drag it off the Dock until **Remove** appears above the icon, release, and poof, the stack disappears. Another option is to secondary click on the stack, select **Options** from the contextual menu, and choose **Remove**.

Volumes Stack

If you have multiple internal or external drives, wouldn't it be cool to see them all in one stack? While macOS allows you to drag each one individually from the **Devices** list in the Finder sidebar, you can use this tweak to see them all in a single stack.

If you like a clean, uncluttered desktop, you probably wish macOS wouldn't show all your disk drives on the desktop. (See Chapter 5 to learn how to disable this feature.) Once macOS no longer displays your hard drives on your desktop, a **Volumes Stack** makes accessing your internal or external hard drives a breeze.

Creating a Volumes Stack is a multi-step process.
1. Open Finder and enter ⇧⌘G (shift+command+G) to open the **Go to the folder** dialog box.
2. Enter **/Volumes** in the dialog box and hit **return** to open the Volumes folder.
3. Click **View** and select **as Columns** in the Finder toolbar. The Volumes folder will be highlighted and grayed out. This is because **Volumes** is a hidden folder.
4. Drag and drop the Volumes folder to the Dock to create a Volumes Stack.

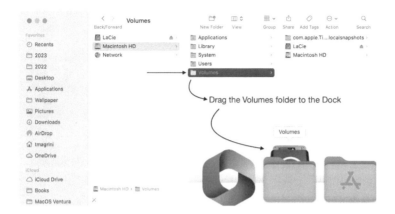

Drag the Volumes folder to the Dock

By default, the contents of a Volumes Stack are sorted by Name, displayed as a Stack, and content viewed as Automatic. Secondary click on the Volumes Stack to set the sort, display, and content viewing options.

To remove a Volumes Stack, drag it off the Dock until **Remove** appears above its icon. Release your hold to remove the stack. Another option is to secondary click on the stack, select **Options** from the contextual menu, and choose **Remove**.

Open Stacks with a Two-Finger Swipe

Typically, a stack is opened using a single click or click and hold when using temporary highlighting. Another method is to scroll up with one finger on a mouse or use two fingers on a trackpad.

To enable this feature, launch Terminal and enter the following commands.

```
defaults write com.apple.dock scroll-to-open -bool true
```

```
killall Dock
```

Once enabled, you can open a stack by moving the pointer to the stack and swiping up with a single finger on a mouse or two fingers on a trackpad. Swipe down to close the stack. An additional benefit of this feature is that it also activates App Exposé when you use the same swipe gesture on an application icon in your Dock.

Enter the following commands to disable this feature.

```
defaults delete com.apple.dock scroll-to-open
```

```
killall Dock
```

10

Spotlight

Spotlight is a powerful and versatile search utility integrated into macOS. At its core, Spotlight is a system-wide search engine that indexes the content of your Mac's drive. This indexing process enables Spotlight to deliver lightning-fast search results. With its user-friendly interface and robust search capabilities, Spotlight is an invaluable tool to locate and instantly access almost anything on your Mac. In addition to files and applications, Spotlight extends its search capabilities to include a variety of other types of information. Contacts, emails, and messages are easily accessible through Spotlight.

Spotlight's search functionality extends beyond the boundaries of your Mac, allowing you to perform web searches directly from your desktop. By typing a query into Spotlight, you can initiate a web search using your default search engine, providing a quick way to access information on the internet without opening a browser. Spotlight searches 20 different categories of data, configurable in the Spotlight settings. To make suggestions more relevant, Spotlight includes your location in its search request to Apple.

Spotlight is accessed using keyboard shortcut ⌘space (command+space). If you decided to keep Spotlight's icon on your Menu Bar, it is in its usual spot in near the upper-right corner next to Control Center. Clicking on the Spotlight icon opens the Spotlight search window.

Spotlight

As you type in the Spotlight search field, Spotlight offers results it thinks are probable matches, refining them as you type and organizing them into categories. The **Top Hit**, the result Spotlight determined to be the most likely, is highlighted at the top of the list. Pressing **return** opens the Top Hit.

Clicking on any item in the search results opens the item. To see an item's location, hold down the ⌘ (command) key while clicking on it. Spotlight will open a Finder window with the item highlighted.

Categories

By default, Spotlight searches 20 categories: apps, contacts, definitions, documents, events and reminders, folders, fonts, images, mail and messages, movies, music, PDF documents, presentations, Siri suggestions, spreadsheets, System Settings, plus an other category for those things not listed above. Spotlight can even do calculations and conversions, so you never have to remember the formula to convert temperatures in Celsius to Fahrenheit.

Depending on your perspective, this could be pretty darn awesome or just a lot of information overload. If you are leaning towards information overload, you can exclude categories in Spotlight settings.

To exclude Spotlight search categories, open System Settings and select **Siri & Spotlight** in the sidebar. Scroll down to the Spotlight section of the settings window. By default, all categories are included. Uncheck the checkbox next to any category you want to exclude from your Spotlight searches.

Privacy Settings

Some information is sent to Apple to make search results more relevant. When you perform a search, your Mac sends your search query, suggestions you have selected, and related usage data. This could include generalized topics of interest to you. If you have Location Services enabled, your location is sent to Apple to provide localized recommendations. Apples states that it uses "privacy-friendly techniques" to ensure that this information is not associated with you.

If sending your personal information and location data to Apple creeps you out, you can disable this feature in System Settings.

To stop Spotlight from sending your location to Apple when you do a Spotlight search, open System Settings, and select **Privacy & Security** in the sidebar. Scroll down to find **Spotlight** in the settings window and flip the switch off. Enter your password when prompted.

Exclude Folders or Disks

By default, **Spotlight** searches everything on your Mac. macOS lets you exclude specific folders or volumes from being searched.

To exclude a folder or volume, open System Settings and select **Siri & Spotlight** in the sidebar. Scroll down to the Spotlight section in the settings window. Click the **Spotlight Privacy...** button at the bottom of the window to reveal a configuration sheet. Click the **+** (add) button to open a **Finder** window. Browse to the folder you want to exclude and click on it to highlight it. Click the **Choose** button. Your selection will be added to the exclusion list.

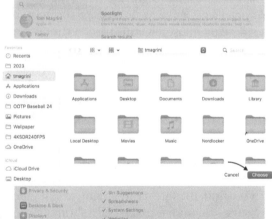

You can also drag a folder or volume directly into the exclusion list.

To remove a folder previously excluded, highlight it in the excluded folders list and click the **–** (delete) button. Click **Done** to finish.

Keyboard Shortcut

The default keyboard shortcut for Spotlight is ⌘space (command+space). macOS lets you change it to any keyboard shortcut you desire.

To change the keyboard shortcut for Spotlight, open System Settings, scroll down in the sidebar, and select **Keyboard**. Next, click the **Keyboard Shortcuts...** button in the Keyboard settings window to reveal a configuration sheet. Select **Spotlight** from the sidebar. You can choose any combination of keys for Spotlight's shortcut.

Click on **Show Spotlight search** to highlight it and click on the **⌘space** keyboard shortcut. You can now enter your custom shortcut in the field. Be sure to select a shortcut that is not already in use. If you select a shortcut already in use, a warning triangle appears next to your keyboard shortcut and the message, "Shortcut used by another action" will appear next to a **Restore Defaults** button that will revert the shortcut to the macOS default.

To revert all keyboard shortcuts on in the configuration sheet to their macOS defaults, click the **Restore Defaults** button at the lower left. Click **Done** when finished.

Status Menu

If you find it more convenient to use the **⌘space** (command+space) shortcut to invoke Spotlight, you may want to reclaim the valuable space the Spotlight icon takes in your Menu Bar.

To remove the Spotlight icon from your Menu Bar, open the System Settings app and select **Control Center** from the sidebar. Scroll to the bottom of the Control Center settings window to the **Menu Bar Only** section. Using the pop-up menu next to **Spotlight**, choose **Don't Show in Menu Bar** to remove Spotlight's Menu Extra.

If you ever change your mind, open the Control Center settings, and choose **Show in Menu Bar** from the pop-up menu next to **Spotlight** in the Menu Bar Only section.

Metadata Attributes

Spotlight allows you to narrow your search using metadata attributes. For example, if you are looking for a specific file type, such as a spreadsheet created in Excel, you can enter **kind:excel** followed by the filename. Spotlight limits the search results to only Excel files. If you are not sure if you created that spreadsheet in Microsoft Excel or Apple Numbers, you could search using the metadata attribute **kind:spreadsheet** followed by the filename.

The following list of metadata attributes can be used to improve your Spotlight searches. Entering an attribute alone without a search term items that match that metadata attribute.

`author:name`	Searches for items created by the author's name.
`from:name`	Searches for email sent by name.
`kind:alias`	Returns results that are aliases.
`kind:app`	Used to locate applications.
`kind:audio`	Returns search results that are audio files.
`kind:avi`	Returns results that are AVI files.
`kind:bookmark`	Used to search Safari bookmarks.
`kind:chat`	Used to search the Messages logs.
`kind:contact`	Searches Contacts.
`kind:developer`	Returns results from the developer category.
`kind:document`	Used to search for document files.
`kind:email`	Used to search Mail.
`kind:event`	Searches Calendar events.
`kind:excel`	Returns spreadsheets created in Microsoft Excel.
`kind:folder`	Finds folders.
`kind:font`	Used to search for fonts.
`kind:gif`	Returns images in GIF format.
`kind:history`	Searches your Safari history.
`kind:image`	Returns results that are image files.
`kind:jpeg`	Used to search for images in JPEG format.
`kind:keynote`	Finds presentations created in Apple Keynote.
`kind:mail`	Used to search Mail.
`kind:message`	Returns results from Messages.
`kind:movie`	Returns results that are movies.
`kind:music`	Used to search for music.
`kind:numbers`	Searches for spreadsheets created in Apple Numbers.
`kind:pages`	Returns documents created in Apple Pages.
`kind:pdf`	Used to locate PDF files.
`kind:powerpoint`	Finds presentations created in Microsoft PowerPoint.
`kind:preferences`	Used to search for System Settings.
`kind:presentation`	Returns files that are presentations.
`kind:quicktime`	Used to locate QuickTime movies.
`kind:reminder`	Used to search for Reminders.

`kind:spreadsheet`	Returns files that are spreadsheets.
`kind:tiff`	Returns images in TIFF format.
`kind:webpage`	Searches your Safari history.
`kind:word`	Returns documents created in Microsoft Word.
`Tag:color`	Searches for files tagged by the color.
`Tag:name`	Searches for files tagged with the name.
`title:name`	Searches for items by name.

Searching by Tag

If you use Finder tags, Spotlight allows you to search for files based on their tag's color using the search metadata attribute **tag**. For example, to find files with a red tag, you would enter **tag:red** into the Spotlight search field. Valid tag colors are red, orange, yellow, green, blue, purple, gray, and white.

Once you have tagged files, you may want to rename the tags to something more descriptive. macOS allows you to search for tags based on their color or their name. Let's say you renamed the green tag to "vacation." Either of the following searches would return all your files tagged with the green tag "vacation." For more information on using tags, see the chapter on Finder.

`tag:green`

`tag:vacation`

Searching by Author

Spotlight allows you to use the search keyword **author** to search for documents written by a specific author. For example, to search for documents written by myself, I would enter the following into the Spotlight search field.

`author:Magrini`

Searching by Date

Spotlight can search for files based on the date they were created or modified using the search metadata attribute **date**. The date can be a specific date, a range, today, or yesterday. The following search will return files created or modified on July 4, 2023.

`date:7/4/23`

Spotlight also allows you to search for ranges. The following search would return all files created or modified in July 2023.

`date:7/1/23-7/31/23`

You can use greater than and greater than or equal to find files created or modified on or after a specific date. The following search would return all files created or modified after September 1, 2023.

```
date:>9/1/23
```

This search returns all files created or modified on and after September 1, 2023.

```
date:>=9/1/23
```

You can also look for files created or modified before a specific date. In this example, Spotlight returns all files created or modified before September 1, 2023.

```
date:<9/1/23
```

This search returns all files created or modified on and before September 1, 2023.

```
date:<=9/1/23
```

Spotlight also allows you to search for files created or modified yesterday or today.

```
date:yesterday
```

```
date:today
```

Spotlight understands yesterday and today. What about tomorrow? Yes, Spotlight does understand what tomorrow means. However, results are limited to Calendar events and Reminders. While macOS is intelligent, it cannot predict the files you will create or modify in the future.

```
date:tomorrow
```

In addition to the **date** search keyword, Spotlight understands **created** and **modified**.

```
created:<=10/1/23
```

```
modified:7/1/23
```

Searching Comments

Adding Comments to your files is a convenient way to organize related content without creating folders in Finder. The Comments feature allows you to enter descriptive metadata into a file's **Get Info** window, which facilitates searches.

To add comments to a file, locate the file in Finder. Next, highlight it, secondary click, and select **Get Info** or press ⌘**i** (command+i). This opens the Get Info window. Expand the Comments section by clicking on the little triangular-shaped caret to the left of **Comments**. Enter your comments in the field provided.

To search for comments in Spotlight, use the metadata attribute **comment:** followed by one of your comments. To search for files tagged with multiple comments, type **comment:** into the Spotlight search field before each comment.

Combining Metadata Attributes

Any of the metadata attributes can be used together to narrow your search. For example, the following Spotlight search would find all Microsoft Word documents I created or modified in September 2023.

```
kind:word date:9/1/23–9/30/23 author:Magrini
```

This search looks at Safari's history and returns any webpages about Sonoma that I visited after August 1, 2023.

```
kind:history created:>8/1/23 Sonoma
```

Boolean Searches

By default, Spotlight searches the same way Google searches. If you enter two search terms, say **vacation** and **florida**, Spotlight will return results that include both search terms. Therefore, results will contain vacation AND florida. The "AND" is what is known in Boolean algebra as a logical operator. The only valid search results must contain both vacation and florida.

Another logical operator is "OR," which will find results that contain either search term. For example, searching for **vacation OR florida** will provide an entirely different set of results than search for vacation and florida, as shown in the images above.

Results Shortcuts

Spotlight features some useful keyboard shortcuts. Use any of the following shortcuts after Spotlight displays search results.

esc	Clears the Spotlight search box.
⌘B	Opens Safari and searches the internet for the terms listed in the Spotlight search field.
⌘B	Opens web browser and searches the internet for the terms listed in the Spotlight search field.
⌘D	Opens the Dictionary application and looks up the word in the Spotlight search field.
⌘delete	Clears the Spotlight search box.
⌘down	Jumps down and highlights the first result in the next category of search results.
⌘I	Get info for the selected result.
⌘K	Opens Safari and searches Wikipedia.
⌘L	Jump to the definition category.
⌘O	Opens the currently highlighted search result, the same as pressing **return**.
⌘R	Launches the app or opens the containing folder of the currently highlighted result.
⌘T	Launches the Top Hit.
⌘up	Jumps up and highlights the first result in the previous category of search results.

Math Tools

Spotlight is quite handy performing calculations and unit conversions. The integration of mathematical calculations and unit conversions adds a practical dimension to Spotlight's functionality. You can type mathematical expressions or unit conversions directly into the search bar, and Spotlight provides instant results. The calculator functionality eliminates the need for a separate calculator app and enhances the efficiency of performing quick calculations.

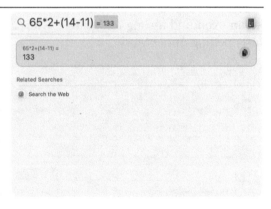

Spotlight can also perform unit conversions, allowing you to convert temperatures, measurements, and currencies. This seamless integration of unit conversions provides convenience and a clutter-free experience. By consolidating these features into the

Spotlight search bar, macOS ensures that you have quick access to these essential tools without the need to switch between apps.

Searching for Other Information

Spotlight is also quite good at providing information, literally at your fingertips. What to know the weather in Boston or what time a flight arrives and whether it is on time. And speaking about time, what time is it in Boston? How about the price of Apple stock. Spotlight can serve up sports scores, nearby restaurants, and movie showtimes.

Spotlight also serves as a knowledge tool by providing dictionary definitions and quick access to Wikipedia. Spotlight is so versatile; it can even find a song and play it without first opening Apple Music.

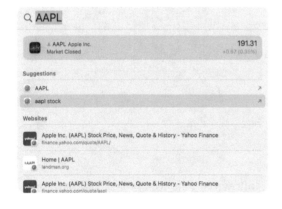

App Launcher

Spotlight is a handy application launcher. This is an excellent feature if you're trying to launch an application that is not in the Dock or if you're running your Dock in taskbar mode where it only displays running applications. The best part is that your fingers never have to leave the keyboard to launch an app.

Launch Spotlight and begin typing the name of the application into the search field. Spotlight zeroes in on the application after you enter a few letters of its name. The application appears as the Top Hit. You can launch the application by pressing **return**, entering **⌘T** (command+T), or clicking on the app within the search results. While you can use the metadata attribute **kind:app**, it is not necessary to find and launch an app. Spotlight learns which applications you launch and often finds your target application after you've typed just a few letters.

Rebuild the Spotlight Index

Sometimes Spotlight won't find a file you know is on your Mac or an external drive. You're not crazy. Sometimes the Spotlight index becomes corrupt, causing inaccurate searches. When this happens, it is time to rebuild the index.

You must be logged into your Mac with an administrator account to run the **sudo** command in Terminal. To rebuild the Spotlight index, launch Terminal and enter the following command. The command erases the existing Spotlight index, forcing Spotlight to reindex the drive. Enter your password into Terminal when prompted.

```
sudo mdutil -E /
```

```
● ● ●                    tmagrini — -zsh — 80×24
Last login: Tue Feb 21 12:49:30 on ttys000
[tmagrini@Toms-M2-MacBook-Pro-13 ~ % sudo mdutil -E /
[Password:
/:
        Indexing enabled.
tmagrini@Toms-M2-MacBook-Pro-13 ~ %
```

The rebuilding process takes some time and depends on the size and speed of your drive and the number of files it contains. Once the rebuilding process is complete, Spotlight will provide more accurate search results.

11

Siri

Siri is Apple's intelligent virtual assistant application, familiar to anyone who owns an iPhone or iPad. It works just like it does on your iPhone or iPad and features the same natural language interface, which adapts to your language usage and search preferences.

Like many features in macOS, there are several ways to invoke Siri. You can click the Siri icon in the Dock, which Sonoma may have conveniently placed there during its installation. If the Siri icon is not in your Dock, I'll show you how to add it later in this chapter.

Siri

You can also click on the Siri icon in your Status Menu, located between Control Center and the Date and Time in the Menu Bar.

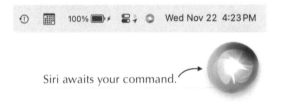

Siri awaits your command.

If you prefer to use a keyboard shortcut, the default shortcut for Siri is **⌘space** (command+space). But wait, isn't **⌘space** (command+space) the keyboard shortcut for Spotlight? Yes, it is. To use Siri, you will need to hold down **⌘space** (command+space) until the Siri icon appears in the upper-right corner of your desktop as shown in the image above. That's where Siri will provide its respons e. Siri also provides voice feedback and will speak its response as well. Dismiss the Siri window using the keyboard shortcut **⌘space** (command+space) again or press the **esc** key.

You don't have to hold the **⌘space** (command+space) key until you have finished speaking; however, I find doing so useful in case I pause. Releasing **⌘space** (command+space) lets Siri know you are finished speaking and that it should execute your command or search for your answer.

Dock Icon

If you customized your Dock in a previous release of macOS, the upgrade to Sonoma may not have installed the Siri icon in your Dock. To  add Siri to your Dock, open your Applications folder. Find the Siri icon and drag it to your Dock and macOS will create an alias for it.

Menu Extra

If you find it more convenient to use the **⌘space** (command+space) keyboard shortcut to invoke Siri, you may want to remove Siri from your Menu Bar to reclaim valuable space. To remove Siri's Menu Extra, open the System Settings app and select **Control Center** from the sidebar. Scroll to the bottom of the Control Center settings window to the **Menu Bar Only** section. Using the pop-up menu next to **Siri**, choose **Don't Show in Menu Bar** to remove Spotlight's Menu Extra.

If you ever change your mind, open the Control Center settings, and choose **Show in Menu Bar** from the pop-up menu next to **Siri** in the Menu Bar Only section.

Hey Siri

Siri responds when you say, "Hey Siri," just like it does on an iPhone and iPad. New in macOS Sonoma is the ability to drop the "hey" and simply say "Siri" to invoke Siri. You can configure Siri to respond to "Hey Siri," "Siri," respond to both, or disable listening.

Open System Settings and select **Siri & Spotlight** in the sidebar. Using the pop-up menu next to **Listen for** select what macOS will listen for to invoke Siri. If you select **Off**, you will have to click the Siri icon in the Menu Bar, launch Siri from the Dock, or enter the Siri keyboard shortcut to use Siri.

Siri when Locked

By default, Siri is available even when your Mac is locked or asleep. Simply say "Hey Siri" or "Siri" to invoke Siri to make your request. Depending on what you ask Siri to do, you may need to unlock your Mac. You have the option of disabling this feature.

To disable Siri when your Mac is locked or asleep, open System Settings and select **Siri & Spotlight** in the sidebar. Flip the switch next to **Allow Siri when locked** off. Once disabled, Siri will no longer be available when your Mac is sleeping or locked.

Keyboard Shortcut

By default, Siri's keyboard shortcut is to hold down ⌘**space** (command+space). However, macOS allows you to select another keyboard shortcut or use a custom keyboard shortcut.

If you want to change Siri's keyboard shortcut, open System Settings, and select **Siri & Spotlight** from the sidebar. Select one of the standard keyboard shortcuts from the pop-up menu next to **Keyboard shortcut**. You have the option of **F5**, ⌘**space** (command+space), ⌥**space** (option+space), or ⊕ **space** (function/globe+space).

You can create your own Siri keyboard shortcut by selecting the **Customize...** option. A text field will replace the pop-up menu. Enter your desired Siri keyboard shortcut into the text field.

Language & Voice

Siri supports over 20 different languages and multiple regional dialects for Chinese, Dutch, English, French, German, Italian, and Spanish.

To change Siri's language, open System Settings and select **Siri & Spotlight** from the sidebar. Select your desired language from the pop-up menu next to **Language**. Once you have selected a language, you can choose the Siri voice by clicking the **Select...** button next to **Siri voice**. From the configuration sheet, choose your desired voice under **Voice Variety** and **Siri Voice** options. As you select each voice, Siri will play a short sample. Click **Done** to finish.

For example, when the language is set to English (United States), you have the option of 5 different male and female voices. You also have the option of selecting from Australian, British, Indian, Irish, or South African female or male voices.

History

When you make a Siri request, Siri sends data about you to Apple to process and respond, including what you say to Siri, which is sent and processed on Apple servers. Your Mac will send other data to Apple, including contact names and relationships, music, podcasts, names of your and Family Sharing members' devices, Apple TV user profiles, names of people in Photos, and apps installed on your Mac.

Siri data collected by Apple also includes computer-generated transcripts of your Siri requests, which are used to help Siri better understand you. Apple anonymizes your data using a random, device-generated identifier that is not linked to your Apple ID, email, or other data Apple may possess about you. Your Siri request history is associated to this random identifier and stored for up to 6 months.

You can delete your Siri request history in the Siri & Spotlight settings. Open System Settings and select **Siri & Spotlight** from the sidebar. Click the **Delete Siri & Dictation History** button next to **Siri history**. Click **Delete** in the next window. Note that deleting your Siri history also deletes your Dictation history.

Privacy Settings

According to Apple, Siri processes your searches on your Mac to provide personalized suggestions and better search results. Siri uses information on your Mac to personalize your user experience, including your Safari browsing history, email, text messages, and contacts as well as information from other applications installed on your Mac. Apple synchronizes across your Apple devices to ensure a consistent user experience.

Some information is sent to Apple to make search results more relevant. This could include generalized topics of interest to you that Siri has learned. When you perform a search, your Mac sends your search query, suggestions you have selected, and related usage data to Apple. You can configure the applications from which Siri is allowed to make suggestions and whether you want to allow Siri to learn how you use them.

Open the Systems Settings app and select **Siri & Spotlight** in the sidebar. Click the **Siri Suggestions & Privacy...** button. The next window lists all the apps from which Siri is collecting information.

When Siri Suggestions is enabled, macOS will suggest actions in some apps even before you ask. For example, when you receive an invitation in the Mail app, macOS will ask if you want to add the event to your calendar. You can disable Siri suggestions on a per app basis. To disable Siri suggestions for an app, click on the app in the sidebar and flip the switch next to **Show Siri Suggestions in application** off.

To disable information collection for an application, flip the switch next to **Learn from this application** off. Click **Done** when finished.

To learn more about how Apple uses your data, click the **About Siri & Privacy...** button. You can read more information at https://www.apple.com/privacy/.

Responses

macOS allows you to configure how you want Siri to respond to you. By default, Siri will speak its response, a feature is called **Voice feedback**. You can also have Siri to provide the text of its response to your desktop. This feature is called **Siri captions**. Another feature, called **show speech**, provides a transcription of what you asked Siri.

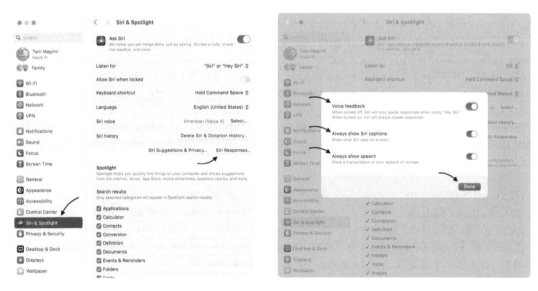

To configure how Siri should respond, open System Settings, and select **Siri & Spotlight** in the sidebar. Click on the **Siri Responses...** button to reveal a configuration sheet.

When the switch next to **Voice feedback** is on, which is the default, Siri will provide a spoken response. If you want to disable this feature, because you are in a quiet office environment, flip this switch off. Siri's response will be shown in a window but not spoken aloud unless you said "Hey Siri" to start your request.

When the switch next to **Always show Siri captions** is on, Siri will show you what it said in a window on your desktop. When the switch next to **Always show speech** is on, Siri will provide a transcription of your request in addition to its response.

Type to Siri

You can type your Siri requests instead of speaking. This feature is useful if you are in an office environment and don't want to disturb your office mates or have your Siri requests overheard. Speaking to Siri could be disruptive in a quiet office environment or difficult if you are in a noisy environment like a Starbucks. You also may want to enable the type to Siri feature when you are listening to music on your Mac and don't want Siri to interrupt your music.

To enable type to Siri, open the System Settings app and select **Accessibility** in the sidebar. Scroll down to the bottom of the Accessibility settings window to the **General** settings and click **Siri**. Flip the switch next to **Type to Siri** on to enable.

If you are typing your questions or commands, you may also want to read Siri's responses rather than having Siri speak its response. macOS allows you to disable voice feedback in the **Siri** settings window. Open System Settings and select **Siri & Spotlight**. Click the **Siri Responses...** button to reveal a configuration sheet. Flip the switch next to **Voice feedback** off.

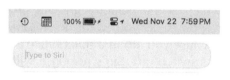

When type to Siri is enabled, you can activate Siri using its keyboard shortcut, holding down **⌘space** (command+space) until the Type to Siri dialog box appears in the upper-right corner of your desktop. Type the question you want to ask Siri and press the **return** key. If you disabled voice feedback, Siri's responses will be shown below the Type to Siri dialog box. If voice feedback is enabled, Siri will speak its response.

Disable Siri

Don't like or want Siri? Concerned about privacy? macOS allows you to disable Siri.

To disable Siri, open System Settings and select **Siri & Spotlight** in the sidebar. Flip the switch next to **Ask Siri** off. A dialog box appears warning that your Siri and Dictation interactions will remain on Apple's servers unless you also disable Dictation. Click **Turn Off** to finish.

12

Notification Center

Notification Center is a hidden panel at the right edge of your desktop where you can catch up on notifications and alerts that you may have missed. Notification Center consolidates notifications from a variety of Apple applications and supports notifications from social media applications like LinkedIn, Facebook, Twitter, and many third-party applications and websites. Like previous macOS releases, you can choose which applications can save notifications and alerts to Notification Center. Notification Center also supports widgets, which means you can have widgets on both your desktop and in Notification Center.

The gesture to open Notification Center seems a little odd at first because you start off the right edge of your trackpad and swipe left with two fingers to reveal Notification Center. You can also open Notification Center by clicking on the Date and Time in the Menu Bar. Click the Date and Time again, press the **esc** key, click on any window, or swipe right with two fingers and Notification Center will slide back under the right edge of your desktop.

At the top of Notification Center, you'll find notifications from apps and websites that have allowed to send notifications to your Mac. Multiple notifications from the same app are stacked and can be expanded by clicking on the top notification. Individual notifications can be dismissed by clicking the **X** (delete) button. You can collapse the stack by clicking the **Show Less** button or dismiss all notifications in the stack by clicking the **Clear All** button. If there are more notifications than can be displayed, macOS will display a button indicating there are more notifications and provide a count. Clicking on this button will display the additional notifications.

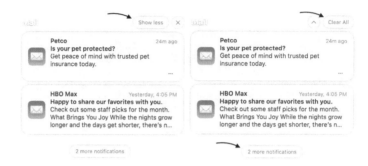

Clicking on an individual notification takes you to the app. For example, if you click on a notification from the Mail app, macOS will open that email message in the Mail app. Similarly, clicking on a weather notification will launch the Weather app.

Below your notifications are customizable widgets, which, for example, allow you to keep track of news headlines, stock prices, the weather, or your calendar.

Widgets

Widgets first appeared in Notification Center in macOS Big Sur. With macOS Sonoma you can now place widgets on your desktop in addition to placing them in Notification Center.

You don't have to settle on either the desktop or Notification Center, macOS lets you have widgets in both locations. However, the process of adding widgets to Notification Center differs slightly from previous versions of macOS. This change was necessary to accommodate macOS Sonoma's Desktop Widgets.

In macOS Sonoma, you will add widgets using the same widget browser used to add widgets to your desktop. To customize Notification Center's widgets, open Notification Center and scroll to the bottom. Click the **Edit Widgets** button to reveal the widget browser from the bottom of your desktop.

The widget browser will appear from the bottom of your desktop. Apps with widgets are listed in the sidebar. Scroll down the sidebar to find your favorite apps or choose a widget from a selection of suggested widgets. You can also search for a widget using the search field. Depending on the app, small, medium, and large widget versions will be available

Select a widget and a size, then look for **Drag widgets here to add them to Notification Center** in the upper right corner of your desktop. Drag the widget from the widget browser onto the text and drop it. If you already have widgets in your Notification Center, you'll see them along the right edge of your desktop. Drag your widget into place. Click the **Done** button in the widget browser when finished.

Another method is to hover over a widget in the widget browser with your pointer until a green **+** (add) button appears. Click the **+** button to add the widget to Notification Center. The widget drops to the bottom of Notification Center. Rearrange widgets by dragging them into place.

Widgets can be edited directly in Notification Center by secondary clicking on a widget or by holding down the **^** (control) key while clicking on a widget. This reveals a contextual

menu that allows you to edit the widget, change its size, remove it from Notification Center, or open the widget browser.

Banners & Alerts

Notifications delivered to the upper-right-hand corner of your desktop appear as a **Banner** or **Alert**, depending on the style chosen in the Notifications settings. **Banners** appear and disappear automatically after a set period. A Music notification with the name and artist of the current song playing is an example of a Banner. **Alerts** stay on your desktop until you dismiss them. Reminders are an example of an Alert, requiring you to take some action such as marking the reminder complete or snoozing it to dismiss the alert. All previous notifications, regardless of style, are stored in Notification Center.

The next series of images demonstrate how you can interact with a notification, in this case, a notification from the Music app. Image 1 shows a notification from the Music app of a song that started to play.

Hovering over the notification with your pointer reveals additional ways you can interact with the notification as shown in image 2. You can click the **X** (delete) button to dismiss the notification, click the **Skip** button to skip the song, or click the **>** (more) button to expand the notification to show the album cover art shown in image 3.

The expanded notification can be closed by clicking the down caret in the upper right corner.

Clicking the ellipsis shown in image 4 allows you to mute or disable notifications from the Music app and access the Notifications settings. Finally, clicking on the notification launches the Music application.

Notifications differ depending on the application that sourced the notification. For example, a notification from the Mail application will offer options to reply, mark the message as read, or delete it. Clicking the **X** (delete) button dismisses the notification. Clicking on a Mail notification opens the message in the Mail application.

Similarly, a notification from the Messages application offers options to show more or mark the message as read as well as the **X** (delete) button to dismiss the notification.

A notification from the Reminder app offers options to mark the reminder complete or to snooze it. Clicking the **X** (delete) button dismisses the notification. Clicking on the notification opens the Reminders application.

macOS allows you to customize which applications can send notifications to your desktop and Notification Center. To customize notifications, open the System Settings app and select **Notifications** in the sidebar.

Four configuration options at the top of the settings window control when notifications are sent to your desktop. The pop-up menu next to **Show previews** controls when notification previews are allowed – always, when unlocked, or never. Selecting always will allow notifications to be shown on your desktop even when you are not logged into your Mac, presenting a potential privacy issue. When unlocked, which is the macOS default setting, only displays notifications when you are logged into your Mac, and it is unlocked.   Never disables notification previews. Note that the setting you choose becomes the default for all notifications from all apps and websites. You will have to configure previews individually by application to override this setting.

The next three settings control previews when your Mac is sleeping, locked, and when your display is mirroring. When the switch next to **Allow notifications when the display is sleeping** is on, notifications will be sent to your desktop even when your Mac is asleep. Similarly, when the switch next to **Allow notifications when the screen is locked** is on, notifications will be sent to your desktop even when your Mac is locked. When **Allow notifications when mirroring or sharing the display** is enabled, notification previews will be sent to your desktop when you are mirroring or sharing your display to another device.

The next section of the Notifications settings window allows you to control notifications from apps and websites that support notifications. Alert styles and options such as history, previews, badging, and sound are configured on a per-app and pre-website basis in the Notifications settings. Click on an application or website to start.

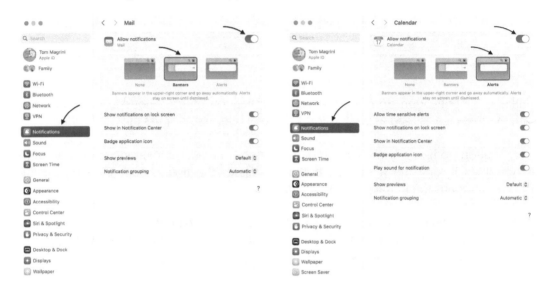

The switch next to **Allow notifications** toggles notifications on or off. If you do not want to receive notifications from a particular app, flip this switch off.

You can customize the notification type used by each application. Notifications can be configured as a Banner or an Alert by clicking on the notification type at the top of the settings window. A Banner is a notification that appears on your desktop and disappears after a set amount of time. An Alert stays on your desktop until you respond or dismiss it. The current notification type is bordered in blue. Click on Banners or Alerts to change the type. If you choose **None**, the application's notifications will no longer appear on your desktop.

Once you have selected the notification type, you can configure the options. The options available vary by application. Common options for application notifications are **Show notifications on lock screen**, **Show in Notification Center**, and **Badge application icon**. All these options are enabled by default. Flip the switch off to disable any of the options.

Notifications received when your Mac was asleep will appear on the login window when you wake your Mac, creating a potential privacy issue. If you want to disable this feature, flip the switch next to **Show notifications on lock screen** off.

By default, the **Show in Notification Center** option is enabled, allowing notifications to be saved in Notification Center. You have the option of disabling this feature by flipping the switch off. If you do, you will only see messages on your desktop and only if the alert style is set to Banners or Alerts. Selecting none for the notification style and setting the **Show in Notification Center** switch to off, completely disables notifications from the selected app.

The **Badge app icon** option displays the number of notifications in a red circular badge on the app's icon in the Dock. The app must be in the Dock for badges to appear. If you don't want the app icon badged, flip this switch off.

The pop-up menu next to **Show Previews** controls whether previews for the app will be sent to the desktop. When set to the default, the setting you chose in the main Notifications settings window will be used. Selecting always will allow notifications to be shown on your desktop even when you are not logged into your Mac, presenting a potential privacy issue. When unlocked, which is the macOS default setting, only displays notifications when you are logged into your Mac, and it is unlocked. Never disables notification previews for the selected application or website.

Some notifications play a sound when they appear. If you prefer silent notifications, flip the switch next to **Play sound for notifications** off.

Another option available with some applications include time-sensitive notifications for events that require your immediate attention. You can enable or disable this feature using the switch next to **Allow time sensitive alerts**.

Notification grouping allows you to organize how an app's notifications are grouped in Notification Center when multiple notifications are received. The pop-up menu offers three options – automatic, which is the default, by app, or off. macOS groups notifications in stacks by app or website. When **by app** is selected, multiple notifications are grouped by application with the app or website with the most recent notification listed first in Notification Center. When set to **off**, notifications are not grouped.

Banner Time

Banners delivered to the upper-right-hand corner of your desktop automatically disappear after a few seconds. Often this is not enough time to read them. This tweak allows you to set the amount of time that Banners stay on your desktop before disappearing.

To increase the Banner time, launch Terminal and enter the following command. This command increases the Banner time to 20 seconds. You can change the 20 in the command below to any whole number. You need to log out and log back in for the change to take effect.

```
defaults write com.apple.notificationcenterui bannerTime 20
```

If you want Banners to stick around until you dismiss them, replace 20 with 86400.

To return to the macOS default, enter the following command in Terminal. Log out and log back in for the change to take effect.

```
defaults delete com.apple.notificationcenterui bannerTime
```

Keyboard Shortcut

By default, there isn't a keyboard shortcut for Notification Center. If you would like to assign a keyboard shortcut to open Notification Center, open System Settings and select **Keyboard** in the sidebar. Click the **Keyboard Shortcuts...** button to reveal a configuration sheet. Select **Mission Control** from the sidebar.

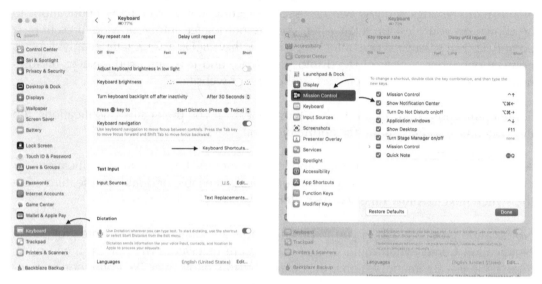

To assign a keyboard shortcut, ensure the checkbox next to **Show Notification Center** is checked. Enter your desired keyboard shortcut in the field provided. If you'd like to use the keyboard shortcut used by previous versions of macOS, enter ⌥⌘left (option+command+left arrow). Otherwise, be sure to select a key combination that is not used by another function.

To disable, uncheck the checkbox next to **Show Notification Center**. If you want to restore all keyboard shortcuts to their macOS defaults, click the **Restore Defaults** button.

Click **Done** when finished.

13

Launchpad

Launchpad is a macOS feature that blurs the line between iOS, iPadOS, and macOS. Like the home screen on iPhone and iPad, Launchpad allows you to see every application installed on your Mac on one or more pages. From Launchpad, you can search, launch, organize, and delete applications on your Mac.

To open Launchpad, click on its icon in the Dock, pinch your thumb and three fingers together on the trackpad, or tap the Launchpad icon in your Touch Bar. Your desktop background blurs and the Menu Bar and windows disappear to reveal Launchpad's grid of application icons. The Dock, if hidden, reappears.

Launchpad provides a search field at the top center allowing you to quickly find applications, particularly ones that are hidden in a folder. Small dots at the bottom center represent pages. You can swipe left or right with one finger on a mouse or two fingers on a trackpad or hold down the ⌘ (command) key while pressing the left or right arrow keys to navigate between pages. You can also click on one of the dots to jump directly to that page. You can use your mouse, trackpad, or the four arrow keys to move up, down, left, or right within the grid to highlight an application. Clicking an app icon launches the app, as does pressing the **return** key when an app is highlighted.

Folders are created the same way they are on an iPhone or iPad, by dragging one icon on top of another. Once a folder is created, it can be renamed, and you can drag other applications into it. Folders are opened by clicking on them. Close an open folder by clicking anywhere outside it.

You can close Launchpad using the Show Desktop gesture by spreading your thumb and three fingers apart on your Mac's trackpad, the opposite gesture used to open Launchpad. You can also click on a blank space in Launchpad, press the **esc** key, click the Launchpad icon in your Touch Bar, or by launching an application from the Dock.

App Icons

The application icons in Launchpad can be rearranged by dragging them into the order you desire. To move an icon between pages, drag it to the edge of the screen and hold it there until the page changes. Drop the icon on the desired destination page by releasing your hold.

Deleting Apps

Some applications can be deleted from your Mac in Launchpad. To delete an app, click and hold on an icon until all the app icons begin to jiggle. An **X** (delete) button appears in the upper-left corner of some of the app icons. Clicking the **X** deletes the app.

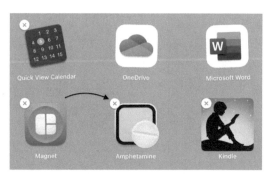

If an app can't be deleted from Launchpad, you'll need to use an app like AppCleaner or select the uninstall option in the installer you used to install the app.

Finder Icon

Open **Launchpad**. Now type **Finder** in the search field. No Results. Noticeably absent from Launchpad is one of the most critical apps in macOS, Finder.

To add Finder to Launchpad, open **Finder**. Enter ⇧⌘G (shift+command+G) to open the **Go to the folder** dialog box. Enter the following into the field and click **Go**.

`/System/Library/CoreServices/`

Locate **Finder** in this folder and drag and drop it onto the **Launchpad** icon in the Dock. Now, check out Launchpad, and there's Finder.

Apps per Page

On my 13-inch MacBook Pro display, macOS lays out a 7-column by 5-row grid in Launchpad, displaying 35 icons per page.   If you want more application icons to appear on each Launchpad page, you do so by adding more columns and rows.

For example, if you want Launchpad to display 60 application icons per page, you will need to resize the grid to 10 columns by 6 rows. To resize Launchpad, open Terminal and enter the following commands.

```
defaults write com.apple.dock springboard-columns -int 10
```

```
defaults write com.apple.dock springboard-rows -int 6
```

```
killall Dock
```

I suggest you experiment, trying different combinations of column and row sizes until you find the right combination. Replace the number after **–int** in each command with an integer to find your perfect size.

Increasing the size of the grid decreases the size of each icon. With Launchpad displaying more icons per page, it takes fewer pages to display your applications. In the image below, I configured Launchpad to display 60 icons in a 10-column by 6-row grid. Why aren't there 60 icons on this page? macOS doesn't automatically rearrange the icon layout when you change the number of rows and columns. You must rearrange the icons manually.

Conversely, you can configure Launchpad grid smaller with fewer columns and rows, so that fewer, larger application icons are displayed on each page.

For example, if you want Launchpad to display 20 application icons per page, you need to resize the grid to 5 columns by 4 rows. To resize Launchpad to show 20 icons per page, enter the following commands in Terminal.

```
defaults write com.apple.dock springboard-columns -int 5
```

```
defaults write com.apple.dock springboard-rows -int 4
```

```
killall Dock
```

With Launchpad displaying fewer icons per page, it takes more pages to display all your applications. The image at the bottom of the previous page now requires 5 pages to display all the app icons that previously required only 3 pages.

To revert to the macOS default, enter the following commands.

```
defaults delete com.apple.dock springboard-columns
```

```
defaults delete com.apple.dock springboard-rows
```

```
killall Dock
```

You probably noticed macOS spread your application icons across multiple pages as you changed the Launchpad grid size. Launchpad does not automatically rearrange the icons for you as you experimented with different grid sizes. Unfortunately, you must rearrange the app icons manually or revert Launchpad to its default.

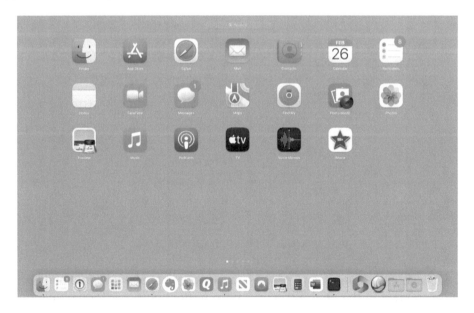

Page Scrolling Delay

macOS introduces a short delay when scrolling between pages in Launchpad. If you prefer pages to appear immediately, enter the following commands in Terminal.

```
defaults write com.apple.dock springboard-page-duration -int 0
```

```
killall Dock
```

You can increase the delay by replacing 0 in the first command with another integer. Let's try 5 to see the Launchpad animation in slow motion. Enter the following in Terminal.

```
defaults write com.apple.dock springboard-page-duration -int 5
```

```
killall Dock
```

To restore the default scroll delay, enter the following commands in Terminal.

```
defaults delete com.apple.dock springboard-page-duration
```

```
killall Dock
```

Keyboard Shortcut

If you would like to assign a keyboard shortcut to open Launchpad, open System Settings, scroll down and select **Keyboard** in the sidebar. Click on the **Keyboard Shortcuts...** button to reveal a configuration sheet. Select **Launchpad & Dock** from the sidebar.

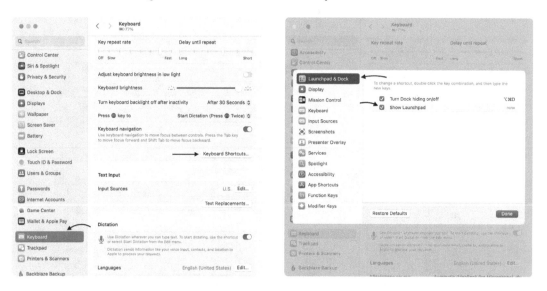

To assign a keyboard shortcut, ensure the checkbox next to **Show Launchpad** is checked and enter a shortcut in the field provided. Be sure to choose a key combination that is not used by another function.

To remove the keyboard shortcut, uncheck the checkbox next to **Show Launchpad** or click the **Restore Defaults** button.

Click the **Done** button when finished.

Add to Dock

If you have a new Mac with macOS Sonoma pre-installed, the Launchpad icon should be in the Dock. If you upgraded from a previous version of macOS and the Launchpad icon is not in the Dock, adding it is simple.

Open the **Applications** folder in Finder and scroll down to find the **Launchpad** application icon. Drag it to your Dock.

Revert to Default

If you need to revert to the macOS Launchpad defaults, enter the following commands in Terminal. All tweaks, including folders you created, will be reset to their defaults.

```
defaults write com.apple.dock ResetLaunchPad -bool true
```

```
killall Dock
```

Note that if you added Finder to the Launchpad, resetting to the default settings will remove it.

14

Finder

One of the most integral parts of the macOS experience is Finder, which serves as the macOS file manager. Finder provides you with a powerful, flexible, and user-friendly tool to access and manage your files, folders, drives, iCloud, apps, and shared folders and files. A Finder window has numerous components, which include the Toolbar, Sidebar, Path Bar, Status Bar, Search Bar, Preview Pane, and the main Finder window as shown in the image below.

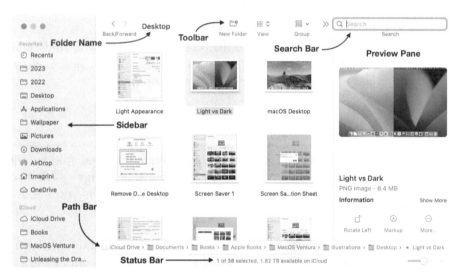

At the top of the Finder window is the **Toolbar**, which contains various icons for common tools such as creating a new folder, viewing folder contents, grouping files, deleting files, and searching. The name of the current folder, whose contents are displayed in the main Finder window, appears on the Toolbar.

The **Sidebar** on the left-hand side of the window provides quick access to frequently used folders such as the Desktop, Documents, Downloads, and iCloud Drive. You can customize the Sidebar by adding or removing folders. The Sidebar is divided into four sections. **Favorites** lists shortcuts to your favorite or frequently accessed items such as your Home, Desktop, Applications, Documents, Movies, Music, and Pictures folders. The

Favorites category also provides access to AirDrop, which allows you to transfer files between Macs, iPhones, and iPads. Underneath Favorites is **iCloud**, which lists the contents of your iCloud Drive. Below iCloud is **Locations**, which lists internal and external drives and network shares connected to your Mac. The final section is the list of **Tags**, which are used to organize files.

The **Path Bar** is located at the bottom of the Finder window and displays the path to the currently selected file or folder. You can click on any of the folder icons shown in the path to quickly navigate to that folder.

The **Status Bar** is located at the bottom of the Finder window and displays information about the currently selected file or folder, such as the file size, and for folders, the number of items.

The **Search Bar** is located at the top-right corner of the Finder window and allows you to search for files and folders by name, date modified, kind, or content. Search results are displayed in a separate window, and you can easily preview files by pressing the space bar to invoke Quick Look or open files by double-clicking them.

The **Preview Pane** is located on the right-hand side of the Finder window and provides a preview of the currently selected file. You can view a variety of file types including images, PDFs, and Microsoft Office documents.

The contents of a folder are displayed in the main Finder window. The view options are in the Toolbar and allow you to choose between Icon, List, Column, and Gallery views. You can also group files and folders by name, date, size, or kind.

Sidebar

The Finder Sidebar offers one-click access to your frequently used folders and files, organized into four categories – **Favorites**, **iCloud**, **Locations**, and **Tags** – saving you time and effort by allowing you to easily navigate to the files and folders you need without having to search for them.

Like most features in macOS, Finder's Sidebar is customizable. macOS gets you started with a default selection of folders. You can rearrange the folders in your Finder's Sidebar and can add or remove folders and locations. To add a folder to the Sidebar, secondary click on the folder to reveal a contextual menu. Choose **Add to Sidebar**. Alternatively, you can drag a folder onto the Sidebar to add it.

To remove a folder from the Sidebar, drag it off until a gray circle containing an **X** (delete) button appears. Release, and the item disappears. You can also remove a folder from the Sidebar by secondary clicking on it and choosing **Remove from Sidebar** from the contextual menu. Items in the Sidebar can be rearranged by dragging them.

The **Favorites** category provides quick, single-click access to folders and files that you access frequently. Secondary clicking on an item reveals a submenu allowing you to open the folder in a new tab, show the enclosing folder, remove the folder from the Sidebar, get info, or add it to your Dock.

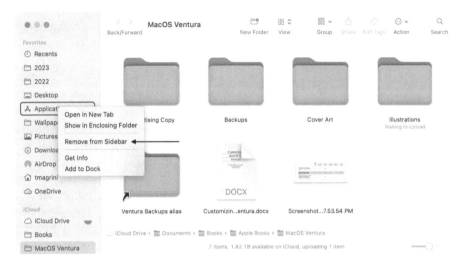

The **iCloud** section lists the contents of your iCloud Drive. Secondary clicking on an item in the iCloud list opens a submenu allowing you to open the folder in a new tab, show the enclosing folder, download it, remove it from your Sidebar, get info, rename the folder, or add it to your Dock.

The **Locations** category includes internal drives, external drives, or other devices connected to your Mac. A secondary click on items in the list of **Devices** provides a different set of options allowing you to open the drive in a new tab, remove the drive from your Sidebar, or get info.

The **Tags** category lists the Finder Tags. Clicking on a Tag populates the Finder window with all files tagged with the selected tag. Secondary clicking offers options to open tagged items in a new tab, remove the tag from your Sidebar, delete the tag, or change its color.

You can also customize your Sidebar by choosing which items you want to display from a predefined list available in Finder's settings. Select **Finder > Settings…** from the Menu Bar or use the keyboard shortcut ⌘, (command+comma). Click **Sidebar** from the set of four icons at the top of the window. Checked items are displayed in Sidebar, while unchecked items are hidden. Hidden items can be unhidden by checking their checkbox. Using the checkboxes, you can configure Sidebar to your liking.

By default, macOS sets the size of the icons in Finder's Sidebar to medium. If you have many items in the Sidebar, you may want to set the icons to a smaller size to limit or avoid the need to scroll. Conversely, you may want the Sidebar to display larger icons to make the items easier to read.

To change the icon size in Sidebar, open System Settings and select Appearance in the sidebar. Use the pop-up menu next to **Sidebar icon size** to select Small, Medium, or Large. Changing the Sidebar icon size also changes the size of the text.

To hide the Sidebar, choose **View > Hide Sidebar** or use the keyboard shortcut ^⌘S (control+command+S). The Sidebar can be toggled on and off by selecting **View > Show Sidebar** or with the ^⌘S (control+command+S) keyboard shortcut.

Another method is to hover over the dividing line between the Sidebar and the main Finder window with your pointer. When the resizing pointer appears, slide it left or right to make the Sidebar smaller or larger. You can hide the Sidebar by moving the resizing pointer to the left until the Sidebar disappears.

Path Bar

The Path Bar provides a visual representation of the current folder hierarchy. It is located at the bottom of the Finder window and displays the path to the current folder or file. To display the Path Bar, select **View > Show Path Bar**. The Path Bar can be toggled on and off with the keyboard shortcut ⌥⌘P (option+command+P).

The Path Bar supports drag and drop functionality, allowing you to move files and folders into any of the folders in the Path Bar. If you want to copy the file instead, hold down the ⌥ (option) key while dragging. To create an alias, hold down ⌥⌘ (option+command) keys while dragging. A folder can even be dragged within the Path Bar to move it to a new location. You can even drag between different Finder windows. If you change your mind while dragging, press the **esc** key to cancel. If you change your mind after completing the move, copy, or alias creation, select **Edit > Undo** or use the keyboard shortcut ⌘Z (command+Z).

You can click on any folder in the Path Bar to quickly navigate to that location and view its contents. The folder's contents will replace the items displayed in the main Finder window. If you hold down the ⌘ (command) key while double-clicking, the folder opens in a new tab. Holding down the ⌥ (option) key while double-clicking opens the folder in a new Finder window while simultaneously closing the source window or tab.

Sometimes a path is so long that it cannot fit in the Path Bar. In that case, macOS truncates the folder names. Hover your pointer over a truncated folder name to expand it.

macOS lists the path from the root of the disk drive to the current directory, which, depending on the depth of your directory structure, could result in ridiculously long paths and truncated folder names. If most of your file browsing is done in your Home folder, you can shorten the path to reflect your location relative to your Home folder.

To shorten the path shown, enter the following commands in Terminal.

```
defaults write com.apple.finder PathBarRootAtHome -bool true
killall Finder
```

To revert to the macOS default and show the full path, enter the following commands.

```
defaults delete com.apple.finder PathBarRootAtHome
killall Finder
```

Title Bar

If you don't want to display the Path Bar, macOS allows you to configure Finder's Title Bar to display the path. By default, the Title Bar displays the name of the current folder or file. If you would like it to show the path instead, open Terminal and enter the following commands.

```
defaults write com.apple.finder _FXShowPosixPathInTitle -bool true
```

```
killall Finder
```

Longer paths will be truncated. To see the entire path, hover your pointer over the path in the Title Bar to expand it.

To revert to the macOS default, enter the following commands.

```
defaults delete com.apple.finder _FXShowPosixPathInTitle
```

```
killall Finder
```

You can also see the path to the currently displayed folder by pressing the ⌘ (command) key while clicking on the folder name in the Title Bar. The path will be displayed in a pop-up window as shown in the image on the next page.

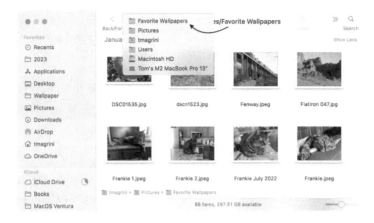

Status Bar

The Status Bar displays important information about the current folder or file. It is located at the bottom of the window and provides details such as the number of items in a folder, the size of a selected file or folder, and the available disk space.

To view the Status Bar, select **View > Show Status Bar** or use the keyboard shortcut ⌘/ (command+/). When the Status Bar is enabled, every Finder window will display the Status Bar at the bottom, below the Path Bar.

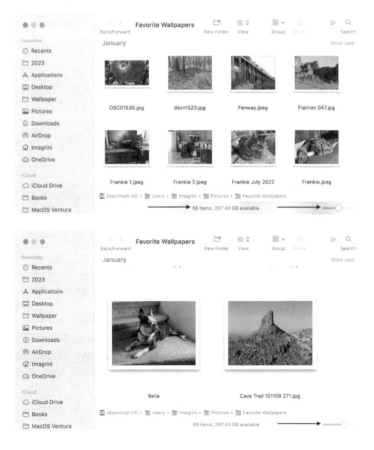

Another handy feature of the Finder Status Bar is that it provides a slider in the lower-right corner that you can use to change the size of the icons displayed in the Finder window. Slide the slider left or right to change the size of the icons.

To hide the Status Bar, select **View > Hide Status Bar** or use the keyboard shortcut ⌘/ (command+/).

Tab Bar

The Tab Bar appears just below the Toolbar when you have multiple tabs open. You can easily switch between different folders, add new tabs, and close existing ones. The Tab Bar also supports drag and drop functionality, allowing you to move files between tabs, even across different windows. When you have a single tab open, the Tab Bar is hidden.

If you prefer to see the Tab Bar all the time, select **View > Show Tab Bar** or use the keyboard shortcut ⇧⌘T (shift+command+T). When the Tab Bar is enabled, every Finder window will display the Tab Bar below the Toolbar.

To hide the Tab Bar, select **View > Hide Tab Bar** or use the ⇧⌘T (shift+command+T) keyboard shortcut. Note that you can only hide the Tab Bar when you have a single tab open. When multiple tabs are open, the Tab Bar will automatically appear, and the option to hide it will be grayed out.

When you have multiple tabs open, you can see a thumbnail of all tabs by selecting **View > Show All Tabs** or using the keyboard shortcut ⇧⌘\ (shift+command+\). The Show All Tabs command allows you to quickly switch between open tabs. All open tabs are displayed as thumbnails, making it easy to visually locate the desired tab. You can add a new tab from this view by clicking on the gray thumbnail containing an **+** (add) button.

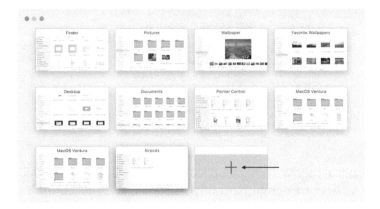

Toolbar

The Toolbar is a powerful and customizable feature that allows you to quickly access frequently used tools and functions. It sits at the top of your Finder window. You can customize the Toolbar by adding, removing, and rearranging icons.

To customize the Toolbar, secondary click in an open area of the Toolbar to reveal a contextual menu. Select **Customize Toolbar…** to open Finder's tool palette. You can also access the tool palette by selecting **Customize Toolbar…** from the **View** menu. Drag and drop the tools from the palette into the Toolbar.

Existing tools located on the Toolbar can be rearranged by dragging them. A tool is removed by dragging it off the Toolbar and back onto the tool palette.

The additional tools available include the **Path** tool, which displays the full path to the location shown in Finder's right-hand pane. You can also see the path by holding down the ⌘ (command) key while clicking on the folder name in the Toolbar.

Eject will eject optical media from the optical drive. It will also unmount any removable media, such as a USB or external hard drive. **Burn** is used to burn files and folders to optical media.

Space and **Flexible Space** are used to space out the tools in the toolbar by adding blank space between them.

New Folder does what its name implies, creating a new folder in the folder displayed in the main Finder window.

Delete sends the selected items to the Trash.

Connect is used to connect to network servers and shared drives.

Get Info opens the Get Info window, which displays information about the selected file such as its tags, kind, size, location, date created, date modified, its file extension, Spotlight comments, the default application that opens the file, and a file preview.

Quick Look opens a preview of the selected file without launching the application in which it was created. Quick Look allows you to preview a file before deciding to open it. The Quick Look window provides an **Open with** button, allowing you to launch the application that created the file, a **Share** button, and if the application is Preview, **Rotate** and **Markup** tools. You also can open Quick Look by clicking on a file and pressing the spacebar.

Preview toggles the Preview Pane on and off.

AirDrop lets you send selected files to another person's Mac, iPad, or iPhone using Apple's AirDrop file transfer feature.

iCloud lets you share a file using through Mail, Messages, Airdrop, or third-party extensions.

To configure the third-party extensions available in iCloud, select a file and click the iCloud icon in the Toolbar. Next, select **Edit Extensions...** from the contextual menu to open the Extensions settings window in System Settings. Use the checkboxes to select which extensions you wish to make available when sharing files using the iCloud icon in Toolbar.

You can choose how the tools will be displayed – **Icon and Text**, **Icon Only**, or **Text Only** – using the pop-up menu next to **Show** at the bottom of the window.

Did you notice when you secondary clicked in the Toolbar to reveal the contextual menu that it also allowed you to select how you wanted the tools displayed? The same choices offered in the Finder tool palette – **Icon and Text**, **Icon Only**, or **Text Only** – are available from the Toolbar with a secondary click. The current setting has a checkmark next to it.

Icons on the Toolbar can be rearranged without having to use the tool palette. To move an icon, hold the ⌘ (command) key down while dragging the icon to its new location. You can also use the ⌘ (command) key to remove an icon. Hold down the ⌘ (command) key while dragging the icon off the Toolbar.

To revert to the default set of tools, drag the default set to the Finder Toolbar.

Click **Done** when finished editing the Toolbar to close the tool palette.

Want to hide the Toolbar? Select **View > Hide Toolbar** or by using the keyboard shortcut ⌥⌘T (option+command+T). This command will also hide the Sidebar. Note that you can only hide the Toolbar when you have a single tab open. This option will be grayed out when your Finder window contains multiple tabs.

Add a Folder or File to the Toolbar

Do you have a folder you frequently access and would like it prominently displayed in Finder? You have several options. You can add your folder to the Sidebar. You also can configure Finder to always open that folder in new windows and tabs. (See New Windows and Tabs later in this chapter to learn how to do this). Another option is to add an alias of your folder to Finder's toolbar.

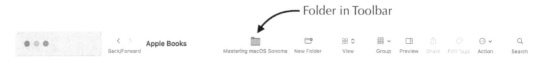

To add a folder to the Toolbar, open a Finder window and secondary click in an open area of the Toolbar. Select **Customize Toolbar...** to open the tools palette. Next, open a new Finder window by selecting **File > New Finder Window** or by using the keyboard shortcut **⌘N** (command+N). Navigate to the folder you want to add to the Toolbar in the new Finder window. Drag that folder from the new window to the one with the Finder tools palette and drop it onto the Toolbar when you see the green **+** (add) icon.

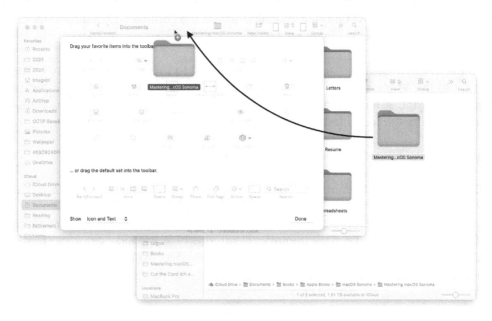

The folder in your toolbar is an alias. You can click on it to open the folder and can even drag files and other folders onto the alias to move them into your folder.

You can also add a file or app alias to Finder's Toolbar using the same method.

To remove a folder, file, or app alias from Finder's toolbar, hold down the **⌘** (command) key and drag it off the Finder Toolbar or open the tools palette and drag it off the toolbar.

Preview Panel

The Preview Panel is an incredibly useful feature that lets you preview various types of files without opening them. The Preview Panel provides a quick glimpse of the contents of a file, including images, videos, audio files, and documents. When you select a file, the Preview Panel displays a thumbnail of the file, along with information about the file's type, size, and modification date.

To show the Finder Preview Panel, select **View > Show Preview**, use the keyboard shortcut ⇧⌘P (shift+command+P), or click the Preview icon in the Toolbar. Select any file to see it in the Preview Panel. Once you have enabled the Preview Panel, it is enabled for all new Finder windows. To hide the Preview Panel, select **View > Hide Preview** or use the keyboard shortcut ⇧⌘P (shift+command+P).

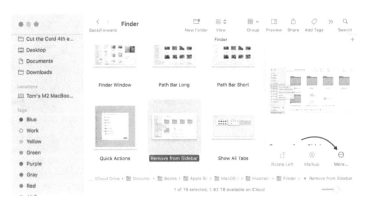

You can customize the data shown in the Preview Panel by choosing **View > Show Preview Options**. Select the items you want to display in the Preview Panel using the checkboxes.

In addition to previewing files, the Preview Panel provides access to **Quick Actions**, which allow you to perform basic editing functions, such as rotating images, cropping photos, and trimming videos. This is incredibly useful for making quick edits to files without having to open them. Quick Actions are accessed by clicking the ellipsis above the **More** icon in the lower right corner of the Preview Panel to reveal a pop-up menu.

To customize the **More** pop-up menu, select **Customize...** to open the Extensions settings window in System Settings. Add or remove Quick Actions using the checkboxes. Click **Done** when finished.

Gallery View

Gallery is a Finder view that allows you to see a large preview of a file's content. Gallery View is accessed directly from the Toolbar using the **View** pop-up menu. Gallery View is perfect for viewing and working with image files. It also provides access to Quick Actions from the ellipsis icon above **More.**

You can customize the Gallery View by using the keyboard shortcut ⌘J (command+J) to reveal the Gallery View customization panel. If you want to always open folders in Gallery View, check the checkbox next to **Always open in gallery view**. Files in Gallery View can be sorted by name (the default), kind, date modified, date created, date last opened, date added, size, and tags. The **Thumbnail** size controls the size of the file thumbnails at the bottom of the window.

Check the checkbox next to **Show preview column** to add the Preview Column to Gallery View. The Preview Column allows you to see file metadata and access Quick Actions.

Show icon preview is enabled by default and displays the file content in the thumbnails along the bottom of the Gallery View. **Show filename** adds the filename to the thumbnails at the bottom of Gallery View. Click the **Use as Defaults** button to save your changes as the default when viewing files in Gallery View.

Tags

Tags are a useful organizational tool, providing a way to label files and folders with descriptive keywords, making it easy to find and group files. Tags were introduced in macOS Mavericks in 2013 and they have been improved in subsequent macOS releases.

Tagging files is a significant departure in the way you work with the macOS file system. When using tags, files no longer need to be saved in a specific folder to create a relationship between them. Tags remove the need to have deeply nested folders within the file system to create relationships between different files. It doesn't matter where files are saved because Tags can be used to relate files to each other. The tags section in Finder's Sidebar and the macOS Spotlight search feature allow you to immediately locate files based on their Tag regardless of where they reside in the file system.

One of the benefits of using tags is that they are customizable. You can create your own tags to suit your needs and preferences and can assign multiple tags to a single file. Tagging files is a convenient way to organize related files, such as files from a project, without having to create a special folder or modify the locations of the files. You can customize the name to "Kitchen Remodel" or "Budget." You can choose the color of a tag to help visually distinguish it from other tags. This makes it easy to quickly find files related to a specific project or task, regardless of where they are in the macOS file system.

There are several methods to tag an item in Finder. The first is to select the item, click the **Add Tags** icon in the Toolbar, and select the appropriate tag. Another method is to select the file, secondary click on it to reveal a contextual menu, and choose a tag. Another method is to select the file or files you want to Tag and select a tag from the **File** menu.

If you have a MacBook Pro with a Touch Bar, you can select a tag from the Touch Bar.

To change or remove a tag from an item, select the file and click the **Edit Tags** tool in the Toolbar. An alternate method is to secondary click on an item to remove or change any existing Tags using a contextual menu. A third method is to use **File > Tags…** to remove existing Tags.

You can rename Tags and choose which tags you want displayed in the Sidebar. Select **Settings…** from the **Finder** menu. You can also access the Finder settings using the keyboard shortcut ⌘, (command+comma). Once the settings window appears, make sure **Tags** is selected from the set of four icons at the top of the pane.

You can rename a tag by selecting it and entering its new name.

To add a new Tag, click the **+** (add) button. To remove a Tag, highlight it and click the **−** (delete) button or secondary click on the Tag and choose **Delete**. You can also rename a tag by secondary clicking on it and choosing **Rename**.

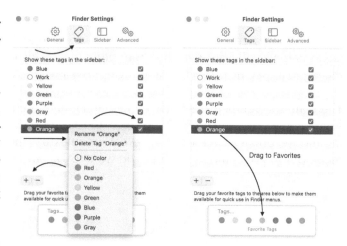

Use the checkboxes under **Show these tags in the sidebar** to choose which Tags appear in the Finder sidebar. Drag the Tags to rearrange their order. At the bottom of this pane are your **Favorite Tags**, which appear in Finder menus. To remove a Tag, drag it off. To add a Tag, drag it from the list into the **Favorite Tags** at the bottom of the window.

All files associated with a Tag can be quickly retrieved using the Sidebar. If tag files with multiple tags, you can perform search for them using Spotlight or the search field in Finder window. You then can create a Smart Folder and add it to the Sidebar. To search for a file tagged with both a blue and a purple tag, open Spotlight and enter the following search parameters.

```
tag:blue tag:purple
```

You can also search for tagged files by the Tag name. For example, if I rename the blue tag "macOS" and the purple tag "Apple." The following Spotlight search will return the same result as the search above.

```
tag:macOS tag:Apple
```

Smart Folders

Smart Folders are dynamically updated virtual folders that you create based on a set of pre-defined search parameters. The beauty of Smart Folders lies in their ability to automate the process of organizing and accessing documents and files. Instead of manually searching through a vast collection of files and folders, you can create a Smart Folder that automatically gathers relevant files based on specific criteria, such as file type, date modified, keyword, or tags.

The advantage of Smart Folders is that they are dynamic and update in real-time. As new files are added to the system that meet the Smart Folder's search criteria, they will automatically be added to the Smart Folder. This means that you can always stay on top of your files and documents without having to manually create and organize folders.

To create a Smart Folder, select **File > New Smart Folder**. You will then specify the search criteria, such as file type, date range, or specific keywords. The Smart Folder will automatically populate with all the relevant files that meet the specified criteria.

To add additional search criteria, click the **+** button next to **Save**. You can choose the search scope with **This Mac** being the default. You also have the option of only searching within the current folder. That option is to the right of **This Mac**. Any search line can be removed by clicking the **−** button. Select **Other...** to reveal a list of over 100 search attributes against which you can search. Use the checkboxes to add search attributes.

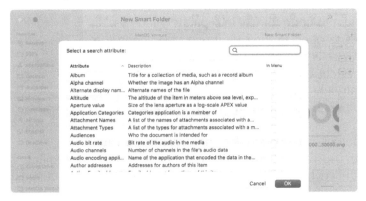

macOS offers several other ways to create a Smart Folder. You can select **File > Find**, use the ⌘**F** (command+F) keyboard shortcut, or type search criteria into the **Search** field of an open Finder window. Another method is to execute a search using Spotlight, then click **Search in Finder...** to open a Finder window with the search results. You then can adjust the search parameters and click the **Save** button when finished.

Smart Folders are dynamically updated and remain current as you add and delete items matching the search criteria. All items are conveniently displayed in a Smart Folder as if they were in a single folder, regardless of where they reside in your file system. While the items only appear to be in one folder, they remain safely tucked away in the folders in which you saved them.

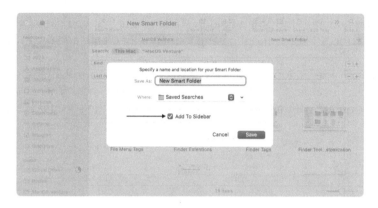

Once you have perfected your search criteria, click the **Save** button to reveal a configuration sheet allowing you to name your Smart Folder, save it to a folder, and add it to the Sidebar.

By default, all Smart Folders are saved to the **Saved Searches** folder. However, you can choose where to save your Smart Folder. The checkbox next to **Add to Sidebar** is checked by default. Uncheck it only when you do not want your Smart Folder to appear in the Sidebar. Otherwise, your Smart Folder will appear at the bottom of your list of Favorites.

Open Folders in New Windows

By default, macOS opens folders in a new tab. Sometimes it is more convenient to open folders in separate windows. If you want folders to open in their own windows, open the Finder settings by selecting **Finder > Settings...** or by using the keyboard shortcut **⌘,** (command+comma). Next, select **General** if not already highlighted. Uncheck the checkbox next to **Open folders in tabs instead of new windows**.

Changing how folders are opened does not disable the Tabs feature. You can use Tabs when needed or when it is more convenient. You can open a new Tab using the keyboard shortcut **⌘T** (command+T) or by selecting **File > New Tab**.

When you disable opening folders in tabs, you also change another macOS behavior. Double-clicking to open a folder while holding down the **⌘** (command) key now opens the folder in a new window instead of a new tab.

Holding down the **⌥** (option) key while double-clicking on a file or folder will open the file while simultaneously closing the Finder window. You can also accomplish the same thing with the keyboard shortcut **⌥⌘O** (option+command+O).

If you have multiple Finder windows open, you can merge them into one window with each window becoming a Tab. To merge all windows, click on any Finder window then select **Window > Merge All Windows**.

Any of the Tabs can be used to create a new Finder window. Secondary click on the tab you want to move to a new window and select **Move Tab to New Window**. Alternately, you can drag and drop a tab out of a Finder window onto your desktop to make it open in a new window.

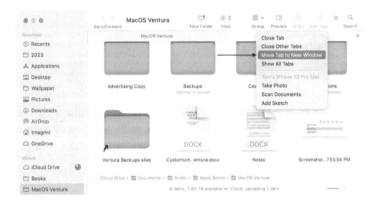

The contextual menu revealed when secondary clicking on a Tab allows you to close the tab, close other tabs and leave the selected tab open, or move the tab to a new window.

Display Options

The default icon size in macOS is 64 x 64 pixels. While this is good for most applications, you may find it too small when trying to preview documents, pictures, or movies. macOS allows you to change the default icon size.

To change the default icon size, secondary click any open space in a Finder window to reveal a contextual menu. Choose **Show View Options**. You can also select **View** > **Show View Options** or use the keyboard shortcut ⌘J (command+J). The Finder View Panel appears with the name of the folder located in its Title Bar. If the checkbox next to **Always open in icon view** is checked, this folder will always open in icon view.

Grouping and sorting options in the section allow you to change the arrangement of the icons and how they are sorted. Use the pop-up menus to set your options.

In the next section, you can change the icon size and grid spacing using the sliders. Icons can be made as small as 16 x 16 pixels or as large as 512 x 512 pixels. The largest size is handy when sorting through a folder containing pictures or movies. Grid spacing lets you choose how close (or far apart) icons are spaced in Finder.

The next section allows you to change the text size of the label shown at the bottom of files and folders. The default text size is 12 points. Supported text sizes are 10, 11, 12, 13, 14, 15, and 16 points. The default label position is at the bottom of the files and folders. macOS lets you choose to display the label at the bottom or to the right of an item.

Show item info will display the size of the file or the number of items a folder contains. The second checkbox, **Show icon preview**, is checked by default, and will render a preview of the file content. If you uncheck it, macOS will display default icons which denote the app in which each file was created rather than rendering file content previews.

The next section allows you to change the background in Finder. The default is white when in Light Mode and black in Dark Mode, but you have the choice of another color or a picture. If you want a color background, click the square to the right of **Color** to open a color wheel. If you chose **Picture**, drag a picture into the square.

Clicking on the **Use as Defaults** button located at the bottom of the window makes your selections the default for the current folder and all its sub-folders.

Library Folder

macOS allows you to toggle a switch to make the Library folder, which is usually hidden, visible. To make the Library folder visible, open Finder and navigate to your Home directory. Secondary click any open space in the window and select **Show View Options** from the contextual menu. You can also select **View > Show View Options** or use the keyboard shortcut ⌘J (command+J). Check the checkbox next to **Show Library Folder**.

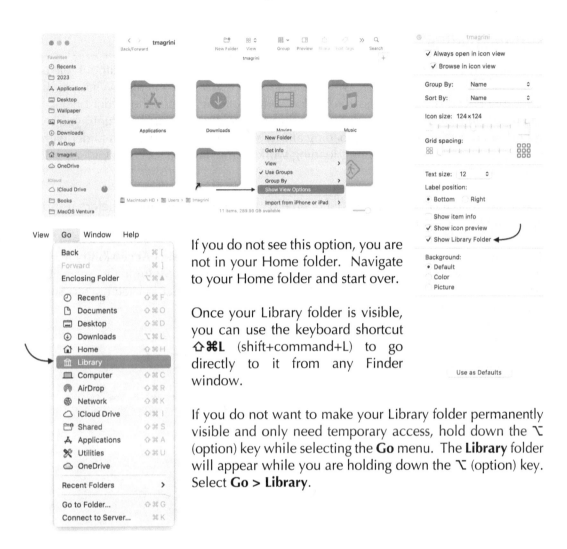

If you do not see this option, you are not in your Home folder. Navigate to your Home folder and start over.

Once your Library folder is visible, you can use the keyboard shortcut ⇧⌘L (shift+command+L) to go directly to it from any Finder window.

If you do not want to make your Library folder permanently visible and only need temporary access, hold down the ⌥ (option) key while selecting the **Go** menu. The **Library** folder will appear while you are holding down the ⌥ (option) key. Select **Go > Library**.

Hidden Files

macOS hides any file or folder when its name begins with a "." If you need to see the hidden files in Finder, open Terminal and enter the following commands.

```
defaults write com.apple.finder AppleShowAllFiles true
```

```
killall Finder
```

To revert to the default where these files are hidden, enter the following commands.

```
defaults write com.apple.finder AppleShowAllFiles false
```

```
killall Finder
```

Spring-Loading

Try dragging a file or folder onto another folder, pausing for a moment without releasing your hold. Suddenly the folder will spring open to reveal its contents. What you have just experienced is a macOS feature called spring-loading. Once the folder opens, you can repeat the same gesture to drill down through the directory structure until you reach your desired destination. Spring-loading allows you to drag an item into a folder without having to open the folder. Spring loading works throughout macOS, in folders, stacks, disks, and iCloud.

The spring-loading delay, the amount of time you must pause on a folder before it springs open, can be tweaked, or disabled entirely.

To adjust the spring-loading delay, open System Settings and select **Accessibility** from the sidebar. Next select **Pointer Control,** which can be found under **Motor** in the Accessibility settings window. Adjust the spring-loading delay using the slider located next to **Spring-loading speed** from slow (turtle) to fast (rabbit).

If you are in a hurry and don't want to wait for the spring-load delay timer to expire, press the **spacebar** to bypass the delay and open a folder or tab immediately.

Like macOS folders, Finder tabs are also spring-loaded. The tab will expand if you drag a file or folder and hover over it until the spring-load delay timer expires.

If you want to disable the spring-loading delay, flip the switch next to **Spring-loading** off.

If you hold down the ⌥ (option) key while dragging and hovering, you will copy the file instead of moving it. Holding down ⌥⌘ (option+command) will create an alias.

New Windows and Tabs

By default, macOS will open your Documents folder when launching a new Finder windows or tab. If you prefer macOS open another folder, macOS lets you select which folder opens when new Finder windows and tabs are opened.

To change to another folder, launch the Finder preferences by selecting **Finder > Settings...** or use the keyboard shortcut **⌘,** (command+comma) to open the Finder settings window. Next, click **General** at the top of the window.

Use the pop-up menu under **New Finder windows show** to set your desired location. You can choose from your Home, Desktop, Documents, iCloud Drive, or Recents folder. Selecting **Other...** opens a Finder window, allowing you to choose another folder.

Close All Windows

Sometimes you end up with a lot of open Finder windows on your desktop. Wouldn't it be great if there was an easy and quick way to close all of them? Hold down the ⌥ (option) key while clicking the red close window button in the upper left-hand corner of any Finder window. All Finder windows will close. Another option is to use the keyboard shortcut ⌥⌘W (option+command+W) to close all Finder windows.

You can also minimize all open Finder windows by holding down the ⌥ (option) key while clicking the yellow minimize window button in the Title Bar of any Finder window.

Backspace & Delete

The **delete** key on a Mac keyboard acts like the backspace key on a Windows PC. So how do you delete? On a Mac, the **delete** key works both ways – forward and backward. Hold down the **fn** 🌐 (function/globe) key while pressing **delete** to have the key act like a delete key on a Windows PC.

File Extensions

By default, macOS doesn't display file extensions, proving that learning the difference between those 3- and 4-letter extensions in Windows was a terrible waste of your time. For those of you switching from a Microsoft Windows PC to a Mac and are worried because you miss the comfort of seeing those file extensions after every filename, macOS allows you to show file extensions.

Open the Finder settings by selecting **Finder > Settings...** or use the keyboard shortcut ⌘, (command+comma), and click **Advanced** at the top of the window. Check the checkbox next to **Show all filename extensions**.

macOS will warn you when you change a file extension. You can disable this warning by unchecking the checkbox next to **Show warning before changing an extension**. Note that changing a file extension can make a file unusable.

iCloud Drive Warning

macOS will warn you when you remove a file from iCloud. You'll see this warning if you move a file from iCloud to the local storage on your Mac or to an external drive. If you feel this warning is unnecessary, you can disable it.

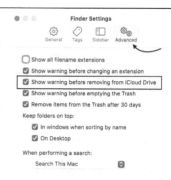

Open the Finder settings by selecting **Finder > Settings...** or use the keyboard shortcut ⌘, (command+comma). Click **Advanced** at the top of the window. Uncheck the checkbox next to **Show warning before removing from iCloud Drive**.

Empty Trash Warning

Every time you empty the Trash, macOS asks you to confirm that you want to erase the items in the Trash. If you find this warning unnecessary, you can disable it.

To tell macOS to stop asking if you want to empty the Trash, open the Finder settings by selecting **Finder > Settings...** or use the keyboard shortcut ⌘, (command+comma). Click **Advanced** at the top of the window. Uncheck the checkbox next to **Show warning before emptying the Trash**.

Empty Trash After 30 Days

macOS can automatically delete items that have been in the Trash for 30 days. This is a handy feature that ensures old files in the Trash can are not left hanging around indefinitely.

To enable this feature, open the Finder settings by selecting **Finder > Settings...** or by using the keyboard shortcut ⌘, (command+comma). Click **Advanced** at the top of the window. Check the checkbox next to **Remove items from the Trash after 30 days**.

Keep Folders on Top

You can configure macOS to display folders at the top of the directory when sorting by name in a Finder window. This feature ensures that Finder windows are better organized with folders on top followed by files.

To enable this feature, open the Finder settings by selecting **Finder > Settings...** or by using the keyboard shortcut ⌘**,** (command+comma). Click **Advanced** at the top of the window. Check the checkbox next to **Keep folders on top when sorting by name**. To keep folders on top of your desktop, check the checkbox next to **On Desktop**. You can enable either or both options.

When enabled, Finder will sort folders by name, placing them all at the top of the list. Files will be sorted next and placed after the list of folders.

Search Scope

When searching in Finder, macOS searches your entire Mac. You can change the search scope to limit it to the current folder or a previous search scope.

To change the search scope, open the Finder settings by selecting **Finder > Settings...** or by using the keyboard shortcut ⌘**,** (command+comma). Click **Advanced** at the top of the window. Use the pop-up list under **When performing a search** to select your desired search scope.

Scroll Bars

In macOS, scroll bars only appear while you are scrolling. This is very different from Windows, where scroll bars are an ugly blight on the right and bottom edges of every window. If you are a former Windows user and miss your scroll bars, macOS can be configured to permanently tack those ugly scroll bars on the right and bottom edges of every macOS window.

To change the behavior of the scroll bars, open System Settings and select **Appearance** from the sidebar. Under **Show scroll bars**, choose from the three options by selecting one of the radio buttons.

When set to **Automatically based on mouse or trackpad**, scroll bars will not appear unless the document requires scroll bars, and you have placed either one finger on the mouse or two fingers on a trackpad in preparation to scroll. This is the macOS default. If you like your scroll bars hidden until you are scrolling, choose the **When scrolling** option. The scroll bars disappear when you are finished scrolling. If you are a former Windows user suffering from scroll bar separation anxiety, select **Always**.

You have two options for clicking within a scroll bar. When **Jump to the next page** is selected, clicking within the scroll bar will page up or page down a single page at a time. When **Jump to the spot that's clicked** is selected, clicking within the scroll bar will take you to that spot in the document. For example, clicking ¼ of the way down the scroll bar will allow you to jump about a quarter way through your document. This feature is quite handy when you need to navigate quickly through a long document.

If you hold down the ⌥ (option) key while clicking within a scroll bar, macOS will temporarily toggle to the other option. For example, if you have configured macOS to **Jump to the next page**, holding down the ⌥ (option) key when clicking in the scroll bar will temporarily enable the **Jump to the spot that's clicked** option.

Scrolling Inertia

A neat macOS scrolling trick is to flick your fingers at the beginning or end of your scroll. This engages a feature called Scrolling Inertia, which is enabled by default. macOS mimics the scrolling experience of an iPhone or iPad, where a flick of your finger causes a window to scroll rapidly, gradually slowing to a stop. Scrolling inertia allows you to scroll past content rapidly to get to the content you want to see.

Start your scroll by moving two-fingers in the direction you want to scroll (i.e., up, down, left, or right) on and flick your fingers at the beginning of the scroll. The content scrolls rapidly and will gradually slow to a stop. Flicking your fingers at the end of a scroll causes the content to accelerate, jumping past content until the scroll gradually slows and stops. How fast the content scrolls by is proportional to how quickly you flick your fingers.

If you don't care for scrolling inertia, macOS allows you to disable it. Open the System Settings app and select **Accessibility** from the sidebar. Next select **Pointer Control,** which can be found under **Motor** in the Accessibility settings window. Click the **Trackpad Options...** button to reveal a configuration sheet. Flip the switch next to **Use inertia when scrolling** off. Click **OK** when finished.

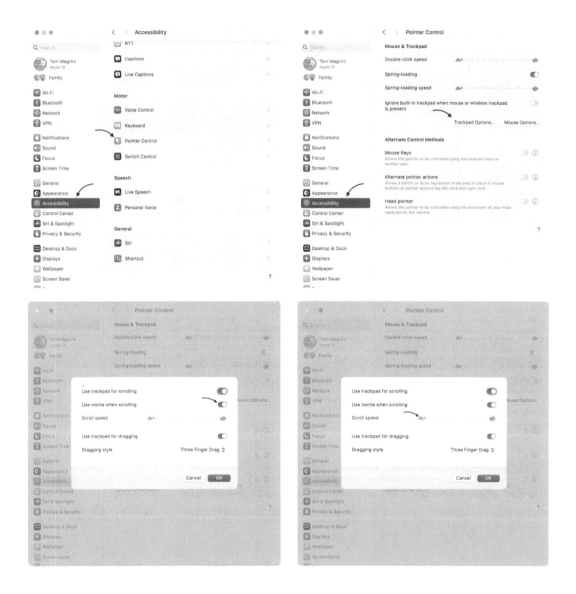

Scrolling Speed

If you find the default scrolling speed too slow or too fast, you can adjust it until you get it just right.

Open the System Settings app and select **Accessibility** from the sidebar. Next select **Pointer Control,** which can be found under **Motor** in the Accessibility settings window. Click the **Trackpad Options...** button to reveal a configuration sheet. Use the slider next to **Scroll speed** to adjust the scrolling speed from slow (turtle) to fast (rabbit). Changes take place immediately. Click **OK** when done.

To adjust the scrolling speed on a Magic Mouse, open System Settings and select **Accessibility** from the sidebar. Next select **Pointer Control,** which can be found under **Motor** in the Accessibility settings window. Click the **Mouse Options...** button to reveal a configuration sheet. Use the slider next to **Scroll speed** to adjust the scrolling speed from slow (turtle) to fast (rabbit). Click **OK** when done.

Rubber band scrolling is a macOS feature where your content scrolls a little further past the end of a document or webpage and then snaps back like a rubber band. This animation lets you know you've reached the end of your document and is the same animation used on the iPhone and iPad.

Search Keyboard Shortcut

You can change the keyboard shortcut for a Finder Search. The default macOS keyboard shortcut is ⌥⌘**space** (option+command+space). macOS lets you configure any keyboard shortcut you desire.

To change the keyboard shortcut for a Finder Search, open System Settings, scroll down and select **Keyboard** in the sidebar. Next, click the **Keyboard Shortcuts...** button to reveal a configuration sheet.   Select **Spotlight** from the sidebar.   Click on **Show Finder search window** to highlight it and click on ⌥⌘space. You can now enter your custom shortcut in the field provided. Be sure to select a shortcut that is not already in use. Click **Done** when finished.

To revert to the macOS defaults for the Finder Search Window, click the **Restore Defaults** button. Note that if you changed the keyboard shortcut for Spotlight search, it will be reverted to its default as well.

List View

macOS displays the following three columns in the **Finder List View**: Date Modified, Size, and Kind. The Finder List View also supports other attributes such as iCloud status, date created, last opened, and added, size, kind, version, comments, and tags.

To change the columns shown in the Finder List View, open a Finder window and select **as List** from the pop-up menu that appears when you click **View** in the Toolbar.

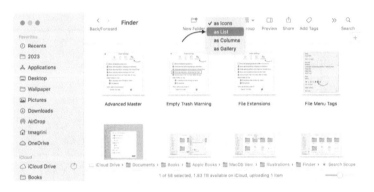

Next, use the keyboard shortcut ⌘J (command+J) to display the View Options settings.   Check the checkboxes next to the items you want to display. Be sure your Finder window is in List View. Otherwise, you will not see these options.

Click **Use as Defaults** to set your choices as the default when opening Finder windows. You can also configure Finder to **Always open in list view**, choose group and sort options, icon size, and text size.

When you're viewing items in **List View**, you will notice that only files have an entry under the **Size** column. You will see a pair of dashes in the size column for folders as macOS does not calculate the size of folders.   If you would like to see the amount of disk space your folders are using, check the checkbox next to **Calculate all sizes**. This attribute is set on a per-folder basis. So, if you would like to make this the default for all folders, click the **Use as Defaults** button.

Quiet the Trash

You'll hear a sound that sounds like you a dumping a trash can when you empty the trash. This can be annoying if you're working in a quiet office environment or are listening to music. The sound of the trash emptying can disturb your concentration or the concentration of your office mates.

To quiet the Trash when emptying, open Terminal and enter the following commands. This change takes effect immediately.

```
defaults write com.apple.finder FinderSounds -bool false
```

```
killall Finder
```

Enter the following commands in Terminal to revert to the macOS default.

```
defaults delete com.apple.finder FinderSounds
```

```
killall Finder
```

Quit Finder

Finder is the one application that you can't quit. This is because Finder is responsible for managing the macOS file system and must run all the time. If you check the **Finder** menu, you will not find a **Quit** command. That is because other than relaunching Finder through **Force Quit** or with a **killall Finder** command, Finder must run continuously.

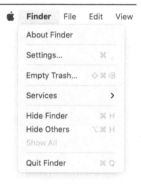

Why would you want to add a Quit command to the Finder menu? Adding a Quit command is a quick and easy way to execute the **killall Finder** command to restart Finder.

Open Terminal and enter the following commands to add a Quit command to Finder.

```
defaults write com.apple.finder QuitMenuItem -bool true
```

```
killall Finder
```

To revert to the macOS default and remove the Quit command from the Finder menu, enter the following commands.

```
defaults delete com.apple.finder QuitMenuItem
```

```
killall Finder
```

15

iCloud

iCloud is seamlessly and securely integrated into Apple's technology and applications, making secure online storage part of the macOS operating system instead of an add-on app like Dropbox, Box, or OneDrive. Working invisibly in the background, iCloud allows you to store data, such as photos, documents, passwords, and contacts, in the cloud and automatically synchronizes them across all your Apple devices. The data you store in iCloud is encrypted, and if you enable two-factor authentication, your data can be accessed only on your trusted devices.

One of the advantages of using iCloud is that it works natively across all your Apple devices. iCloud Photos, Backup, and iCloud Drive synchronize automatically when you sign into a new Apple device with your Apple ID. You can easily access your data and files across all your devices without having to manually transfer data between them. You can even access your data and files from a Windows PC. This feature is huge for those who work on multiple devices throughout the day.

iCloud is integral to the communication between your Apple devices, supporting Handoff, which lets you switch devices, continuing the task you started on one device on another device. For example, you can start a text message on your iPhone and finish and send it on your Mac. iCloud is also a vital component of the Find My app, which allows you to find a misplaced or lost Apple device.

With iCloud, you can easily share files with others, collaborate on documents in real-time, and keep your data secure and backed up. iCloud also makes restoring your Mac or migrating to a new Mac a snap.

Apple gives you 5 GB of storage for free when you sign up for an Apple ID. It's like having your own 5 GB external hard drive in the cloud. Because your documents are stored in iCloud, they are accessible anywhere in the world using your Mac, iPhone, or iPad or at iCloud.com.

If you need more storage, you can upgrade to iCloud+, Apple's premium subscription cloud service. I'll show you how to upgrade to iCloud+ later in this chapter.

Desktop and Documents

When you enable this feature, your Desktop and Documents folders will be safely and securely stored in iCloud, easily accessible from any other device signed in with the same Apple ID. You can start a document on your MacBook and finish it on your iPad without having to manually transfer the file between the two devices. Your files are stored securely and automatically synchronized in iCloud, so you don't have to worry about losing important files if your Mac is lost or stolen.

To enable iCloud Drive on your Mac, open the System Settings app and click on your name at the top of the sidebar. Click **iCloud** in the next window. Next, click **iCloud Drive** to reveal a configuration sheet. Verify that the switches next to **Sync this Mac** and **Desktop & Documents Folders** are on. If not, flip both switches on. Click **Done** to finish.

Once enabled, your Desktop and Documents folders will be listed in the iCloud section of your Finder's Sidebar. The files contained in these folders use your iCloud storage, and you can store as many files as you want provided you have sufficient storage space. You can access the files in your Desktop and Documents folders on your iPhone and iPad using the Files app. You'll also be able to access your files from icloud.com.

If you have multiple Macs and enable iCloud Desktop and Documents, you'll see those files in the iCloud section of your Finder's Sidebar with the name of each Mac.

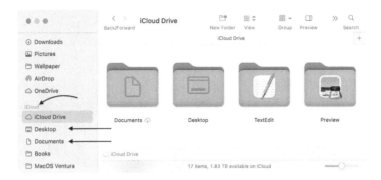

Any time you make a change to a document, it will automatically synchronize in iCloud. If you delete a document in your iCloud Drive on one device, it will be deleted on every device you are signed into with your Apple ID. Files you delete from iCloud go into the **Recently Deleted** folder on icloud.com and in the Files on app on your iPhone or iPad. You can restore deleted items for 30 days. After that, they are permanently deleted.

App Synchronization

You can synchronize more than your Desktop and Documents folders with iCloud. macOS synchronizes data for Apple's apps, including Photos, Passwords, Contacts, Calendars, Reminders, Notes, Safari, News, Stocks, Home, Wallet, Siri, and Freeform.

To choose which apps synchronize with iCloud, open the System Settings app, and click on your name at the top of the sidebar. Click the **Show More Apps...** button to see a complete list of Apple apps that are being synchronized with iCloud. You can enable or disable apps using the switch next to the name of each application. Apps with an **On >** button open a configuration sheet with a switch to disable synchronization with your Mac. Click the **Done** button when done.

iCloud Storage

Apple gives you 5 GB of free storage to store your photos, videos, documents, backups and more. You can easily check how much iCloud storage you are using and how much you have left in the System Settings app.

To manage the contents of your iCloud storage, open the System Settings app, and click on your name at the top of the sidebar. Next, click **iCloud**. The bar chart at the top of the window details your usage of your iCloud storage.

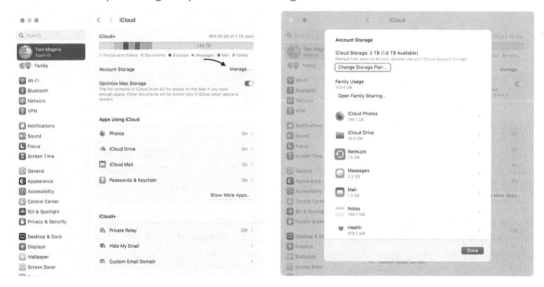

To see the apps using your iCloud storage, click the **Manage...** button, which populates a configuration sheet with a list of the applications utilizing iCloud storage. Click on any app to manage its data.

You may find data in iCloud for applications you no longer use. In that case, you can delete the data and free up storage space by selecting the app and clicking the **Delete All Data** button. Another window will appear asking you to confirm that you want to delete all files. Click **Delete All Data** to delete the data or **Don't Delete** to cancel.

One application you should check is the **Backups** app. You may find backups of devices you no longer own. Delete these old, unneeded backups to free iCloud storage space. Click on the backup to highlight it and click the – (delete) button to delete it.

Devices

When you sign into an Apple device using your Apple ID, the device becomes associated with your Apple account as a trusted device. If you find old devices listed that you no longer own or have handed down to other family members, you should remove the device from your Apple account.

To remove a device from your account, open the System Settings app, and click on your name at the top of the sidebar. Look for a list of trusted **Devices** in the Apple ID settings window. If you see an old device or one you do not recognize, click on the device to open the Device Details window. To remove the device from your account, click the **Remove from Account...** button. A dialog box will appear asking you to confirm the removal or cancel it.

iCloud+

If you need more storage than the 5 GB Apple provides for free, you can upgrade to an iCloud+ subscription to get 50 GB, 200 GB, or 2 TB of iCloud storage.

To upgrade to iCloud+, open the System Settings app, and click on your name at the top of the sidebar. Next, click **iCloud**. Click the **Manage...** button at the top of the window to reveal a configuration sheet. Click the **Add Storage** button. Choose from the three storage upgrade options and click the **Next** button.

If you already have an iCloud+ subscription and want to increase or decrease the amount of iCloud+ storage, click the **Change Storage Plan...** button. You can get up to 2 TB of iCloud storage for $9.99 a month.

If you have an Apple One Plan, you can make changes to it by clicking the **Change Apple One Plan** button.

If you want to downgrade your current plan to one with less storage, your new storage plan must be of sufficient size to accommodate the amount of data you are currently storing in iCloud.

The monthly cost of iCloud+ storage in the U.S. when this book went to press is:

50 GB	99¢
200 GB	$2.99
2 TB	$9.99
6 TB	$29.99
12 TB	$59.99

If you are not in the United States, you can see how much iCloud storage costs in your country at Apple's iCloud Storage page: https://support.apple.com/en-us/HT201238.

iCloud+ is not available in all countries or regions, and features may vary by area. Check Apple's macOS feature availability page at: https://www.apple.com/uk/macos/feature-availability/.

In addition to more storage, iCloud+ adds iCloud Private Relay, Hide my Email, HomeKit Secure Video, a Custom Email Domain, and lets you share the features of your iCloud+ plan with family members.

Private Relay

iCloud Private Relay protects your privacy by hiding your IP address and Safari browsing activity on your Mac, iPhone, iPad, and iPod Touch. When iCloud Private Relay is enabled, your unencrypted internet traffic is encrypted and sent through two separate internet relays. This stops your Internet Service Provider (ISP) from collecting information on your browsing activity and hides your IP address and location from websites that collect this data. Not even Apple can see your IP address, location, or web browsing history. There is no perceptible performance impact of using iCloud Private Relay. iCloud Private Relay is not available in all countries.

To enable to Private Relay, open the System Settings app, and click on your name at the top of the sidebar. Next, click **iCloud** and then click **Private Relay** to open a configuration window. Flip the switch next to **Private Relay** on. Using the pop-up menu next to **IP Address Location**, select **Maintain general location** or **Use country and time zone**. Maintain general location allows you to see local content while use country and time zone obscures your location.

Hide My Email

Hide My Email allows you to generate a unique, random email address when signing up for online services. The feature keeps your personal email address private by generating a random email address and forwarding email to your real email address, giving you greater control over your personal information. Hide My Email is easy to use and can be managed in iCloud settings.

To use to Hide My Email, open the System Settings app, and click on your name at the top of the sidebar. Next, click **iCloud** and then click **Hide My Email** to open a configuration window. You can manually create a random email address by clicking the **+** (add) button. This will open a new window containing a unique, random email address. If you don't like the email address, click the circular arrow to create another. Click the **Continue** button and enter a **Label** to identify the email address. Entering a **Note** is optional. Click **Continue** and the **Done** button in the next window.

macOS can automatically create a unique, random email address when you are presented with an email field when creating an account on a website. macOS will suggest a random email address in addition to your real email address. Click on **Hide My Email...** to use the random email address suggested by macOS. If you don't like the email address, click the circular arrow to create another in the next window. Once you are satisfied with the random email address, click the **Use** button.

To manage your random email address, open the System Settings app, and click on your name at the top of the sidebar. Next, click **iCloud** and then click **Hide My Email** to open a configuration window. Select the site from the sidebar. You can change the Label, Note, copy the email address, or Deactivate it. If you chose to deactivate the email, you will confirm this in the next window. Doing so will stop email from being forwarded from that random email address.

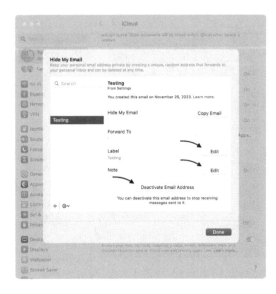 

To reactivate a deactivated email address, open the System Settings app, and click on your name at the top of the sidebar. Next, click **iCloud** and then click **Hide My Email** to open a configuration window. Click the gear at the lower left to reveal a pop-up menu. Select **Show Inactive Addresses** to open a window with a list of inactive email addresses. Select the site from sidebar. You can reactivate by clicking the **Reactivate Address** button or delete the email address by clicking the **Delete Address** button. Click **Done** to finish.

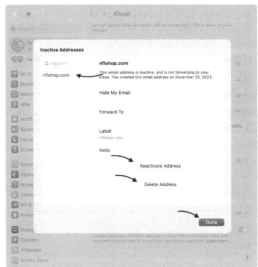

Family Sharing

You can share your iCloud+ subscription with up to 6 family members, each with their own Apple ID. You can share music, movies, TV shows, apps, and books. To setup a Family Sharing group, open System Settings and select **Family** from the sidebar. To add your family members, click **Add Member…** and then **Invite People** in the next window.

To remove someone from your Family Sharing group, click their name to open a new window. Click the **Remove** button to remove them from Family Sharing.

You can also create a more restrictive child account for a child under the age of 13. You must be the child's parent or legal guardian and provide consent to create a child account.

Disable iCloud Desktop & Documents

If you do not want to not save your Desktop and Documents folders in iCloud, instead preferring to save your files locally to your Mac, macOS lets you disable iCloud Drive.

To disable iCloud Drive on your Mac, open the System Settings app and click on your name at the top of the sidebar. Click **iCloud** in the next window. Next, click **iCloud iDrive** to reveal a configuration window. Flip the switch next to **Desktop & Documents Folders** off.

When you disable Desktop & Documents Folders, macOS creates a new folder in your Home folder. Your files remain in iCloud until you move them to your Mac. Select all the files in your Desktop and Documents folders in iCloud Drive and drag them to the corresponding folder on your Mac. New documents you create in your Desktop and Documents folders will be saved locally.

If you disable iCloud Desktop & Documents, I strongly suggest you use Time Machine to back up your files, use another cloud storage solution such as OneDrive, Box, or Dropbox, or sign up with a cloud backup service provider.

___

16

Managing Windows

Stage Manager

One of the coolest features in macOS is Stage Manager, which brings an entirely new approach to how windows are managed. When Stage Manager is enabled, all open windows except the one in which you are working are pinned to the left side of your desktop as thumbnails. Stage Manager helps you focus on a single application window, displayed in the center of your desktop, by minimizing the distractions caused by having multiple windows open.

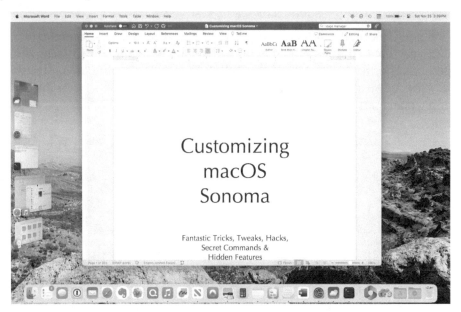

The window you are currently working in appears in the center of your desktop. You can switch between windows by clicking on one of the thumbnails shown on the left side of your desktop. macOS automatically arranges the thumbnails based on recent usage and can show up to six thumbnails, depending on the size of your desktop.

To bring a window to the center without switching applications, hold down the ⇧ (shift) key while clicking on the thumbnail. The thumbnail will expand and move to the center of your desktop to create a group. You can also drag a thumbnail onto your desktop to create a group. You can see two groups in the image below, the first group is in the center of the desktop and consists of Word and Finder. A second group containing Safari and Music is in the bottom thumbnail.

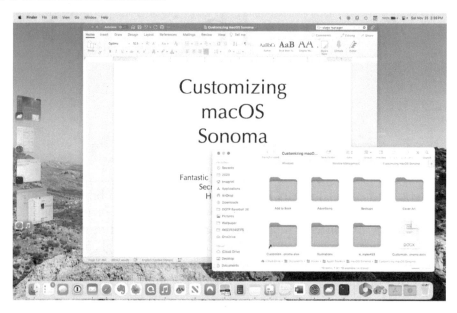

To remove any window from the center group, drag it back to the thumbnail area. A window can be sent to the thumbnail area by dragging it, minimizing it using the yellow minimize button in the left corner of the Title Bar, or by using the ⌘M (command+M) keyboard shortcut. If you minimize all windows, they will all be sent to the thumbnail area as individual apps or groups as shown in the image below.

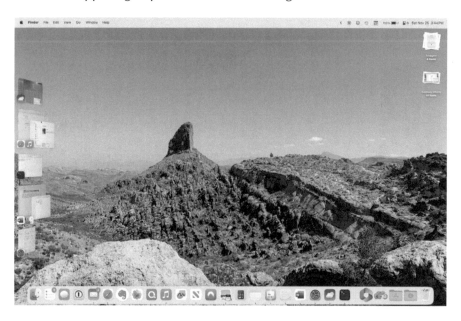

You can remove a window from a group in a thumbnail by dragging it to the center. Apps that haven't been used recently will drop off the thumbnail area as they are replaced with more recently used apps. Hiding an app removes it from the thumbnail area.

To enable Stage Manager, open System Settings, select **Desktop & Dock** from the sidebar. Scroll down to **Desktop & Stage Manager** section of the settings window. Flip the switch next to **Stage Manager** on. Stage Manager can also be toggled on and off in Control Center. Its module is directly below the Focus module.

The switch next to **Show recent apps in Stage Manager** controls whether the thumbnails are shown or not. Switch it on and the recent app thumbnails will always appear on the left side of your desktop. When switched off, the thumbnails are hidden. You must move your pointer to the left edge of your desktop and pause momentarily to make the thumbnails appear.

The images below compare Stage Manager's thumbnails when recent apps are enabled and disabled. In the left image, recent apps are enabled. In the center and right images, recent apps are turned off. They are hidden in the center image while the right image shows the thumbnails when the pointer is moved to the desktop's left edge. Notice the difference between the thumbnails in the left and right images.

You can also use the app switcher or Dock to switch between apps in Stage Manager when thumbnails for recent apps are turned off. The app switcher's keyboard shortcut is **⌘tab** (command+tab).

The pop-up menu next to **Show windows from an application** allows you to choose which windows to show when you use an app. When set to **All at Once**, all available windows for an app will be shown when you switch to it while **One at a Time** only shows the most recently used window. When configured for one at a time, you'll need to click the thumbnail again to open the next available window from the app.

You can choose when to show desktop items, such as your Desktop folder and disks, using the checkboxes next to **Show Items**. When the checkbox next to **On Desktop** is checked, desktop items will always be displayed on your desktop. When this box is unchecked, they will be hidden. To see your desktop items, you will need to perform the Show Desktop command by clicking anywhere on your desktop wallpaper (if enabled), performing the Show Desktop trackpad gesture, or pressing **fn F11** or **F11**.

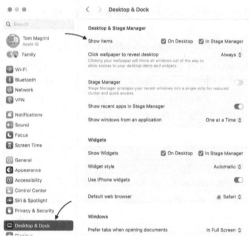

When the **In Stage Manager** checkbox is checked, items will appear on your desktop when Stage Manager is enabled. When this checkbox is unchecked, they are hidden. To see your desktop items in Stage Manager, you must show the desktop by clicking anywhere on your desktop wallpaper (if enabled), performing the Show Desktop trackpad gesture, or pressing **fn F11** or **F11**.

If you want your desktop items to always be displayed on your desktop, check both checkboxes.

Stage Manager's Desktop Items feature is not compatible with the Pristine Desktop tweak from the Desktop chapter. You must disable this tweak for the desktop items checkboxes to work.

The pop-up menu next to **Click wallpaper to reveal desktop** offers 2 options. When you select **Always**, clicking your desktop performs the show desktop command. All windows will be cleared from your desktop. When **Only in Stage Manager** is selected, clicking your desktop to clear windows only works when Stage Manager is enabled.

There appears to be no way to completely disable clicking the desktop to perform the show desktop command unless you do not use Stage Manager. You can disable this feature by turning Stage Manager off and selecting only in Stage Manager in the pop-up menu next to **Click wallpaper to reveal desktop**.

Window Resize Area

Application windows can be resized by hovering your pointer over any of the window's edges until the resizing pointer, a double-headed black arrow, appears. Dragging the resizing pointer resizes the window.

The area in which the pointer changes to the resizing pointer is quite small. It is sometimes difficult to get the pointer in the precise spot to make the resizing pointer appear.

This tweak increases the size of the area in which the pointer will change into the resizing pointer. Open Terminal and enter the following command. You will need to log out and log back in for the change to take effect.

```
defaults write -g AppleEdgeResizeExteriorSize 15
```

Feel free to try different numbers at the end of the command to make the area larger or smaller.

To revert to the macOS default, enter the following command. You will need to log out and log back in for the change to take effect.

```
defaults delete -g AppleEdgeResizeExteriorSize
```

Window Snapping

 One feature I miss when switching between my Windows PC and my MacBook Pro is Microsoft's window snapping feature. Luckily there is a great, low-cost app in the Mac App Store that offers window snapping functionality. Like everything on a Mac, window snapping is more powerful and more fully featured than Microsoft Windows.

Magnet is a simple, easy to use, elegant, and highly intuitive third-party app. It supports window snapping by dragging, keyboard shortcuts, or through a pop-up menu in its Menu Extra. Magnet keeps your desktop organized by letting you snap windows to use a quarter, third, half, two-thirds, or your entire desktop. Neatly aligning your windows side-by-side eliminates having to switch apps constantly. I especially like the capability to maximize a window to full screen without losing the Menu Bar and Dock, although macOS Sonoma now allows you to set Menu Bar auto-hiding to never.

If you are looking for Windows-like snapping features, Magnet delivers them in a powerful, customizable, and easy to use application. Because Magnet packs so many powerful features in a simple to use package, it is my recommended window snapping app for macOS. As I write this sentence, Magnet is the #2 rated productivity app in the Mac App Store with a rating of 4.9 stars with over 154,000 reviews. Magnet is available from the Mac App Store for $4.99 at the time of this writing. https://apps.apple.com/us/app/magnet/id441258766?mt=12.

Privacy & Security Settings

The first time you launch Magnet, you must authorize the application in the Privacy & Security settings. Open the System Settings app, select **Privacy & Security** in the sidebar. Scroll down in the settings window and click **Accessibility**. Flip the switch next to **Magnet** on to authorize it.

Launch Magnet at Login

To ensure you can always take advantage of Magnet's powerful window snapping capabilities, verify that Magnet will launch when you start your Mac.

From the Magnet Menu Extra, select **Preferences...** to open Magnet's settings. By default, the checkbox next to **Launch at login** should be checked. If you prefer to launch Magnet manually, uncheck this checkbox.

The checkbox next to **Snap windows by dragging** should be checked too. When unchecked, you must use Magnet's keyboard shortcuts and Menu Extra to resize windows. **Unsnap to original size** does what its name implies. When unsnapping a window, it returns to its original size before you resized it. Unchecking disables this feature.

Sides Do Halves

The simplest method of rearranging and resizing the windows on your desktop is to drag them. Window snapping is accomplished by dragging a window to a location at the edge of your desktop.

Let's say you want to compare two documents side-by-side. Drag one document to the left edge of your desktop. The left half of your desktop dims, previewing the result of the window snap. Release your hold on the window, and it resizes to the left half of your desktop. Drag the other document to the right edge, and the right half of your desktop dims. Release and the window, and it resizes to the right half of your desktop.

Perhaps you'd prefer to compare the documents with one occupying the top half of your desktop and the other the bottom half. To snap a window to the top half of your desktop, drag it to the left or right side, just below either of the top corners. The top half of your desktop dims to preview the snap. Release your hold on the window, and it resizes to the top half of your desktop.

For the bottom half, drag the window to the left or right side, just above either of the bottom corners. The bottom half of your desktop dims to preview the resize. Release your hold on the window, and it resizes to the bottom half of your desktop.

You just learned the first rule of Magnet. **Sides do halves**.

If you prefer to use keyboard shortcuts, the default shortcut to snap a window to the left half of your desktop is **^⌥left** (control+option+left arrow). To snap a window to the right half, use the keyboard shortcut **^⌥right** (control+option+right arrow).

A window can be snapped to the top half of your desktop with the keyboard shortcut **^⌥up** (control+option+up arrow). To snap a window to the lower half, use the keyboard shortcut **^⌥down** (control+option+down arrow).

If you need another option, Magnet features a Menu Extra with a pop-up menu from which you can select **Left**, **Right**, **Up**, or **Down**.

Corners for Quarters

Dragging a window to any of the four desktop corners snaps it to that corner and resizes it to a quarter of your desktop.

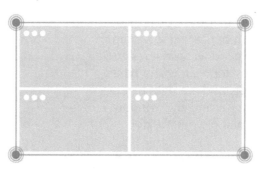

The second rule of Magnet is **corners for quarters**.

If you prefer to use keyboard shortcuts, the default shortcuts for the four corners of the desktop – top left, top right, bottom left, and bottom right are **^⌥U** (control+option+U), **^⌥i** (control+option+i), **^⌥J** (control+option+J), and **^⌥K** (control+option+K).

From the Magnet Menu Extra, select **Top Left**, **Top Right**, **Bottom Left**, or **Bottom Right**.

Bottoms Make Thirds

Drag a window to the bottom of your desktop, and it snaps to the left, center, or right third. Move your pointer across the bottom edge of your desktop without releasing your hold to preview your options. When you do so, you'll notice you have the option of resizing to a third or two-thirds of your desktop.

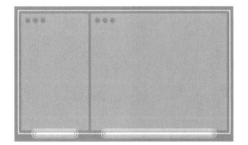
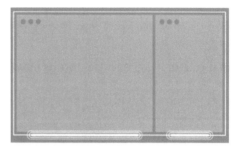
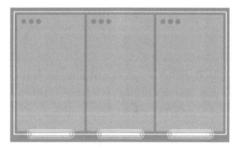

The third rule of Magnet is **bottom makes thirds**.

If you prefer to use keyboard shortcuts, the default shortcut to snap a window to the left third is ^⌥D (control+option+D). Need the window bigger? The keyboard shortcut ^⌥E (control+option+E) snaps a window to the left two-thirds. Use the keyboard shortcut ^⌥F (control+option+F) to snap a window to the center third. The shortcuts for the right two-thirds and right third are ^⌥T (control+option+T) and ^⌥G (control+option+G).

From the Magnet Menu Extra, select **Left Third**, **Left Two Thirds**, **Center Third**, **Right Two Thirds**, or **Right Third**.

Top to Maximize

Magnet supports a full screen mode, called **Maximize**, which differs from the native macOS Full screen mode discussed in the Mission Control chapter. With Magnet, you can take a window to full screen without hiding the Menu Bar and Dock, which is the default behavior when using the native macOS Full screen mode. This feature comes in handy when you're using an application with many controls in the Application Menu, and you don't want to wait for the Menu Bar to unhide in macOS Full screen mode. Similarly,

Magnet's Maximize feature does not hide the Dock, allowing you to access it without waiting for it to unhide. To maximize a window, drag it to the top edge of your desktop.

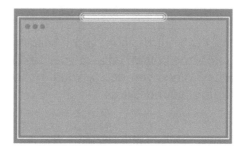

The final rule of Magnet is the **top to maximize**.

If you prefer to use keyboard shortcuts, the shortcut to maximize a window is ^⌥**return** (control+option+return).

From the Magnet Menu Extra, select **Maximize**.

Centering a Window

Magnet features a **Center** option, which centers the active window, both horizontally and vertically, on your desktop. It's accessible through the Magnet Menu Extra or by using the keyboard shortcut ^⌥**C** (control+option+C).

Restoring a Window

To restore a snapped window to its original size and location, drag it away from the edge of your desktop, use the keyboard shortcut ^⌥**delete** (control+option+delete), or select **Restore** from Magnet's Menu Extra.

Multiple Displays

You can use Magnet to move windows between displays. The keyboard shortcut ^⌥⌘**right** (control+option+command+right arrow) moves the active window to the next display. Use the ^⌥⌘**left** (control+option+command+left arrow) keyboard shortcut to move the window back to the previous display. From the Magnet Menu Extra, select **Next Display** or **Previous Display**.

Ignoring an App

An **Ignore** option, accessible from Magnet's Menu Extra, lets you tell Magnet to ignore the currently active application. This option is handy if you are manipulating an application's windows and don't want Magnet's snapping features to engage.

Keyboard Shortcuts

If you want to change any of the default keyboard shortcuts, select **Preferences...** from the Magnet Menu Extra to open the Magnet settings. Click on the **X** (delete) button next to the keyboard shortcut you want to change or click on the keyboard shortcut itself to reveal **Type New Shortcut**. Enter your desired keyboard shortcut in this field. To return to the previous entry, click the circular restore button, which replaces the **X** shown to the right of the keyboard shortcut after you have changed the shortcut.

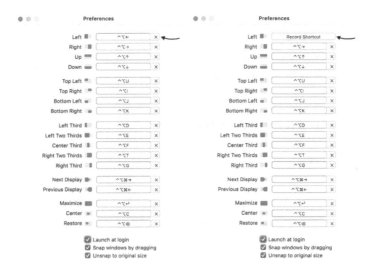

Vertical Screens

If you have your display set up vertically, which is great for editing documents using Microsoft Word or Apple Pages, Magnet easily adapts. Note the change in the snap areas when using a vertical screen, as shown in the image below.

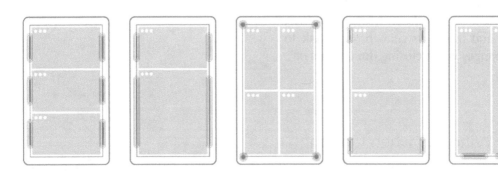

If your display is set up vertically, thirds use the sides, as shown in the first two images. Corners are still for quarters. Horizontal halves still use the sides. However, vertical halves now use the bottom.

Open Windows in Tabs

You can configure macOS to open documents in a tab instead of a new window. When set to open in a tab, new documents will open in a tab inside a single instance of an app window. This feature cuts down on the desktop clutter that occurs when each document is opened in a new window.

To configure documents to open in tabs, open the System Settings app. Select **Desktop & Dock** from the sidebar. Scroll down to the **Windows** section. Using the pop-up menu next to **Prefer tabs when opening documents**, choose from **Never**, **Always**, and **In Full Screen**.

Save Changes Automatically

By default, macOS asks you if you want to save any unsaved changes when you close a document. You can disable this behavior and have macOS automatically save unsaved changes when you close a document's window.

To enable automatic saving of documents when closing them, open the System Settings app. Select **Desktop & Dock** from the sidebar. Scroll down to the **Windows** section and flip the switch next to **Ask to keep changes when closing documents** off.

Close Windows when Quitting

A handy feature of macOS is that it can reopen windows that were open the last time you quit an application. This a useful feature if you're working on a document and want it opened each time you launch the app. However, this feature can be annoying if you want to start fresh each time you launch an application and must close the old windows first. To stop closed windows from reopening when you launch an application, open the System Settings app. Select **Desktop & Dock** from the sidebar. Scroll down to the

Windows section and flip the switch next to **Close windows when quitting an application** on.

When this feature is enabled, open windows will close when you quit an app and will not reopen the next time you launch the app.

17

Safari

For most users, Safari requires little customization and can be used out-of-the-box. However, if you have made it this far, you are not like most users. You want to fine-tune the Safari settings, change its appearance, and make it perform better.

Start Page

Safari allows you to change the layout of your Start Page. The default for Safari's Start Page is to display your Favorites, Frequently Visited sites, Share with You, a Privacy Report, Siri Suggestions, Reading List, and iCloud Tabs. Safari will use your Start Page on all your Apple devices.

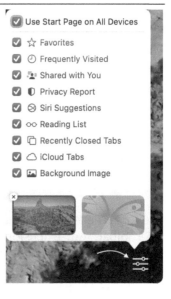

You can customize your Start Page by clicking on the settings icon in the lower right corner of your Safari start page to reveal a contextual menu as shown in the image to the right. Check and uncheck the items listed to configure your Safari Start Page.

✓ Show Favorites
✓ Show Frequently Visited
✓ Show Privacy Report
✓ Show Siri Suggestions
✓ Show Reading List
✓ Show Shared with You
✓ Show Recently Closed Tabs
✓ Show iCloud Tabs

Choose Background...
Clear Background

You can secondary click anywhere on Safari's start page to reveal a contextual menu that offers the ability to configure all but the **Use Start Page on All Devices** option. This contextual menu uses checkmarks to enable features.

Safari allows you to change the background of your Start Page from the default, boring gray to any image you choose. You can change your Safari Start Page background by clicking on the settings icon in the lower right corner of your start page to reveal a configuration menu shown in the image above right. You can select from nine standard backgrounds provided by Apple or choose your own image. To see the standard images, swipe to the left with two fingers. To select your own image, click on the gray background with the **+** (add) button to open a Finder window. Navigate to your desired image and click **Choose**.

You can also select a background by secondary clicking in an open area of Safari's start page to reveal the contextual menu shown in the image to the right. Select **Choose Background...** to launch a Finder window.   Navigate to your desired image and click **Choose**.

Note that you will not see the **Clear Background** option until you have configured Safari to use a background image. This option will clear the current Start Page image and return to Safari's default background.

Toolbar

The Toolbar, located at the top of the Safari window, offers tools to enhance your web browsing experience. You can customize the Toolbar, adding, removing, and rearranging the tools as you see fit. Secondary click in an open area of the Toolbar to reveal a contextual menu with a single option to **Customize Toolbar...**, which opens the Safari tool palette. You can also launch the tool palette by selecting **Customize Toolbar...** from the **View** menu.

The tool palette allows you to add additional tools by dragging and dropping them onto the Toolbar. Any extensions that offer a tool are shown on the tool palette. To add a tool to the Toolbar, drag and drop it on to the Toolbar. Existing tools located on the Toolbar can be rearranged by dragging them. A tool is removed by dragging it off the Toolbar and onto the tool palette.

Available tools include **iCloud Tabs**, which displays the websites open in tabs on other Apple devices associated with your Apple ID.

The **Share** button lets you share an item via Mail, Messages, Airdrop, or through third-party extensions.

The **New Tab** tool does what you would expect it to do – opens a new Safari tab. The **Show/Hide Tab Overview** tool toggles the tab overview, which displays thumbnails of websites open in tabs. This tool lets you quickly jump to a tab by clicking on it.
The **Start Page** tool takes you to your start page. The **Home** tool takes you to your Home page, which is configured in Safari's General preferences.

The **History** tool displays a history of webpages you have previously visited. The **Sidebar** tool toggles the Safari sidebar on and off. Safari's sidebar displays your bookmarks or reading list.

The **Bookmarks** tool toggles Safari's favorites bar on and off. The Favorites Bar conveniently lists the websites in your Favorites bookmark folder in a bar just below the Safari toolbar.

The **Autofill** tool tells Safari to automatically fill website forms with data such as your name, address, email, and phone number.

The **Zoom** tool does what you would expect it to do – zooms in and out.

The **Mail** tool lets you share a webpage via your default mail application. The **Print** tool lets you print a webpage.

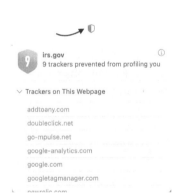

The **Privacy** tool provides a privacy report that shows how many trackers Safari blocked for the website you are visiting. A tracker is a script designed to collect data on you while you visit the site. In the image to the left, you can see how the IRS website uses 9 trackers to track and profile visitors.

Website Preferences let you quickly configure various options for the website you are visiting. You can choose to display the Reader view; enable content blockers; configure settings for page zoom, autoplay, and pop-up windows; and control access to your camera, microphone, screen, and location.

The **Flexible Space** tool is used to space out the tools in the toolbar by adding blank space between them.

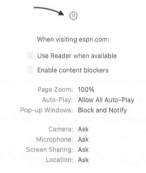

Tools located on the Toolbar can be rearranged without having to use the tool palette. To move a tool, hold the ⌘ (command) key down while dragging it to its new location. You can also use the ⌘ (command) key to remove a tool. Hold down the ⌘ (command) key while dragging the tool off the Toolbar.

To revert to the default set of Safari tools, drag the default toolset onto the toolbar and click **Done**.

Sharing Pages

To configure the third-party extensions available when sharing, click the Share button and select **Edit Extensions…**, which opens the Extensions settings window in the System Settings app. Use the checkboxes to choose how you wish to share content. The choices you make will be available in all apps that offer a sharing feature.

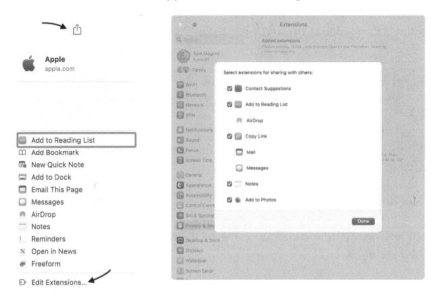

You can also navigate to the Sharing settings through the System Settings application. Open System Settings and select **Privacy & Security** from the sidebar. Next, scroll down to the bottom of the Privacy & Security settings window and click on **Extensions** near the bottom of the window under the **Other** category. Select **Sharing** in the next window.

Default Browser

The default web browser is the browser that launches when you click a web link. For macOS, the default browser is Safari. Safari is extremely fast, easy to use, and is optimized for your Mac. While it may seem odd, Apple allows you to choose another browser installed on your Mac as the default browser.

You must first install other browsers before you can change your default browser. Firefox, Chrome, Opera, and Microsoft Edge are the usual suspects.

Firefox can be downloaded from:
https://www.mozilla.org.

Chrome is available for download at:
https://www.google.com/chrome/.

Another option for a fast and secure browser is Ulaa, which is available at:
https://ulaabrowser.com.

Opera is available at:
https://www.opera.com.

Microsoft Edge, yes you can run Microsoft's internet browser on your Mac without running Windows. Download Microsoft Edge from:
https://www.microsoft.com/en-us/edge.

To change your default web browser, open System Settings and select **Desktop & Dock** from the sidebar. Scroll down until you see **Default web browser** below the Widgets section. Choose your desired web browser from the pop-up menu.

Opening Safari

You can configure how you want Safari to open from the General tab in the Safari settings. Select **Safari > Settings...** or use the keyboard shortcut ⌘, (command+,). Click the **General** button at the top of the window.

You have the option to start Safari with a new window, a new private window, all windows from your last session, or all non-private windows from your last session. Make your selection from the pop-up menu next to **Safari opens with**.

New Windows & Tabs

The default is for Safari to open your start page when opening new windows and tabs. You can change this using the pop-up menu next to **New windows open with**. You can choose from your start page, home page, an empty page, the same page you most recently viewed, or tabs for favorites. To use the tabs feature, you need to select **Choose tabs folder...** to open your bookmarks to select a bookmarks folder.

The pop-up menu next to **New tabs open with** allows you to choose from your start page, home page, an empty page, or the same page you most recently viewed.

Home Page

Your Home page is the page your browser will navigate to when you click the Home button in Safari's toolbar. If you do not choose a Home page, it will default to Apple's website at https://www.apple.com.

To configure your home page, browse to the site you want as your home page. Next, open the Safari settings by selecting **Safari > Settings...** or using the keyboard shortcut **⌘,** (command+,). Click the **General** button at the top of the window. Click **Set to Current**

Page. You can also type the URL of your desired home page in the field next to **Homepage**. If you do not set a home page, the Home tool in your Safari toolbar will be grayed out.

History

Safari maintains a history of all websites you have visited. This is a handy feature if you want to return to a website but forgot to bookmark it. You can view your browsing history organized by date in Safari by selecting **History > Show History** or by entering the keyboard shortcut ⌘Y (command+Y).

The length of time Safari keeps your history is configurable to one day, one week, two weeks, one month, one year, or manually, which will require you to clear your history. Make your selection from the pop-up list next to **Remove history items**.

Favorites

You can choose the bookmarks folder you want on your start page, displayed below the URL smart search field. Select from the bookmarks folders listed in the pop-up menu next to **Favorites shows**. The default is to show the bookmarks in your Favorites folder.
If you always want the bookmarks in your favorites folder available, select **View > Show Favorites Bar** or enter the keyboard shortcut ⇧⌘B (shift+command+B). The Favorites

Bar is located directly below the Safari toolbar. Enter ⇧⌘B (shift+command+B) to toggle the Favorites Bar on and off.

To manage your bookmarks, select **Bookmarks > Edit Bookmarks** or enter the keyboard shortcut ⌥⌘B (option+command+B) to launch the Bookmarks Editor. From the Bookmarks Editor, you can drag, drop, rearrange, delete, and add bookmarks and bookmark folders. To hide the Bookmark Editor when finished, select **Bookmarks > Hide Bookmarks Editor**, use the keyboard shortcut ⌥⌘B (option+command+B), click on a bookmark to go to a website, or enter a URL in the address and search field.

Downloads

By default, Safari saves downloaded files to your Downloads folder. You can change this location to any folder by choosing **Other...** in the pop-up menu next to **File download location**. A Finder window will open. Navigate to your desired save location and press the **Select** button.

You can also configure Safari to ask you for the save location each time you download a file. Choose the ask for each download option from the pop-up menu next to **Save downloaded files to**.

Safari maintains a list of all files downloaded. By default, this list is cleared after one day. You can configure Safari to remove this list after one day, when Safari quits, upon successful download, or manually using the pop-up menu next to **Remove download list items**.

Safari automatically opens movies, pictures, sounds, PDF files, text documents, and archives upon downloading. You can change this behavior by unchecking the checkbox next to **Open "safe" files after downloading**.

Tabs

macOS lets you change how tabs are displayed in Safari. The default is separate, where tabs appear below the Safari toolbar in a separate Tab Bar. macOS offers a compact option, where your tabs appear in the Safari toolbar. The options are shown below with the default in the top image, and the compact option in the second image.

To select how tabs are displayed, select **Safari > Settings...** or enter the keyboard shortcut **⌘,** (command+,). Click on the **Tab** button. Choose between the Separate and Compact options shown next to **Tab layout** by clicking on desired option.

If you want to see website titles on your tabs, check the checkbox next to **Always show website titles in tabs**.

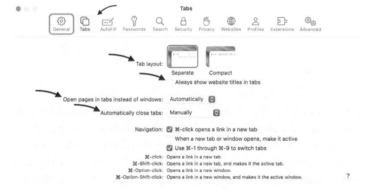

Safari opens new pages in tabs unless the page is designed for a specially formatted window. By default, the pop-up menu next to **Open pages in tabs instead of windows** is set to **Automatically**. Two other configuration options are available – never or always. The never option opens all pages in a new Safari window. If you choose always, Safari creates a new tab even if a website requests a new window.

By default, you must manually close tabs. You can configure Safari to close tabs after 1 day, 1 week, or 1 month by selecting your choice from the pop-up menu next to **Automatically close tabs**.

Navigation

The next section in the Safari settings allows you to control navigation. By default, holding down the ⌘ (command) key while clicking on a link opens a new tab. To disable this feature, uncheck the checkbox next to ⌘-**click opens a new link in a new tab**. Holding the ⇧⌘ keys (shift+command) when clicking on a link opens a new tab and makes it the active tab. Holding the ⇧⌥⌘ keys (shift+option+command) while clicking a link opens it in a new window and makes the window active.

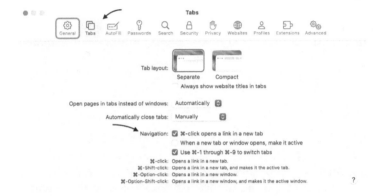

You can choose to make a new tab or new window active when it opens by checking the checkbox next to **When a new tab or window opens, make it active**. This feature is disabled by default.

You can switch tabs using the ⌘ (command) key combined with the numbers 1 through 9. This option is enabled by default.

Autofill

The autofill feature automatically inserts data into online forms. The data includes your name, address, username, password, credit card, or other information you previously entered on a web form. If you need to change this information because you moved, changed your login credentials, or received a new credit card, you can edit the information saved in Autofill from the Safari settings. Click the **Autofill** tab.

Safari autofills information from your contacts card, which consists of your name, address, city, state, zip code, and phone number. This feature is handy when filling out shipping information when making an online purchase. To edit your contact information, click the **Edit** button next to **Using info from my Contacts card**.

Safari securely saves your user credentials and automatically enters your username and password when you revisit a website. To edit your login credentials, click the **Edit** button next to **User names and passwords**. Enter your password, and Safari switches to the **Password** tab where you can see and edit the websites for which your user credentials have or have not been saved.

Safari also saves your credit card number, expiration date, and cardholder name. It automatically enters this information when needed to complete a purchase. To edit your credit card information, click the **Edit** button next to **Credit cards**. Enter your password and double-click on a stored credit card you want to edit. You can also add new credit cards and remove old ones. Click **Done** when finished.

The **Other forms** attribute allows Safari to save the information you entered on a web form and automatically enter the information when you revisit the webpage. To view or edit this information, click the **Edit** button next to **Other forms**. Safari provides a list of all websites where you filled out a web form of some type. You can **Remove** any site or **Remove All**. Click **Done** when finished.

The information stored by Safari is available on your iPhone and iPad and other Macs using the same Apple ID. Information modified on any device is updated via iCloud.

Passwords

Safari automatically stores your login credentials for websites you visit and synchronizes them across all your Apple devices. Safari automatically enters your login credentials, so there is no need to memorize passwords, and you can easily access your passwords through Safari's settings. When you create a new account on a website, Safari offers the option to create and save a strong password for you.

Safari's password feature allows you to implement a security best practice of creating a unique, strong password for every website you visit. Unfortunately, it is far too common for hackers to steal login credentials. If you use the same password on every website, and a website is compromised, hackers can use your stolen credentials to access other websites to steal your credit card data or money from your bank accounts. You should use unique, strong passwords for every website.

Your passwords are accessible from Safari's settings. Click **Passwords** at the top of the window. The window has e sections with the first providing Security Recommendations, identifying weak and reused passwords and Password Options. The second provides the

the ability to Share Passwords With Family. The third section is a list of websites and credentials.

Clicking on **Security Recommendations** opens another window that lists high priority recommendations, which include any passwords exposed in a data leak. By default, Safari will securely monitor your passwords and alert you if they were exposed in a data leak. Other recommendations identify weak or reused passwords. Clicking on the > (more) button will provide additional information and allow you to change the password on the website.

Clicking on **Password Options** opens the Password Options settings window. By default, all options are enabled. Safari will autofill your passwords and passkey to help you sign into apps and websites. Passwords and passkeys are stored in iCloud Keychain. Lastly, Safari will automatically delete the Multifactor Authentication one-time passcodes sent via text message when signing into a website or app.

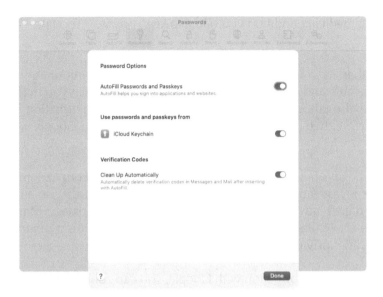

If you want to share your passwords with your family, click the **Get Started** button below **Share Passwords with Family**. Safari will walk you through how to create a new shared group. If any of your devices need to be upgraded, you will receive a warning. You can move passwords to your shared group by checking the checkbox next to each of the passwords you wish to share. Once you have finished moving passwords, you can notify your share group via text message.

Clicking on a website in the third section of the Passwords settings will display a list of all websites where you saved or not saved a password. Clicking on any website in the list will open another window, allowing you to edit your login credentials. Click the **Edit** button to update or change your credentials. You can also click the **Delete Password...** button to delete your credentials. Click **Done** when finished to return to the Safari Password settings.

Help Defeat the Evil Empire

You can help defeat the Evil Empire's plans for galactic domination by configuring Safari to use a search engine other than Google. Google collects a tremendously scary amount of your personal information, more than you probably realize, and without your knowledge, to drive its advertising revenue. I bet you thought Google was a company that provides a free search engine and email. Nothing in this world is free. Google raked in $224.47 billion (yes, billion with a capital "B") in advertising revenue in 2022 making it the largest advertising company in the world. Nearly 80% of Google's revenue is from advertising. And you thought Google was a search engine. Silly rabbit.

Google is the market leader in search with a worldwide market share of 93.37% as of February 2023. The Evil Empire tracks your searches, capturing detailed information on your search topics and which search results you clicked. Have you searched for information on a medical condition you'd like to keep private? Too late. The Evil Empire already knows.

Google states that its mission is "to organize the world's information and make it universally accessible and useful." That includes information that you may prefer to keep private. Google also tailors your search results based on the information it has collected from you. Therefore, two people who enter the same search on Google will see different results.

It's no wonder the attorneys general of 48 states and the District of Columbia and Puerto Rico joined an investigation into Google over possible antitrust violations due to its dominance in digital advertising and its use of consumer data. Many presidential candidates have also called for a breakup of Google, alleging it is a monopoly that hurts competition, invades privacy, and misuses consumer data.

If you prefer not to share information with Google, you can configure Safari to use a search engine that does not collect your personal information. Safari offers DuckDuckGo as an alternative search engine. Google's U.S. privacy policy, as of the writing of this book, is over 5,700 words (https://policies.google.com/privacy?hl=en-US#intro). DuckDuckGo's privacy policy is a mere 7 words, *"We don't collect or share personal information."* (https://duckduckgo.com/privacy). DuckDuckGo does not tailor search results to your previous internet search history. Therefore, you'll receive the same unfiltered results as any other DuckDuckGo user.

To configure Safari to use DuckDuckGo as its search engine, select **Safari > Settings…** or use the keyboard shortcut ⌘, (command+comma). Click the **Search** icon at the top of the settings window and select **DuckDuckGo** using the pop-up menu next to **Search Engine.** Other options are Bing, Yahoo, Ecosia, and of course, the Evil Empire.

New in macOS Sonoma is the ability to select a different search engine when using Safari's private browsing feature. Select your search engine choice from the pop-up menu next to **Private Browsing search engine**. Your choices are DuckDuckGo, Bing, Yahoo, Ecosia, and the Evil Empire.

Checking the checkbox next to **Include search engine suggestions** in the Safari Search settings allows Safari to query your chosen search engine for suggestions as you type your search terms. When the checkbox next to **Include Safari Suggestions** checked, Safari will make suggestions from the internet, Music, App Store, movie showtimes, and nearby locations as you type in Safari's Smart Search field.

Enable Quick Website Search lets Safari record information about your searches to speed up future searches on the same website. With this feature enabled, you can search within a website by entering the site's name, followed by the search term in Safari's search field. You can see and remove a site for which Safari recorded search information by clicking the **Manage Websites...** button. Click on any website to highlight it and click **Remove**. You can remove all websites by clicking **Remove All**. Click **Done** when finished.

When **Preload Top Hit in the background** is enabled, Safari will begin to load the top search hit. Therefore, the website will appear much faster when you click on it. When the checkbox next to **Show favorites** is checked, Safari shows your favorite websites below the search field when you click in the Smart Search field when viewing a webpage.

Security

By default, Safari warns you if a website you are attempting to visit is suspected to be a fraudulent website running a phishing scam. Phishing is an attempt by cybercriminals to trick you into divulging personal information such as your username, password, social security number, credit card number, banking, or other personal information.

Most phishing attempts start as a fake email that appears to be from a bank, credit card company, retailer, delivery service, or streaming site alerting you that you must take care of something immediately; otherwise, your account will be suspended or closed. Urgency is a red flag that the email is a phishing scam as are grammatical errors, misspellings, and strange capitalization. The links in a phishing email direct you to a fraudulent website that appears to be the real thing. If you enter your login credentials or other personal information, they will be captured by a cybercriminal, who will use your information to make fraudulent purchases, steal money from your accounts, or steal your identity.

Safari warns you if you visit a website that has been reported as fraudulent when the checkbox next to **Warn when visiting a fraudulent website** is checked. There is no reason to disable this security feature. Be sure to heed all security warnings from Safari.

Privacy

Apple is serious about safeguarding your privacy. Safari prevents advertisers from tracking your internet travels. When you browse to a webpage, your browser provides information that can be used to identify you – your browser, operating system, browser plugins, ISP, IP address, location, previous webpage's URL, download speed, CPU and GPU info, fonts, screen resolution, social media, and websites you are logged into – all without your permission. All this information taken together forms a digital fingerprint that can be used to identify you.

Apple's privacy features remove and block data that websites can use to track you, making it more difficult for advertisers to gather data about your browsing habits to target you for unwanted advertising. Thank you, Apple!

With prevent cross-site tracking enabled, tracking data from third-party content providers, is periodically deleted. This makes it harder for an advertiser to track you across different websites.

Hiding your IP address from trackers, foils the ability of trackers and websites to identify you and follow you as you travel the internet. Two options are available. You can hide your IP address from known online trackers or from all trackers and websites. The latter option requires an iCloud+ subscription because it uses iCloud Private Relay.

Cookies are small amounts of data that a website sends and stores on your Mac. Cookies can be used to compile records of your browsing activity. Safari allows you to remove and block cookies that websites and third parties use to track you. You probably already have cookies stored on your Mac. Safari lets you see which websites have stored cookies on your Mac and remove some or all of them. Click **Manage Website Data...** to see which websites have stored cookies on your Mac. To remove individual website cookies, select the website and click **Remove**. You also have the option to **Remove All**. Click **Done** when finished. It is a good idea to periodically delete cookies from your Mac.

Reader

Nothing is more annoying than a webpage filled with obnoxiously large amounts of advertising and clickbait. You can fight this by configuring Safari to default to Safari Reader, which will display a clean, readable version of a website article.

To configure websites to default to Safari Reader, open the Safari settings by selecting **Safari > Settings...** or by entering the keyboard shortcut ⌘, (command+,). Click on the **Websites** button and then select **Reader** in the sidebar. The right pane populates with a list of currently open and configured websites. Select **On** or **Off** in the pop-up menu to the right of each website. **On** configures the website to use Reader.

If you want to delete a configured website from the list, highlight it and click the **Remove** button.

To configure Safari to always default to the Safari Reader view, select on from the pop-up menu next to **When visiting other websites**. Website articles will use Reader automatically, allowing you to enjoy cleaner websites and ad-free web browsing.

When the checkbox next to **Share across devices** is checked, your settings will be replicated across all your Apple devices.

Content Blockers

Safari's content blocker enhances your web browsing experience by blocking annoying advertisements and other unwanted content from appearing.

To ensure your content blocker is enabled for all websites, open the Safari settings by selecting **Safari > Settings…** or by entering the keyboard shortcut ⌘, (command+,). Click on **Websites** at the top of the window and select **Content Blockers** in the sidebar. The right pane populates with a list of currently open and configured websites and their content blocker setting. To change a setting, select **On** or **Off** from the pop-up menu next to the website name. The on settings blocks ads and other unwanted content from appearing on the website. Off allows ads and other unwanted content.

If you want to delete a website from the list, highlight it and click the **Remove** button.

To enable your content blocker for all websites, select **On** from the pop-up menu next to **When visiting other websites** in the lower-right corner.

When the checkbox next to **Share across devices** is checked, your settings will be replicated across all your Apple devices.

Auto-Play

There is nothing worse than opening a bunch of tabs in Safari and then being assaulted by a cacophony of sound blaring out of your speakers. You don't have to hunt down each one to kill or mute the annoyance because Safari lets you selectively block auto-play.

To review or change your Auto-Play settings, open the Safari settings by selecting **Safari > Settings…** or by entering the keyboard shortcut ⌘, (command+,). Click on **Websites** at the top of the window and then select **Auto-Play** in the sidebar. The right pane populates with a list of currently open and configured websites and their auto-play settings.

To change any website setting, use the pop-up menu to the right of the website name. You have the choice of **Allow All Auto-Play**, **Stop Media with Sound**, and **Never Auto-Play.**

To block auto-play video for all websites, select **Never Auto-Play** from the pop-up menu next to **When visiting other websites** in the lower-right corner.

If you want to delete a website from the list, highlight it and click the **Remove** button.

When the checkbox next to **Share across devices** is checked, your settings will be replicated across all your Apple devices.

Page Zoom

You can set the page zoom in Safari to make text and images appear larger (or smaller). Page zoom can be set individually by website, or you can set a default page zoom for all websites.

To configure the page zoom, open the Safari settings by selecting **Safari > Settings...** or by entering the keyboard shortcut ⌘, (command+,). Click on the **Websites** icon at the top of the window and then select **Page Zoom** in the sidebar. The right pane populates with a list of currently open websites and those you have configured a page zoom policy. To change any individual setting, use the pop-up menu to the right of the website name. You can choose from the following zoom options: 50%, 75%, 85%, 100%, 115%, 125%, 150%, 175%, 200%, 250%, and 300%.

To set the default page zoom for all websites, select your desired page zoom setting from the pop-up menu next to **When visiting other websites** in the lower-right corner.

If you want to delete a website from the list, highlight it and click the **Remove** button.

When the checkbox next to **Share across devices** is checked, your settings will be replicated across all your Apple devices.

Camera, Microphone, & Screen Sharing

Safari allows you to control access to your Mac's camera, microphone, and screen. To change the camera, microphone, and screen sharing settings, open the Safari settings by selecting **Safari > Settings…** or by entering the keyboard shortcut ⌘, (command+,). Click on the **Websites** icon at the top of the window and then select **Camera**, **Microphone**, or **Screen Sharing** in the sidebar. The right pane populates with a list of currently open websites and those for which you have configured a policy.

Use the pop-up menu to the right of each website and select **Ask**, **Deny**, or **Allow** for the camera and microphone settings. For screen sharing, your options are **Ask** or **Deny**.

If you want to delete a website from the list, highlight it and click the **Remove** button.

To set the default camera, microphone, and screen sharing settings for websites, select your desired setting from the pop-up menu next to **When visiting other websites**.

When the checkbox next to **Share across devices** is checked, your settings will be replicated across all your Apple devices.

Location

Websites can spy on your location. This can be handy if location information is necessary to deliver relevant content like the local weather, news, or nearby businesses or to validate that you are logging into your bank's website from the U.S. and not from North Korea, Iran, China, or Russia. However, beyond those situations, there is absolutely no reason for a website to know your location. Safari can be configured to ask your permission before providing your location information to a website requesting it.

To review and change your location settings, open the Safari settings by selecting **Safari > Settings...** or by entering the keyboard shortcut ⌘, (command+,). Click on the **Websites** icon at the top of the window and then select **Location** in the sidebar. The right pane populates with a list of currently open websites and those for which you have configured a policy. A pop-up menu to the right of each website lets you select a location policy – ask, allow, or deny.

Set the default policy using the pop-up menu next to **When visiting other websites** in the lower-right corner. To stop all websites from snooping on your location, select **Deny** from the pop-up menu. You also have the option of **Ask** or **Allow**. When ask is selected, Safari asks you if you want to provide your location each time a website requests your location.

If you want to delete a website from the list, highlight it and click the **Remove** button.

When the checkbox next to **Share across devices** is checked, your settings will be replicated across all your Apple devices.

Downloads

Safari allows you to control the websites allowed to download content to your Mac. The first time you download content from a website, macOS asks you if you want to allow downloads from the website. If you click allow, your content will be downloaded, and your choice will become the default setting for that website.

You can review or change your download settings in Safari settings by selecting **Safari > Settings...** or by entering the keyboard shortcut ⌘, (command+,). Click on the **Websites** icon at the top of the window and then select **Downloads** in the sidebar. The right pane populates with a list of currently open websites and those for which you have configured a policy. A pop-up menu to the right of each website lets you select a download policy – **Ask**, **Allow**, or **Deny**.

Set the default download policy using the pop-up menu next to **When visiting other websites** in the lower-right corner. Your options are **Ask**, **Deny**, or **Allow**. When ask is selected, Safari asks you to allow a download each time a website tries to download content.

If you want to delete a website from the list, highlight it and click the **Remove** button.

When the checkbox next to **Share across devices** is checked, your settings will be replicated across all your Apple devices.

Notifications

Websites utilizing Apple's push notification service can send notifications of breaking news, sports scores, a new post, or other content directly to your desktop, even if Safari isn't running. By default, Safari notifications appear as a Banner on your desktop and are saved to Notification Center. Clicking on them takes you to the website that sent the notification.

If you recall from the Notification Center chapter, a Banner appears in the upper-right corner of your desktop and disappears automatically after a set amount of time. You can change how Safari notifies you, including disabling notifications entirely. Open the System Settings app and select **Notifications** in the sidebar. Scroll down and select **Safari**.

To disable Safari notifications entirely, toggle the switch next to **Allow notifications** off. Once notifications are disabled, all configuration options in the Notification settings window will gray out.

If you want to customize Safari notifications, ensure the switch next to **Allow notifications** is on. The default alert style is Banners, which is highlighted by a blue border. You can change the style to an Alert by clicking on **Alerts**. An Alert stays on your desktop until you respond or dismiss it. If you do not want Safari to send notifications to your desktop, choose **None**. When configured to None, notifications no longer appear on your desktop, but are saved to Notification Center.

Once you have chosen your alert style, you can configure the other options. The options are **Show notifications on lock screen**, **Show in Notification Center**, **Badge app icon**, **Play sound for notifications, Show Previews**, and **Notification grouping**. All the switches are on by default. Show previews is set to default and notification grouping is set to automatic.

Notifications received when your Mac was asleep appear on the login window when you wake your Mac. If you want to disable this feature, turn the switch next to **Show notifications on lock screen** off.

By default, the **Show in Notification Center** option is enabled, which means Safari notifications will be saved in Notification Center. You have the option of disabling this feature by switching it off. If you do so, you will only see Safari notifications on your desktop if to the alert style is set Banners or Alerts.

The **Badge app icon** option displays the number of notifications in a red circular badge on the Safari icon in the Dock. Safari must be in the Dock for badges to appear. If you don't want the Safari app icon badged, switch this feature off.

Safari notifications can play a sound when they appear. If you prefer silent notifications, flip the switch next to **Play sound for notifications** off.

You have a choice of three options in the pop-up menu next to **Show previews** – always, when unlocked, or never. If you select always, previews of notifications received when your Mac was asleep will appear on the login window when you wake your Mac. The default of when unlocked ensures that notification previews will only be displayed when you are logged in to your Mac. Previews are never shown when the never option is selected.

Notification grouping allows you to organize how Safari's notifications are grouped in Notification Center when multiple notifications are received. The pop-up menu next to Notification grouping offers three options – automatic, by app, or off. Automatic is the default.

Before a website can send you push notifications, you must choose to opt-in. If a website supports push notifications, you'll be asked if you would like to receive notifications when browsing to the website. Whatever your select, you can always change your mind later. If you no longer find notifications from a particular website useful, you can opt-out. Similarly, if you opted out, you could opt in.

To change your Safari notification choice, launch **Safari** and open the Safari settings by selecting **Safari > Settings…** or by using the keyboard shortcut ⌘, (command+comma). Select the **Websites** icon at the top of the window. The websites that have asked for permission to send push notifications are listed in the pane. Next to each website is a pop-up menu with two choices: **Allow** and **Deny** with the current setting displayed. Use the pop-up menu to change your selection.

If you want to delete a website from the list, highlight it and click the **Remove** button.

If you would prefer that websites not ask you to opt-in to their push notification service, uncheck the checkbox next to **Allow websites to ask for permission to send push notifications**. Checking this checkbox stops websites from asking if you want to receive notifications.

When the checkbox next to **Share across devices** is checked, your settings will be replicated across all your Apple devices.

Pop-Up Windows

Safari blocks annoying pop-up windows and notifies you with a small pop-up window icon in Safari's address and search bar. However, some websites use pop-up windows to display essential content. Safari allows you to selectively allow pop-ups from specific websites.

You can configure pop-up blocking from the Safari settings by clicking the **Websites** icon and selecting **Pop-up Windows** from the sidebar. You will see a list of currently open and configured websites. Use the pop-up menu to the right of each website to choose **Block and Notify**, **Block**, or **Allow**.

If you want to delete a website from the list, highlight it and click the **Remove** button.

You can change the default method for handling pop-up windows using the pop-up menu next to **When visiting other websites** in the lower-right corner.

When the checkbox next to **Share across devices** is checked, your settings will be replicated across all your Apple devices.

Safari Profiles

A new feature in macOS Sonoma is the ability to create separate profiles in Safari to separate your browsing, bookmarks, and history between different profiles. For example, you may want to create profiles for work and personal browsing.

By default, Safari has already created a profile for you called **Personal**. To create a new profile, open the Safari settings by selecting **Safari > Settings…** or by using the keyboard shortcut ⌘, (command+comma). Select the **Profiles** icon at the top of the window. Next, click Start Using Profiles button, which will open a window where you can create a new Safari profile.

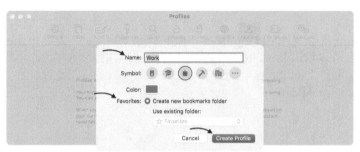

Safari has already created a default profile for you called **Personal**, so technically, you are creating your second profile. Enter the name of your new profile in the **Name** field. Select a symbol from the choices provided or click the **…** button to open a window with 42 more symbols from which to choose. Select a **Color** by clicking on the rectangle. You can create a new bookmarks folder to use as the favorites for your new profile or use an existing bookmarks folder. Using the radio buttons, select **Create a new bookmarks folder** or **Use existing folder**. If you chose to use an existing bookmarks folder, select it using the pop-up menu under **Use existing folder**. Click the **Create Profile** button when done.

You can make changes to your profiles in the next window. First, select the profile from the sidebar. You can change the name, symbol, and favorites. This window allows you configure how new windows and tabs will open. Using the pop-up menu next to **New windows open with**, select **Start Page**, **Empty Page**, **Same Page**, or **Tabs For Work**. If you select Tabs For Work, new Safari windows will open with the sidebar and tab groups open. You can configure how new tabs open using the pop-up menu next to **New tabs open with**. You can choose from **Start Page**, **Empty Page**, or **Same Page**.

You also can create or delete profiles. To create a new profile, click the **+** (add) button at the bottom of the sidebar. If you want to delete a profile, highlight it in the sidebar and click the **–** (delete) button.

To manage the extensions for each of your profiles, click the **Extensions** button. Use the checkboxes next to each extension to choose which will be active for the profile highlighted in the sidebar. Close the Profile settings window when done.

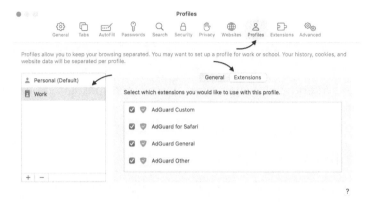

Once you have created a second profile, you'll notice a new pop-up menu in Safari's toolbar. The profile pop-up menu allows you to switch profiles.

Third-party Extensions

Extensions are small applications created by third-party developers to enhance your web browsing experience.

The Extensions settings in the Safari settings window allow you to selectively enable or disable an extension, configure options, and install and uninstall extensions. The Safari Extensions settings window will be empty until you have installed your first extension.

Installed extensions are listed in the sidebar. You can select an extension to show any available options, install, or uninstall it. To disable an installed extension, uncheck its checkbox in the sidebar.

When the checkbox next to **Share across devices** is checked, your settings will be replicated across all your Apple devices.

The **More Extensions…** button in the lower-right opens the Mac App Store, where you can find extensions to add new features to Safari. Extensions can be installed with one click with no need to restart Safari.

Advanced Options

Safari's Advanced options include the ability to configure Safari to show a website's full URL, setting a minimum font size, and saving articles for offline reading. To access Safari's advanced options, open the Safari settings by selecting **Safari > Settings…** or by entering the keyboard shortcut ⌘, (command+,). Click on the **Advanced** icon at the top of the window.

By default, Safari does not display the full URL of a website. If you want Safari to display the full URL of a website, check the checkbox next to **Show full website address**.

Have trouble reading small text on some webpages? Safari lets you set the minimum font size. To set a minimum font size for text on webpages, check the checkbox next to **Never use font sizes smaller than** and select a font size from the pop-up menu. Your options are 9-, 10-, 11-, 12-, 14-, 18- and 24-point fonts. If you are unsure which font size you should choose, start with 12 or 14 points. This feature will change the appearance of some webpages.

Checking the checkbox next to **Press Tab to highlight each item on a webpage** will allow you to use the tab key to move around a webpage with using the mouse or trackpad.

By default, the checkbox next to **Use advanced tracking and fingerprinting protection** is checked. The pop-up menu offers the choice of **in Private Browsing** (the default) and **in all browsing**. This feature prevents advertisers from tracking you using the digital fingerprint of your Mac. When you browse to a webpage, your browser provides information that can be used to identify you – your browser, operating system, browser plugins, ISP, IP address, location, previous webpage's URL, download speed, CPU and GPU info, fonts, screen resolution, social media, and websites you are logged into – all without your permission. All this information taken together forms a digital fingerprint that can be used to identify you.

If you use Apple Pay and want websites that use Apple Pay to check to see if you have Apple Pay enabled on your Mac, check the checkbox next to **Allow websites to check for Apple Pay and Apple Card**. Apple's websites and apps can also check to see if you have an Apple Card. When enabled, websites will offer Apple Pay when you checkout.If you want to stop websites from checking to see if you have Apple Pay enabled, uncheck the checkbox.

You have the option to block all cookies, which stops websites, third-party content providers, and advertisers from storing cookies on your Mac. However, doing so often prevents many websites from working. For example, your bank's website will not recognize you and may ask challenge questions to verify your identity or not work at all.

If you want to save webpages in Safari's Reading List so you can read them when you are offline, check the checkbox next to **Save articles for offline reading automatically**. You can access your saved content from the Reading List in Safari's sidebar. Enter ⇧⌘L (shift+command+L), select **View > Show Sidebar**, or click the Sidebar/Tab Groups icon in the toolbar to display the Safari sidebar. Click the icon that looks like a pair of reading glasses to see your reading list. You can also access your bookmarks, items shared with you, and your iCloud Tabs from Safari's sidebar.

Safari Web Apps

Another new feature in macOS Sonoma is that ability to turn a website into a web app in Safari and add it to your Dock and Launchpad. Google Chrome has had this feature for years, but the downside was that you had to run Chrome. It's great that web apps finally came to Safari.

First, browse to the website. Next select **File > Add to Dock...** to open a new configuration window. You can change the name or URL; otherwise click the **Add** button to add a Safari Web App to your Dock. The web app will also be added to Launchpad.

When you click on a Web App, Safari will open with a minimal set of menu items – no address bar, no favorites, no tabs, only a toolbar with back and forward buttons. The File menu is limited too, allowing you to open a new window, close the window, open it in Safari, share, or print. If you want to get out of the web app, either close it and launch Safari or select **File > Open in Safari**.

Cookies, settings, and website data are unique to each Web App and are separate from the main Safari app. If you open the Safari settings by selecting **Safari > Settings...** or by entering the keyboard shortcut ⌘, (command+,), you'll see a very limited set of options.

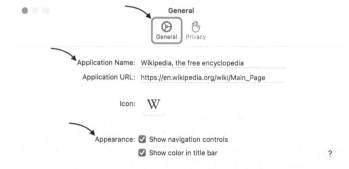

In the General settings, you can change the Web App name, URL, and the appearance. For the **Appearance**, you can choose to **Show navigation controls** (the default) and **Show color in the title bar** (also the default) using the checkboxes next to each option.

Privacy settings are similarly limited, allowing you to clear website data or launch the Privacy & Security settings window in System Settings. If you click the **Clear Website Data...** button, you'll be presented with another window asking for confirmation.

18

Privacy & Security

Anti-Virus Software

Many Mac users think that they do not need anti-virus software. Mac owners are just as likely as Windows PC users to be tricked into installing adware, trojans, and potentially unwanted programs such as Mac Defender, a fake anti-virus app that targets computers running macOS. Mac Defender is also known as Mac Protector, Mac Security, Mac Guard, Mac Shield, and FakeMacDef. Mac owners are just as vulnerable as Windows PC users to platform-agnostic social engineering attacks such as phishing or web-based attacks. The weakest link is not the computer or its operating system. It's the person behind the keyboard, and that is who malicious actors target and exploit.

The bottom line is that you need to install anti-virus software. The good news is that there are many free and paid options available, including Bitdefender, Intego, McAfee, Norton, and Sophos, to name a few. Magazines such as *MacWorld* rate anti-malware software every year.

A good anti-virus application detects and stops malicious software from downloading, installing, and executing. It should scan continuously for threats. Malicious files should be deleted or quarantined automatically, and the file system monitored for changes that appear to be malicious. A good anti-virus application should continuously run in the background using minimal resources, so it doesn't impact your Mac's performance.

Standard User Account

When you set up your Mac for the first time, you created a user account. By default, that account is an administrator account. The administrator account can change any setting on your Mac. Using your Mac for day-to-day work as an administrator poses a security risk. If your Mac becomes infected with malware while you are logged in as an administrator, the elevated privileges of the administrator account could allow malware to change system settings, applications, and other resources. Therefore, it is a best practice to perform day-to-day activities as a standard user and to reserve the administrator account for adjusting system settings and installing applications. If you are using your computer as a standard user and need to make a change that requires administrator access, you can switch to the administrator account using the macOS Fast User Switching feature.

If you have a brand-new Mac and have just set it up, creating separate administrator and user accounts is a breeze. By default, Setup Assistant creates the default administrator account. You can use the Users & Groups settings in System Settings to create a new standard account for your day-to-day computing. However, if you been using your Mac for a while, creating a new standard account won't work for you since all your settings, applications, and data are only accessible from your administrator account. The solution is to create a new administrator account and downgrade your existing account to a standard user.

To create a new administrator account, open the System Settings app, scroll down the sidebar, and select **Users & Groups**. Click on the **Add User...** button to reveal a configuration sheet. Choose Administrator from the pop-up menu next to **New Account**. Enter the Full Name, Account Name, Password, Password Hint, and click **Create User** to finish. Log out and log back in with your new administrator account to see if it works correctly and that you did not fat-finger the password. Since this is a new account, macOS will run through the initial account setup.

Once you have created your new administrator account and have successfully logged in, open the **Users & Groups** settings. Select your old administrator account, the one you want to downgrade to a standard user, by clicking the **i** (info) button to the right of the account name to reveal a configuration sheet. Flip the switch next to **Allow this user to administer this computer** off. Restart your Mac for the change to take effect.

Require Administrator to Change Settings

It's a best practice to require administrator access to make changes to System Settings, particularly if you have multiple people using your Mac. Even if you don't, you should do your day-to-day work as a standard user. Using an administrator account for day-to-day activities such as surfing the web or email poses a security risk. If your Mac becomes infected with malware while you are logged in as an administrator, the elevated privileges could allow malware easier to change system settings, applications, and other resources available only to the administrator.

To require system administrator access to change system-wide settings, open the System Settings app and select **Privacy & Security** from the sidebar. Scroll to the bottom of the Privacy & Security settings window. Click on **Advanced...** button at the bottom of the window.

A configuration sheet appears. Flip the switch next to **Require an administrator password to access system-wide preferences** on. Click **Done** when finished. When this feature is enabled, macOS will ask for your administrator credentials to make changes.

Guest User

The macOS guest user feature allows you to temporarily allow a guest to use your Mac without giving them access to your user account and without having to add them as a new user. A guest doesn't need a password, can't change macOS settings, and can't see your files. A guest can launch apps, and any files the guest creates are stored in a temporary folder, which is deleted when the guest logs out.

To enable the Guest User account, open the System Settings app, scroll down the sidebar, and select **Users & Groups**. Click the **i** (info) button to the right of the **Guest User** to reveal a configuration sheet.

Flip the switch next to **Allow guests to log in to this computer** on. You can prevent guest users from surfing porn sites by flipping the switch next to **Limit adult websites** on. If you flip the switch next to **Allow guest users to connect to shared folders** on, a guest user will be able to access shared folders. Click **Done** when finished.

Automatic Login

With automatic login enabled, anyone can access your Mac by restarting it. They will be automatically logged in with access to all your data. I recommend you disable this feature. If you enabled FileVault disk encryption, macOS automatically disables automatic login.

To disable automatic login, open System Settings, and select **Users & Groups** from the sidebar. Select **Off** from the pop-up menu next to **Automatically log in as**. Once automatic login is disabled, your Mac will always ask for your user name and password when it restarts.

Unlock your Mac with your Apple Watch

You can unlock your Mac with your Apple Watch. Your Mac must be a mid-2013 or later model, your Watch must have watchOS 3 or later installed. You must be logged in to iCloud with the same Apple ID on both devices, and two-factor authentication must be enabled for your Apple ID.

To enable this feature, open System Settings, and select **Touch ID & Password** from the sidebar. Under **Apple Watch**, flip the switch next to the name of your Apple Watch on.

When you wake your Mac while wearing your Apple Watch, your Mac will unlock, and a message will appear on your Apple Watch notifying you that it unlocked your Mac.

Data Protection

Hands down, Apple's Time Machine is the easiest backup application I have ever used. Its simple "set it and forget it" interface quietly backs up all my data regularly without any intervention on my part. And the best part of Time Machine is how quickly and easily it can restore files or your entire Mac. Not only does it back up everything, but Time Machine can also restore your Mac to how it looked on any given day in the past.

To enable Time Machine, open the System Settings app, and select **General** from the sidebar. Click on **Time Machine** to open the

Time Machine settings window. To add a new external disk target, click the + (add) button.

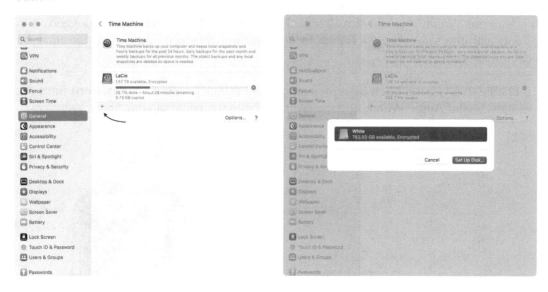

Your external disk should be highlighted on the configuration sheet. If not, click on it. Then click the **Set Up Disk...** button.

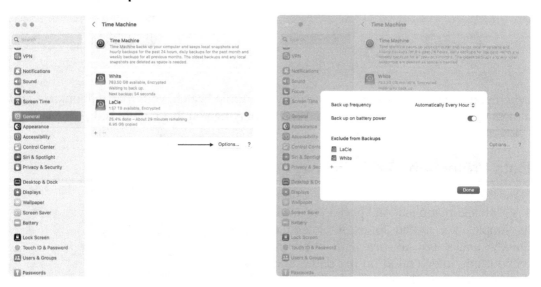

To configure Time Machine back up options, click the **Options...** button in the Time Machine settings window. Select your backup frequency from the options of every hour, every day, every week, or manually using the pop-up menu next to **Back up frequency**. More frequent is better and I suggest hourly.

If you have an Apple laptop, you can choose to back up on battery power by flipping the switch next to **Back up on battery power** on.

You can exclude any folders from being backed up by clicking the **+** (add) button under **Exclude from Backups**. Your target backup disks will be listed in the exclusion list. Click **Done** when finished.

Make Gatekeeper Less Restrictive

Apple's App Store is the safest and most reliable place to download and install applications because Apple reviews each application before it's accepted, checking for malicious or junk software. If an application is later found to be malicious, Apple will remove it. Gatekeeper protects your Mac from malicious software by ensuring it is from a trusted source, an Apple Developer, and verifying the application hasn't been tampered with. Gatekeeper will block the installation of any application that is not signed by a valid Apple Developer ID.

To configure Gatekeeper, open the System Settings app and select **Privacy &** Security from the sidebar. Under **Security**, you will see two options: **App Store** and **App Store and identified developers**. The most secure setting, **App Store**, effectively means you cannot install applications unless they have been downloaded from Apple's Mac App Store. The less restrictive setting, **App Store and identified developers**, ensures that Gatekeeper checks that the application you downloaded is signed with a valid Apple Developer ID. Make your selection using the radio buttons.

If you attempt to install unsigned software, macOS allows you to perform a manual override of Gatekeeper on a case-by-case basis. However, I recommend you only install the applications that have been reviewed by a reputable publication. If you try to install an unsigned application, Gatekeeper blocks it from being installed and displays a warning dialog box.

FileVault Encryption

Encrypting your Mac's disk protects your data in case your Mac is ever stolen. Encryption, combined with the other security customizations covered in this chapter, makes it more difficult for a thief to access your data.

Before enabling FileVault, there are a few things you need to consider. If you are in the habit of forgetting your password and lose your backup recovery key, your data is unrecoverable. This means your data is gone for good. FileVault's encryption is so strong, it's virtually impossible to break it to access your data. You can set up FileVault to use your iCloud password.

If you want a truly secure system, FileVault is the way to go. To encrypt your entire drive with FileVault, open the **Privacy & Security** settings from the System Settings app. Scroll down until you see **FileVault** in the settings window. Click the **Turn On...** button.

You'll be asked if you want to use your iCloud account to unlock your encrypted disk and reset your password if you forget it or use a recovery key instead of your iCloud account. If you choose the recovery code, you'll be presented with your 20-digit recovery code. Make a copy of this code and store it in a safe place, not on the Mac you are encrypting. You can take a screenshot and then drag it to the Photos app where it will be available on your iPhone or iPad. Or copy the recovery key to a secure password manager.

If you lose both your password and the recovery key, you will be unable to access any of the data on your disk drive. It is a terrible idea to keep a copy of your recovery key on your Mac. If you forget your password, you will be unable to access any of the data on your Mac, including the recovery key. Store your recovery key in a safe location.

If there is more than one user account configured on your Mac, you'll be asked to identify the users who are allowed to unlock the encrypted drive. Each user is required to enter his or her password to unlock FileVault.

Virtual Private Network

If you have a MacBook, MacBook Pro, or MacBook Air, you probably use a public Wi-Fi network such as the ones available at Starbucks, hotels, airports, and other businesses. Public Wi-Fi is horribly insecure. It doesn't matter if the service is free or if you must pay a fee. When using public Wi-Fi, your traffic is sent in the clear, allowing anyone to capture the data you send and receive. Sometimes bad guys will camp out in public places and set up their laptops to mimic a legitimate public Wi-Fi service with a tantalizing name such as *FREE Airport Wi-Fi*. All they must do is wait for victims to connect, capture private data, and use it to steal a victim's identity, drain bank accounts, or hack into the victim's computer.

A Virtual Private Network (VPN) protects your data by encrypting it while it travels over public Wi-Fi and the internet. With identity theft dramatically on the rise, it is just plain reckless to use public Wi-Fi without a personal VPN. If you want to protect your privacy and security when online, you should use a personal VPN service.

If you are traveling in a foreign country, you may lose access to Netflix or to social media sites that the local government censors. A personal VPN may allow you to access those services the government considers objectionable.

If your company provides a VPN for business use, don't use it for your personal use. Company VPNs are monitored for misuse. Do you really want your employer to know your personal browsing habits? I think not. That's another reason why you should sign up for a personal VPN service. There are lots of choices available for fees ranging from free to $20 a month. Why not choose one of the free VPN services? The free services are more restrictive regarding maximum bandwidth, the ability to stream video, and are funded by annoying advertising. If you can live with these inconveniences, choose a free VPN service, otherwise better services are available for a nominal monthly or yearly fee.

Find My Mac

If your Mac is ever lost or stolen, you can use the **Find My** app on your iPhone or iPad to locate it in the Maps app, play a sound, lock it, or erase it to keep your data safe. To use this feature, the Find My app must be enabled before your Mac is lost.

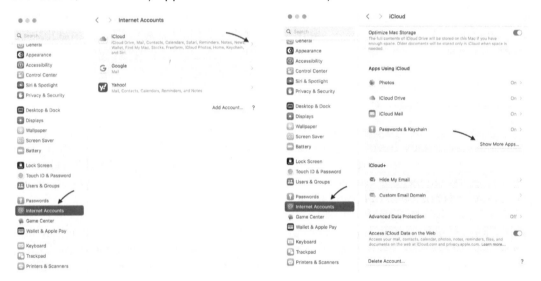

To enable Find My Mac, open the System Settings app. Scroll down and select **Internet Accounts** in the sidebar. Next, click **iCloud** to open the iCloud settings window. Click on the **Show More Apps…** button under **Apps Using iCloud**. Click **Find My Mac** in the next window to reveal a configuration sheet. Click the **Turn On** button next to **Find My Mac** and **Find My network**. A warning dialog box will appear asking, **Allow Find My Mac to use the location of this Mac?** Click the **Allow** button.

If your Mac is lost or stolen, you can use the **Find My** app on your iPhone, iPad, or another Mac to locate it on a map, play a sound, lock it with a passcode, or erase it. If you do not have another Apple device handy, you can log into your iCloud account at icloud.com using your Apple ID to use the **Find My** app to locate, lock, or erase your Mac.

If your Mac is lost or stolen, you should immediately change your Apple ID password as well as passwords for email, financial, and social media sites to prevent someone from accessing your data or using these services. You should also change the passwords on merchant sites, like Amazon.com, where your credit card info is stored. You should also report your lost or stolen Mac and its serial number to local law enforcement.

Password and Passkey Management

Many Apple users pay to utilize a third-party password manager without realizing their Apple devices already have a full-featured password manager that is more secure than many of the popular third-party password managers. Apple provides **iCloud Keychain**, a free password manager that works seamlessly across all your Apple devices, synchronizing your passwords and passkeys using iCloud.

With iCloud Keychain, you can implement a security best practice of creating unique and complex passwords for each website and application. You no longer need to memorize passwords, reuse them, or create weak passwords that you can easily remember. iCloud Keychain will also notify you of password breaches, warn you if you reused a password, and even allows you to share passwords with your family.

iCloud Keychain also supports passkeys, a new authentication method designed to make passwords obsolete. Passkey technology was jointly developed by Apple, Microsoft, and Google to comply with the Fast Identity Online (FIDO) Alliance standards. Instead of using a password to log into a website or app, a passkey uses Touch ID or Face ID. Biometric authentication is more secure that passwords, even if you are using two-factor authentication. Passkeys are stored as encrypted private keys in iCloud Keychain, making them available across all your Apple devices and allowing you to log into a website or app with Face ID or Touch ID. You can see a list of websites and apps that support passkeys and directions how to setup a passkey for each at: https://passkeys.directory.

To use iCloud Keychain, open the System Settings app, and click on your name at the top of the sidebar. Click **iCloud** and then click **Passwords & Keychain** to reveal a configuration window. Flip the switch next to **Sync this Mac** on. Clicking the **Details...** button opens the Password settings window in System Settings.

Once setup, there is very little for you to do to use iCloud Keychain. Pop-ups handle the creation, saving, updating, and entering of passwords. A password generator creates unique, secure passwords when you are signing up for an account on a website. That's it. You are all set.

iCloud Keychain is secured with end-to-end encryption and even Apple cannot access your passwords and passkeys. Caution – if you forget your iCloud password, you will lose access to your passwords.

To see your passwords, view security recommendations or to share passwords, open the System Settings apps and scroll down the sidebar and select **Passwords**. The Password settings are locked, so you will have to enter your password or use Touch ID. There are 4 sections to the password settings.

The top section allows you to search for a password or create a new password by clicking the **+** (add) button. The ellipsis (**...**) reveals a pop-up menu that will let you generate a password, import passwords, or export one or all passwords.

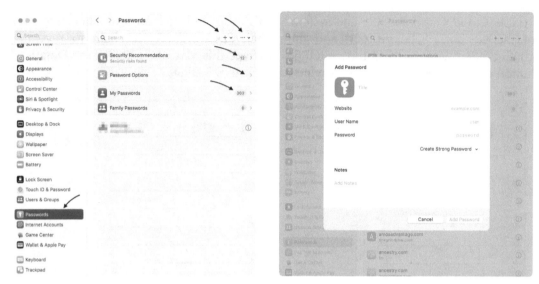

The next section offers security recommendations and lets you configure password options. Clicking **Security Recommendations** opens a new window where macOS will notify you if any of your passwords were leaked in a data breach. This window will also provide recommendations to strengthen your passwords by identifying reused or easily guessed passwords. Clicking on a recommendation will provide additional information and provide a **Change Password on Website** button.

Clicking **Password Options** opens a window with switches to toggle auto filling of passwords and passkeys, iCloud Keychain, and to automatically delete one-time-passcode for 2 factor authentication received in Messages and Mail.

The section containing **My Passwords** and **Family Passwords** lists your passwords and the passwords you shared with your family. The final section is a list of your passwords. Click the **i** (info) button to edit your password. It's in this next window that you will find a little known function of iCloud Keychain, the ability to support 2 factor authentication codes with the use of a separate authenticator app like Microsoft's or Google's Authenticator apps. If the website supports 2 factor authentication, click the **Set Up...** button. You're able to enter a setup key or QR code from the website to set up 2 factor authentication.

macOS Firewall

The macOS firewall blocks unwanted, incoming connections from the internet and other networks (i.e., public Wi-Fi) to your Mac. macOS allows any apps you installed from the Mac App Store and signed apps to receive incoming connections. Other incoming connection attempts will be blocked. The macOS firewall provides another layer of protection against malware.

To enable the macOS firewall, open the System Settings app and select **Network** from the sidebar. Next, click **Firewall** and then flip the switch next to **Firewall** on. Once the firewall is enabled, the **Options...** button becomes available. Click on it to reveal a firewall configuration sheet.

When switch next to **Block all incoming connections** is on, macOS will block all nonessential incoming traffic, only allowing traffic for basic internet services.

The switches next to **Automatically allow built-in software to receive incoming connections** and **Automatically allow downloaded signed software to receive incoming connections** should be on. This allows macOS and apps you downloaded from the Mac App Store and from Apple developers to receive incoming connections.

To allow incoming connections for other apps, click the **+** (add) button, which opens your Applications folder. Select the application you want to receive incoming connections. Note that you do not have to add apps that you downloaded from the Mac App Store as they are already allowed. Nor do you need to add applications that are signed by a valid identified Apple developer. Click the **–** (delete) button to remove an application from the list of exempted applications.

Turning the switch on next to **Enable stealth mode** prevents your Mac from replying to pings and probes from other computers.

Uninstall Unwanted Apps

 It's a best practice to uninstall applications you no longer use because they can have security vulnerabilities. In macOS, you can uninstall an app by dragging it from the Applications folder to the Trash. You also can also uninstall apps in Launchpad by clicking and holding until the apps begin to jiggle, and a **X** (delete) button appears in the upper-left corner of the app's icon. Clicking the **X** (delete) button uninstalls the app.

Apps distribute many files throughout your system. Often applications leave their detritus scattered across your Mac's drive after they are deleted using the above two methods. AppCleaner is an app that will thoroughly uninstall unwanted apps, hunting down their files, and safely deleting their detritus.

AppCleaner is free to download from: http://www.freemacsoft.net/appcleaner/.

19

One More Thing…

In this last chapter, I'll show you a grab bag of tips, tricks, and tweaks that didn't quite fit into the topics of previous chapters.

Transparency

If you are having trouble reading the macOS system font, you can improve readability by reducing transparency. This subtle change reduces the transparent effect used in windows to improve the contrast and readability of text. This setting also eliminates the transparent effect in the Menu Bar and Dock, making both more readable.

To reduce the transparency effect, open System Settings and select **Accessibility** from the sidebar. Click **Display** under the **Vision** settings at the top of the window. Flip the switch next to **Reduce transparency** on. Changes take effect immediately.

Contrast

If you are having trouble reading the macOS system font, you can significantly improve readability by increasing the display contrast. This setting increases the contrast of on-screen items such as borders around buttons and darkens the text and other interface elements without changing the contrast of the screen itself. Increasing your contrast is particularly striking when you have configured the dark mode appearance.

To increase contrast, open System Settings and select **Accessibility** from the sidebar. Click **Display** under the **Vision** settings at the top of the window. Flip the switch next to **Increase contrast** on. You can control the amount of contrast with the slider next to **Display contrast**. Enabling the **Increase contrast** feature also enables **Reduce transparency**. Changes take effect immediately.

Make Help Center Behave

The macOS Help Center has a rather obnoxious habit. It refuses to act like other windows by stubbornly refusing to go to the background when it is not the active window. This tweak forces Help Center to act like all other macOS windows.

First, close the Help Center window if open. Enter the following command in Terminal.

```
defaults write com.apple.helpviewer DevMode -bool true
```

The next time you open Help Center, you'll notice its more polite behavior, no longer blocking other windows when it is not the active window.

To revert to the Help Center's default behavior, enter the following command in Terminal.

```
defaults delete com.apple.helpviewer DevMode
```

Sound

macOS give you a choice of alert sound effects. The alert sound plays when you receive an alert in macOS. The default is the boop alert. You can change the alert sound to anyone of 14 sounds included with macOS. Your options include, breeze, bubble, crystal, funky, heroine, jump, mezzo, pebble, pluck, pong, sonar, sonumi, or submerge.

To change the macOS alert sound, open the System Settings app and select **Sound** from the sidebar. Select your choice from the pop-up menu next to **Alert sound**. The alert sound will play when you select it, so you can hear how it sounds. You can also select the output device through which the alert sound plays using the pop-up menu next to **Play sound effects through**.

The slider next to **Alert volume** controls the volume of the alert sound. This volume slider only controls the volume of the alert sound and is separate from the output volume, which is controlled through the sound function keys, using the Touch Bar, or with the **Output volume** slider found at the bottom of the Sound settings window.

Startup Sound

Apple's iconic Macintosh startup sound returned with the release of macOS, Monterey. While this startup sound tells you that your Mac is starting up properly, it may not be appropriate in a quiet environment. macOS allows you to disable it.

To disable your Mac's startup sound, open the **Sound** settings in the System Settings app. Flip the switch next to **Play sound on startup** off.

User Interface Sound Effects

Your Mac plays various sound effects for actions like dragging and dropping an item into the trash. If you want to disable these sound effects, open the **Sound** settings in System Settings and flip the switch next to **Play user interface sound effects** off.

Volume Feedback

macOS makes an annoying popping sound when adjusting the volume. If you're working in a quiet office environment, the incessant popping can disturb your concentration or the concentration of others. It is also annoying and loud when listening to music using AirPods. You can disable the popping in the Sound settings. This is a blessing to anyone who routinely uses AirPods or headphones. Your office mates will also appreciate not being disturbed by your Mac's popping sounds.

To permanently disable the annoying popping, open the **Sound** settings in System Settings. Flip the switch next to **Play feedback when volume is changed** off.

If you only want to temporarily quiet the popping sound when adjusting the volume, hold down the ⇧ (shift) key while adjusting the sound volume.

Adjust the Volume in Quarter Segments

Sometimes it seems you never can get the volume adjusted to your liking. One segment more is too much. One less is too little. Hold down the ⇧⌥ (shift+option) keys to adjust the volume in quarter-segment increments. This trick also works when adjusting the display brightness and the keyboard backlight.

Output & Input

You can select the output device from the list of sound output devices shown the Sound settings window. Click the **Output** button found under **Output & Input**. The output can be instantly switched to another device by clicking on a device in the list of output devices. You can adjust output volume and the balance between left and right speakers using the sliders in the Sound settings window. A checkbox allows you to mute the sound output.

Click the **Input** button found under **Output & Input** to switch input devices and control input volume. The input can be instantly switched to another device by clicking on a device in the list of input devices. You can adjust input volume using the slider next to **Input volume**.

Login Items

Login items are applications that launch automatically when you log into your Mac. Automating the launch of your frequently used applications saves time, streamlines your workflow, and improves your productivity.

To manage your Login Items, open the System Settings app and select **General** in the sidebar. Next, click on **Login Items**. The applications listed under **Open at Login** will launch when you login to your Mac. To add an item, click the **+** (add) button. Finder will open your Applications folder. Select the application you want to add and click the **Open** button. Repeat for additional apps.

To remove an app, highlight it and click the – (delete) button.

Profile Picture

It's easy to change your profile picture, and you can use any picture for your profile. Apple provides a set of default pictures you can use. If you don't like the defaults, you can choose a picture from iCloud, Photos, a folder on your Mac, or you can take a picture using your Mac's camera.

To change your profile picture, open System Settings and click on your name at the top of the sidebar. Hover your pointer over your current profile picture until **edit** appears. Click

edit. Select your desired profile picture from the selections in the next window. Use the slider to size your picture. Click **Save** when done.

Kill the Spinning Rainbow Pinwheel of Death

Occasionally Finder crashes or gets hung, and you are forced to experience Apple's spinning rainbow pinwheel of death, also known as the beachball of death. Your Mac becomes unresponsive as the rainbow pinwheel defiantly spins and mocks you as you twiddle your thumbs and hope it disappears. Sometimes you must kill the darn thing.

Sometimes it's an app that is hung and is killing the performance of your Mac. If that is the case, you can force quit the offending app by selecting > **Force Quit...** or by using the keyboard shortcut ⌥⌘esc (option+command+escape). Click on the offending app and click the **Force Quit** button.

Sometimes, Finder gets hosed or hung. If that is the case, you can relaunch Finder by selecting > **Force Quit...** or by using the ⌥⌘esc (option+command+escape) keyboard shortcut. Click on Finder to highlight it and then click the **Relaunch** button.

Die spinning pinwheel of death! Pop that rainbow beach ball!

Restore a Previous Version of a Document

macOS automatically saves versions of documents as you are working on them. This safety feature lets you restore a previous version of a document if needed. macOS allows you to browse through various document versions and restore an older version. Versions are typically saved every hour, and when you open, save, duplicate, rename, or revert to an earlier version of the document. If you are actively making changes to your document, macOS saves more frequently.

To restore a previous version of a document, open the document if it is not already open. Select **File > Revert To > Browse All Versions...** to see which versions are available. Browse through the available versions and click the **Restore** button to restore the previous version you selected. You also have the option to revert to the last saved version, which is timestamped by macOS, by selecting **File > Revert To > Previous Save**. This feature may not be available in third-party applications, most notably the Microsoft Office productivity suite. In that case, you can use Time Machine to restore a previous version of an Office document.

Create a Bootable USB Flash Drive Installer

If you own multiple Macs that you want to upgrade to macOS Sonoma, you are facing a lot of downloading from the App Store. A better option is to create a bootable USB flash drive installer. You'll need a copy of the macOS Sonoma installer on your Mac and a USB flash drive with 32 GB capacity. Be sure there is nothing important on that USB drive as you will erase it as part of the creation of the Sonoma installer.

Creating a bootable USB flash drive installer is a multi-step process.

1. Download macOS Sonoma from the Mac App Store.

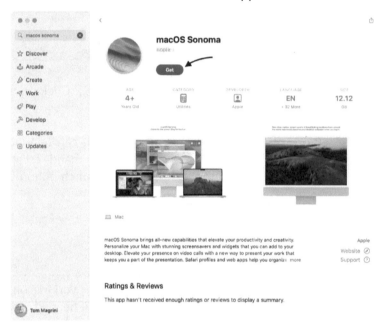

2. While Sonoma is downloading, connect your USB flash drive to your Mac and launch **Disk Utility**. Select your USB drive in the left-hand pane. Click the **Erase** button in the toolbar.

3. Leave the name in the **Name** field as Untitled. When the installer is created, it will rename your USB drive. Select **Mac OS Extended (Journaled)** from the pop-up menu next to **Format** in the configuration window. Click the **Erase** button.

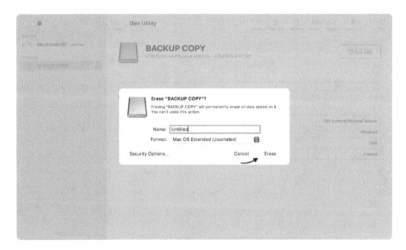

4. When macOS Sonoma finishes downloading, you will see the window below, which asks you to click Continue to start the installation. **STOP HERE!** Exit the installation by quitting using the ⌘Q (command+Q) keyboard shortcut. Confirm that you want to quit in the next window.

5. Open Terminal and enter the following command. All 3 lines are a single command. **Do not** press the **return** key until you have entered the entire command.

If you named your USB disk in step 4, replace **Untitled** with the name you chose. If the name of your USB disk is more than one word, you'll need to put quotes around the name, for example, "Sonoma Installer."

Because this command uses **sudo**, you will need to enter your administrator password when prompted. Don't worry if nothing appears in Terminal as you type your password. This is a security feature.

```
sudo /Applications/Install\ macOS\
Sonoma.app/Contents/Resources/createinstallmedia --volume
/Volumes/Untitled
```

6. Terminal will confirm that you want to erase your USB drive. Enter **Y** and press **return**.

```
●  ●  ●                 🖿 tmagrini — -zsh — 80×24
tmagrini@MacBook-Pro ~ % sudo /Applications/Install\ macOS\ Sonoma.app/Contents/
Resources/createinstallmedia --volume /Volumes/Untitled
[Password:                                                                    ]
Ready to start.
To continue we need to erase the volume at /Volumes/Sonoma Installer.
If you wish to continue type (Y) then press return: Y
Erasing disk: 0%... 10%... 20%... 30%... 100%
Copying essential files...
Copying the macOS RecoveryOS...
Making disk bootable...
Copying to disk: 0%... 10%... 20%... 30%... 40%... 50%... 60%... 70%... 80%... 9
0%... 100%
Install media now available at "/Volumes/Install macOS Sonoma"
tmagrini@MacBook-Pro ~ % █
```

You can quit Terminal when it is done creating your installer disk. Open Finder and check the Locations in the Sidebar. You should see a device called **Install macOS Sonoma**. Eject the device. You are now finished with the creation of your macOS Sonoma USB flash drive installer.

Using Your Bootable Installer Drive

How you use your bootable drive depends on the type of Mac you have. First, ensure that your Mac is compatible with macOS Sonoma. Apple has a list of all compatible Macs on its website at: https://support.apple.com/en-us/105113.

If your Mac is compatible with Sonoma, you'll need to determine if you Mac has Apple silicon or an Intel processor. Select > **About this Mac**.

If the chip is an Apple M series (i.e., M1, M2, or M3), your Mac has Apple silicon, and you'll need to follow the directions in the Mac with Apple Silicon section.

If the About this Mac window shows that your Mac has an Intel, processor, you'll should follow the directions in the Mac with Intel Processor section.

Mac with Apple Silicon

Ensure your Mac is connected to the internet. Although your bootable installer doesn't download macOS Sonoma, an internet connection is required to download firmware and other data specific to your Mac.

1. Shutdown your Mac and plug your bootable USB drive into one of your Mac's USB ports.
2. Press and continue to hold the power button until you see the startup options window showing available bootable drives.
3. Select your USB installer – Install macOS Sonoma – and click **Continue**.
4. Once the installer has opened, follow the installation instructions.

Mac with Intel Processor

Ensure your Mac is connected to the internet. Although your bootable installer doesn't download macOS Sonoma, an internet connection is required to download firmware and other data specific to your Mac.

1. Shutdown your Mac and plug your bootable USB drive into one of your Mac's USB ports.
2. Hold down the ⌥ (option) key while starting your Mac.
3. Release the ⌥ (option) key when the screen listing your bootable volumes appears.
4. Select your bootable installer drive and click **Return**.
5. Choose your language, if prompted.
6. Select Install macOS from the Utilities window and click **Continue**.
7. Follow the installation instructions.
8. It should take about 45 minutes to an hour to complete the installation.

If your Mac has a T2 Security chip, ensure the Startup Security Utility is configured to allow booting from an external removable drive. See this support article on Apple's website for more information: https://support.apple.com/en-us/102522.

Hidden macOS Power Chime

When you connect your iPhone or iPad to their chargers, they emit a chime to let you know they are connected to power. By default, your Mac does not sound a power chime when you connect it to a power source. This tweak configures macOS to play the power chime when you connect your MacBook to AC power.

To enable the power chime, first disconnect your MacBook's power connector. Launch Terminal and enter the following commands.

```
defaults write com.apple.PowerChime ChimeOnAllHardware -bool true

open /System/Library/CoreServices/PowerChime.app
```

Now reattach the power connector, and your MacBook will emit an iPhone-like power chime to tell you it is connected to AC power. Be sure the sound volume is not muted and is turned up so you can hear the chime.

To disable the power chime, enter the following commands in Terminal.

```
defaults write com.apple.PowerChime ChimeOnAllHardware -bool false
```

```
killall PowerChime
```

Caffeinate Your Mac

Sometimes you need to keep your Mac awake, overriding its energy-saving features. For example, you may need to keep your Mac awake if you subscribe to a cloud backup service. Typically, cloud backup services run more efficiently when you are not using your Mac. Depending on the size of your backup, you may need to run your cloud backup application for a couple of hours. Your initial cloud backup may even take days to complete! Unfortunately, when you are not actively using your Mac, macOS will put it to sleep after the inactivity timer set in the Energy Savings settings expires.

To keep your Mac awake, you can use the following command in the Terminal app to override the macOS inactivity timer.

```
caffeinate
```

If you want to keep your Mac awake for a set period, you can set a timer when issuing the caffeinate command. For example, the following command keeps your Mac awake for 12 hours. The time is measured in seconds; therefore, 12 hours equates to 43,200 seconds (12 hours x 60 minutes x 60 seconds).

```
caffeinate -t 43200
```

Once you issue the caffeinate command, your Mac will not sleep, dim its display, or play the screen saver until you end the command.

You can terminate a session using the keyboard shortcut ^C (control+C) in the Terminal app.

Amphetamine

Amphetamine is a free app available from the Mac App Store that will do what the caffeinate command does, but in a graphical user interface with easily configurable options accessible from a status menu in your Menu Bar. You can choose one of the preset timers from 5 minutes to 24 hours listed under **Minutes** and **Hours**, keep your Mac awake indefinitely, until a specific time, or while an application is running, or a file is downloading.

Amphetamine is available from the Mac App Store for free at the time of this writing at https://apps.apple.com/gb/app/amphetamine/id937984704?mt=12.

Restart or Shut Down Immediately

When restarting or shutting down, a dialog box appears asking for confirmation. The advantage of this dialog box is that it gives you 60 seconds to cancel in case you change your mind. Clicking the **Restart** or **Shut Down** button in this dialog box overrides the times and restarts or shuts down your Mac immediately.

If you want to skip this dialog box and restart or shutdown immediately, hold down the ⌥ (option) key while selecting > **Restart** or > **Shut Down**. Your Mac will skip the dialog box and restart or shut down immediately.

343

Index

About the Author

Tom Magrini has written 15 books about computers and technology. He has authored 12 editions of the best-selling *Customizing macOS* series, which helps Mac users completely customize their macOS user experience with hundreds of tweaks, hacks, secret commands, and hidden features. Tom is also the author of 3 editions of *Cut the Cord: How to Watch TV without Paying a Cable or Satellite TV Bill*. *Cut the Cord* shows readers how to save money by ditching expensive cable and satellite TV for streaming video over the internet.

During the day, Tom is an information technology executive with over forty years of experience as a network engineer, systems engineer, consulting systems engineer, network architect, IT manager, IT director, Deputy Chief Information Officer, and Assistant Chief Information Officer. Tom has worked with Macs since 1984 and still fondly remembers his first Apple Macintosh computer with its 8 MHz Motorola 68000 processor, 9-inch 512 x 342-pixel black-and-white screen, 128 kB of RAM, and built-in 400 kB 3½-inch floppy drive. Tom has worked with NeXT computers and the NeXTStep operating system, the forerunner to Apple's macOS. And yes, he has even crossed over to the dark side and has worked extensively with Windows PCs.

During the week, Tom leads a team of IT professionals who maintain two data centers and the data network, telephony, Wi-Fi, Microsoft 365, Microsoft Azure, server, storage, operating systems, service desk, desktop support, IT service management, and inside and outside plant fiber optic and copper cable infrastructure for a large municipality. Tom has also taught programming, operating systems, Cisco Networking Academy, and wireless technology courses as a Computer Information Systems professor at two colleges. He has worked for numerous technology companies, including SynOptics Communications, Bay Networks, FORE Systems, 3Com, and Cisco Systems. Tom is also a certified ITIL® Expert and has achieved eleven Cisco networking certifications and a GIAC Security Leadership Certification (GSLC).

When Tom isn't working, writing books, or hanging out with his family and dogs, he enjoys reading, writing, movies, and the beautiful Arizona weather with its 300+ days of sunshine.

Books by Tom Magrini

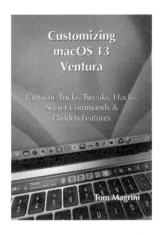

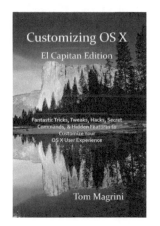

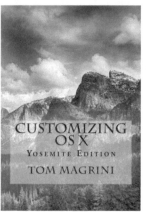

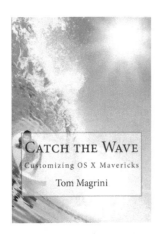

CATCH THE WAVE
Customizing OS X Mavericks
Tom Magrini

TAMING THE PRIDE

CUSTOMIZING OS X
MOUNTAIN LION

TOM MAGRINI

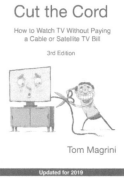

Cut the Cord
How to Watch TV Without Paying
a Cable or Satellite TV Bill
3rd Edition

Tom Magrini

Updated for 2019

Cut the Cord
How to Cut Your Cable or Satellite
TV Cord & Save Big Bucks
2nd Edition

Tom Magrini

Updated for 2018

TOM MAGRINI

Cut the Cord
How to Cut Your Cable or Satellite
TV Cord & Save Big Bucks